JAGUAR
XK120

In Detail

JAGUAR
XK120

In Detail

1948-54

BY ANDERS DITLEV CLAUSAGER

Herridge & Sons

Published in 2006 by
Herridge & Sons Ltd
Lower Forda, Shebbear,
Beaworthy, Devon EX21 5SY

Reprinted 2016

© Copyright JDHT 2006

Designed by Ray Leaning
Special photography by Rowan Isaacs

ISBN 978-0-9549981-0-3
Printed in China

Contents

Introduction

"A thing of beauty…"

In its heyday, the XK 120 was quite simply *the* car to have. From the moment of its sensational debut at the 1948 Motor Show, it attracted rave reviews and easily lived up to its billing as "the fastest production car in the world". In its early years, no other car in regular series production would beat the 120mph-plus the XK 120 repeatedly clocked in reliable independent road tests. The few models that did outrun it were almost invariably semi-racing cars that cost a great deal more money.

Since even today the XK 120 is such a glamorous car, we can scarcely begin to appreciate how extraordinary it must have appeared to contemporary observers almost 60 years ago, set against the drab background of impoverished early post-war Britain. Back then, many everyday necessities were still on ration and what was available was so often utilitarian in nature. It was the age of austerity when, in its effort to build a brighter future, the nation had imposed a Spartan regime upon itself. To escape from dreary, foggy, autumnal London for a few hours – even if only into the Earls Court exhibition hall – must have seemed like travelling to another world. And when you were then confronted with the new Jaguar "Super Sports", you might well think that you had entered automotive heaven.

Apart from its promise of high performance, the immediate appeal of the XK 120 rested on two factors. Its price was surprisingly low – less than £1000 from the factory, in keeping with the by-now-established Jaguar tradition. That wasn't cheap in absolute terms but it was affordable for what the car offered, and like most Jaguars before or since, it meant that the XK 120 was a car that many people could aspire to. Then there was the sheer beauty of its design, reflecting the styling mastery of William Lyons. This, above all, is what made the XK 120 the icon that it remains.

But that's not all. The XK 120 has many other claims to fame, and its beauty is more than just skin deep. Importantly, it was a milestone in Jaguar history, being the first car to feature the revolutionary new XK engine, and the car that would eventually lead its brand to becoming one of the most outstanding manufacturers of sports cars in the world. Before the XK 120, Jaguar was just one of many British specialist manufacturers of quality middle-class saloons, like a more sporting version of Armstrong-Siddeley, Daimler or Rover, without any particular recognition outside the UK. After the XK 120, the name Jaguar became one of the most coveted automotive brands worldwide. In particular, this car began the enduring love affair of the American public with the "Jagwah". And where the USA led, the world followed.

Even if we had not had the C-type and the D-type, the XK 120 would in itself have put Jaguar into the motor sport hall of fame although, as events unfolded, it was only granted a fairly short lifespan in first-rank events, being quickly eclipsed by the other, even faster Jaguars. In 1950-52 almost anyone who was – or wanted to be – somebody in motor sport, had to get an XK 120. Astonishing numbers were seen in British races and rallies and, even when the car became outclassed in the big races, the flame was kept alive in club events and latterly in historic racing. Given the right sort of development some XK

120s were, and still are, amazingly competitive.

Not only did the car offer outstanding performance, it also broke new ground for such a powerful machine by offering unheard-of refinement and comfort. It was completely docile (and in mechanical terms, remarkably bullet-proof) and would happily potter around town or dawdle along at low revs in top gear without making a fuss or fouling its plugs. Many contemporary commentators actually found it difficult to come to terms with this side of its character and were inclined to label it as a fast tourer rather than an out-and-out sports car. This was less of a problem in the USA! There were, however, aspects of the car that were a little less than perfect. The suspension was tuned for comfort so the car tended to roll on corners, although this always looked more dramatic than it actually was, and the handling was still sure-footed. The brakes were prone to fade and wore quickly, and the steering could have been faster and more precise. *In extremis*, overheating was a problem, mostly experienced in the warmer USA.

Despite all this, it is the XK 120's looks which have ensured its continued popularity. Beauty or elegance is not the only factor in deciding what becomes a sought-after classic (who would call the homely Morris Minor or a VW Beetle things of beauty?) but, like select other classics, many of them Jaguars, the breathtaking elegance of the XK 120 alone would have secured it a place in the pantheon of motoring. And it is a classic, timeless beauty. Unlike some of the extravagant styling of yesteryear, the purity and simplicity of the design has always had, and continues to have, a strong appeal.

That does not mean to say that the XK 120 has always led a charmed life. In the 1960s, the XKs in general became eclipsed by the E-type. They were neglected and maltreated, and since the quality of their bodywork was no better than that of other cars of the 1950s, they were often reduced to an appalling condition through the ravages of corrosion. They also fell victim to the Ministry of Transport's then-new

This is the sight that greeted visitors to the Jaguar stand at the 1948 Motor Show – the low sleek bronze-coloured "Super Sports" model, a remarkable contrast even to the many other new post-war models on show.

ADVANCE PARTICULARS

OF THE NEW

JAGUAR

Type XK

"100" AND "120" SUPER SPORTS MODELS

FITTED WITH TWIN OVERHEAD CAMSHAFT ENGINES OF 2 LITRE OR 3½ LITRE CAPACITY

JAGUAR   CARS   LTD   COVENTRY   ENGLAND

... and this is what you got to take way with you: The first simple brochure, "Advanced Particulars", whose sole illustration was a much retouched photo of the bumper-less mock-up. (Jaguar)

test for roadworthiness. They depreciated rapidly and it wasn't long before you could buy an XK for less than £100. This was the period when strange things began to happen to XKs, sometimes blurring their original identities.

The tide turned gradually in the 1970s when the idea of post-war "classic cars" took root in the UK. It became fashionable, and economically viable, to preserve and restore such cars. The XK was a prime candidate and became sought-after once again. Values began to rise. The network of support, through clubs and specialist suppliers or restorers, grew. When it became clear that large numbers of XKs and other classic British sports cars could be found in the USA, often in better condition or at lower prices than in the UK, the import boom of the 1980s got under way. For a time, classic car prices spiralled almost out of sight until the collapse of the market in the early 1990s. Although painful for some, the crash had the

great advantage of putting classic cars back within reach of enthusiasts rather than being considered predominantly as investment objects. Throughout the various ups and downs of the market, the XK 120 has continued to retain and expand its following.

The popularity of the XK 120 as a classic car over the last 30 years has prompted numerous books and magazine articles devoted to this car, not only in the UK but internationally too. It was therefore with some trepidation that I ventured into writing the present volume, but over the last few years I have undertaken a great deal of research in the original records, which are in our care in the Jaguar Daimler Heritage Trust archive, and I hope that even knowledgeable XK 120 experts will find the result of interest. I have also consulted a wide body of published works in preparation for writing this book, and I freely acknowledge the debt that I owe to those who covered the ground before me and who have set such high standards for

others to emulate. Many of my fellow historians and writers still pursue their researches and will, in due course, present their findings, so I cannot expect my book to be the last word on the subject. Indeed, I look forward to other XK books.

It remains only for me to thank John Maries, executive director of the Jaguar Daimler Heritage Trust, and our board of Trustees chaired by Roger Putnam, who have been extremely supportive throughout the long and some times difficult period of research and gestation. I must remember to tell Roger that I found a couple of XK 120s in the records which were originally delivered to owners called Putnam! Colleagues at the JDHT have been equally understanding, despite my somewhat irregular timekeeping, and Karam Ram helped me to find the best images in our photo archive, and did all the scans. Derek Boyce, Richard Soans and Howard Snow from our group of JDHT volunteers were kind enough to read parts of the type-

script and give me the benefit of their comments. The Jaguar historian and author Paul Skilleter read all of the typescript (and was very nice about it!) and provided many erudite comments; he also lent a large number of photos. So did Terry McGrath in Australia, with whose help I completely re-wrote chapter 10. A fuller list of all those who assisted may be found in the appendix. My grateful thanks to all of you.

I also thank my publishers, Charles, Bridgid and Ed Herridge. I have worked with them for a long time now and we have more or less got used to each other. Finally, on the home front, my partner David has once again been a "book widower", a cross he has borne with habitual stoicism; thank you.

Anders Ditlev Clausager
Birmingham and Coventry – 1 November 2005

Jaguar quickly improved on the quality of the XK 120 brochure, and included this composite rendering. The artwork was based on photos taken of the first prototype, HKV 455, some of which will appear later in this book. (Jaguar)

Chapter One

XK 120 Genesis

I don't think that William Lyons set out to become a sports car manufacturer. What his early products offered was distinctive style at an affordable price. The activities of the Swallow Coachbuilding Company were well in tune with the times during a period of steady demand in the British home market for specialist machinery and thus for special body-work, even on small chassis. The number of coachbuilders exhibiting at the annual Motor Show at Olympia peaked at 61 in 1926,[1] the year before Lyons offered his first Swallow body.

Lyons apparently objected to the photo of him at his desk when it was published in The Autocar *in 1948.* (JDHT)

The Swallow company was also spot-on in respect of the chassis that Lyons chose to put his bodies on. He concentrated his efforts on small cars of low tax horsepower ratings which were therefore not only relatively cheap to buy, but also had lower annual running costs. At the time of the depression in particular there was a marked increase in the sale of 8hp cars, the 10hp class of family cars began to outsell the traditional 12hp and some manufacturers downsized their products with a lower hp rating and thus lower tax. Where Lyons and Swallow were perhaps ahead of their time was in the fact that many of the Swallow-bodied cars and the later SS models seem to have been designed with a female audience in mind. This approach was occasionally confirmed by the company's publicity and advertising, and it is irrefutable that the early car records contain quite a high proportion of lady owners. As Lord Montagu has said, the Swallow bodies "appealed to the aesthetically sensitive of both sexes".[2]

The original Austin Seven Swallow was an immediate hit, backed as it was by the efficient distribution network of the motor trader Henlys. The not-very-sporting two-seater was quickly followed by a saloon, the design of which became the prototype for larger saloons fitted to Fiat, Swift and Standard chassis. These cars shared a distinctive style, were typically available in a wide array of bright colour schemes, and had pleasantly luxurious appointments and fittings – sometimes including a "ladies' companion" in the glovebox – but they cost only a little more than ordinary saloon bodies on the same chassis. Yet they had no particular pretensions to performance, nor any

Dramatis personae. *The photo of Bill Heynes was taken much later, but does show him with the XK engine. Walter Hassan is seen outside the Foleshill factory in the 1940s, and the portrait of Claude Baily is also from this period. (JDHT)*

sporting character.

In April 1930, the Wolseley company in Birmingham (owned since 1927 by Morris) introduced a new small car which was unusual in having a six-cylinder engine, of only 1271cc, with a single overhead camshaft following traditional Wolseley practice. This engine was, in fact, one-and-a-half of the Wolseley-designed Morris Minor engine, and the rest of this new Wolseley Hornet also followed the design of the Morris, having a similar two-door saloon body (either fabric-covered or steel-panelled) and a Minor chassis lengthened by 12 inches. For as little £175 the original Hornet offered a top speed of over 60mph (over 96km/h) and cruised easily at 50 (80km/h). There was clearly some further potential in the design and soon there was a brisk trade in converting Hornets using sportier bodywork. Indeed, it seems that a Swallow-bodied Hornet two-seater was offered already by January 1931 at £220.[3]

For the 1932 season, Wolseley began officially to offer the Hornet in chassis form – what they called "chassis supplied to coachbuilders" – as it seems that sales of this version were restricted to selected approved coachbuilders, and Swallow was one of the chosen. The Swallow two-seater was now supplemented by a four-seater, and both models cost £225. Then, halfway through the model year, in April 1932 Wolseley introduced a more powerful version – the Hornet Special – which had a twin-carburettor engine and was normally fitted with centre-lock wire wheels. It was priced in chassis form at £175, and the Swallow two- and four-seater versions were £255. The Swallow-bodied Hornets continued in produc-

tion until August 1933, and while it is not known how many were built in the early part of 1931, a total of 530 were made over the two seasons 1931-32 and 1932-33.

The significance of the Swallow Hornet is that it was the first six-cylinder car that William Lyons had offered in the Swallow range. It was arguably the first sports car he had made, and also the last non-SS model to go out of production. In one sense, the Swallow Hornet was replaced by the SS1 tourer, which was new during the 1933 model year, and with which there was an overlap in production of about six months.

The Wolseley Hornet with Swallow two-seater body was Lyons's first sports car design. This is one of the early Hornet Specials of 1932, with centre-lock wheels and distinctive mascot. (JDHT)

Meanwhile, Lyons had taken the first step on the road to graduating from coachbuilder to car manufacturer. At the 1931 Olympia Motor Show he introduced two new models, called respectively the SS1 and the SS2. The SS1 featured a new purpose-designed chassis supplied by Standard exclusively to Swallow, who contracted to take 500 for the first year, and had the sidevalve Standard six-cylinder engine, rated at either 16 or 20hp (2054 or 2552cc). Even if not all that Lyons had hoped for, the styling was distinctive, complete with long bonnet, closely fitting helmet wings, and short two-door cabin with a fabric roof and blind rear quarters, which featured false hood irons. The SS2 was not nearly as clever as it simply had a similarly styled body, looking rather stunted on the much shorter, unmodified Standard Little Nine chassis. But prices were extremely reasonable at £310 and £210 respectively, and performance was nothing to be ashamed of, with top speeds of over 70mph (113km/h) and around 60mph (96km/h) for the two cars.

A much-improved and better-looking SS1 was offered a year later, with a lengthened wheelbase, the chassis underslung at the rear and flowing wings merging into running boards. Engines were fitted with aluminium alloy cylinder heads. There was now room for four, and the car's top speed was reckoned to be closer to 80mph (128km/h). The price had increased by a modest amount to £325 for the 16hp car, and another £10 for the 20hp model. While at least one SS1 had been entered in the 1932 RAC rally to Torquay, the modified 1933 cars were to compete both in the Monte Carlo Rally and the RAC Rally. The 1933 model was at first offered only in coupé form, but in the spring of 1933 an alternative bodystyle appeared in the form of an open four-seater tourer. The tourer quickly appeared in British rallies, and a team of four, together with a privately entered coupé, were bravely entered in the tough European Alpine Trial. Three cars completed the rally, with a 14th place overall for Austrian importer Koch and his co-driver in one of the tourers. In 1934, the SS1 tourers took a team prize in the Alpine Trial, and the company also put a tourer version of a revised SS2 on the market. The tourer bodystyle was continued for the first two years of production of the new SS Jaguar 2½-litre model from 1935 to 1937, but it was then replaced by a more contemporary and civilised drop-head coupé model.

By 1935, Lyons must have felt that the company's

In the spring of 1933, the SS1 tourer appeared as an additional model to the coupé. In that year's Alpine Trial, the Austrian importer Koch (on the left) managed a sixth place in class. (JDHT)

The SS Jaguar 100 was the first real Jaguar sports car. This example, posed at the main entrance of the Foleshill factory, was supplied to HRH Prince Michael of Rumania. (JDHT)

development was satisfactory enough for him to bring out a first attempt at a proper sports car based on the SS1. The SS90 had a shortened SS1 chassis, the wheelbase being the same as on the SS2, and the 20hp engine (now of 2663cc) with a Weslake improved cylinder head was fitted. The original body design featured a swept tail with inset spare wheel not unlike the abortive Triumph Dolomite straight-eight, or some of the Riley sports cars. This was found only on the first example; the following 23 had a more conventional rear end with a slab Le Mans-type tank and a vertical spare wheel, after the pattern established by MG. The SS90 was offered at £395, and as an SS1 20hp tourer was tested by *The Motor*[4] to have a top speed of almost 85mph (136km/h), it may be speculated that the SS90 would indeed, as suggested by its name, have a maximum speed of 90mph (145km/h) – a fact already taken for granted by *The Autocar*.[5] The first SS90 was driven by Brian Lewis in the 1935 RAC Rally. This particular car, splendidly restored, has for many years been owned by the well-known Swiss Jaguar collector Dr Christian Jenny.

It is entirely possible that a major reason for introducing the SS90 at the unusual time of March was to have the car in the RAC Rally (where it suffered from clutch problems and was not listed among the finishers). It does seem a little odd, however, for SS to introduce the new model with the existing side-valve engine when, surely, by March 1935 the new overhead valve engine to be introduced six months later must have been well under way. SS was also going against the prevailing trend in the British car market, which was generally seeing a move away from out-and-out two-seater sports models towards sports saloons and drophead coupés, especially in the higher-horsepower classes. The SS90 barely had time to establish itself before the model was replaced by the more exciting SS Jaguar 100 and, as indicated, the production figure remained modest.

In September 1935, SS Cars took the biggest step forward in product evolution since the launch of the original SS1 four years earlier. There was a much-revised chassis and a new overhead-valve six-cylinder engine. There was a strikingly good-looking four-door saloon body, the first for the company, and there was a new model name; Jaguar. The new engine was still of 2663cc but now developed over 100bhp – up almost 50 per cent from the sidevalve unit – and offered much better performance, with a top speed of 85-88mph (137-142km/h) for the saloon. Yet the price was only £395. The same figure was asked for an updated version of the SS90, the "competition" version, which was now called the SS Jaguar 100. While the name implied 100mph, the original 2½-litre version did not quite live up to this but came close with a top speed of 94-96mph (151-154km/h),[6] and the later 3½-litre version broke through the barrier with a top speed of 101mph (162.5km/h).[7] Even this still cost only £445, the cheapest genuine 100mph car available in Britain at the time.

The SS 100 had the looks, the panache and style, and the performance. It was completely in the mould of the traditional British sports car, its basic design redolent of an earlier period. It did well in road rallies, winning the Alpine Trial in 1936 and the RAC Rally in 1937 and 1938. Tommy Wisdom, in a much-modified stripped car, won the long handicap race at

Brooklands in October 1937 at almost 112mph (180km/h). Even after World War II, SS 100s did rather well in rallies, notably with Ian Appleyard's performances in the Alpine and Tulip Rallies. The SS 100 had its limitations, however, and it is said that Lyons persuaded the would-be entrants from starting an SS 100 in the Tourist Trophy at Donington Park in 1938. With its old-fashioned hard suspension and flexible chassis, the car could be skittish and it was easy to lose the rear end. Its handling has been called "unpredictable".[8] It was, perhaps, simply too fast for its chassis.

A total of 309 SS 100s were made from 1935 to 1940, although production slowed drastically in the final two years. In the same period, a staggering 14,000 were made of the various saloon, tourer and drophead coupé models, just over half of them of the four-cylinder 1½-litre types, the rest the 2½- and 3½-litre six-cylinder types, and the 1938-39 model year

The SS 100 was most at home in road rallies. Here five of them are filling up during the Scottish Rally in the Coronation Year 1937. (JDHT)

saw more than 5000 cars produced. SS Cars had "arrived" and the company was, in terms of output, among Britain's leading independent specialist car makers. As a limited production sports car model, the SS 100 had its niche and had few competitors. The Railton Light Sports of 1935 with its Hudson 4.2-litre engine offered a top speed of over 100mph (161km/h) at an eye-watering £878, and even more impossibly expensive was the Squire, with prices starting around the £1000 mark but for which a top speed of 100mph was guaranteed, from a supercharged 1½-litre twin ohc engine. They built seven, and there were not that many more Railton sports models. There were even fewer of Triumph's £1225 Straight-Eight Dolomites or its HSM successor, and these had gone by the time the SS 100 got into its stride. Alvis, Bentley and Lagonda in the late 1930s made wonderful and extremely fast cars but these were all in the Grand Tourer class, with corresponding prices.

The most serious rival for the SS 100 was the German BMW 328, promoted and sold in Britain as the Frazer Nash BMW for a not-impossible £695 (including import duty of 33 per cent). In its German home market it cost RM7400, approximately the equivalent of £620 (using the rate of RM12 to the £). It lost out to the SS 100 on sheer muscle, having only 1971cc and 80bhp, but its top speed, aided by better aerodynamics and lighter weight, was about 95mph

(153km/h) in standard form, and a Frazer Nash BMW covered 102 miles (164km) in an hour at Brooklands. With its rigid tubular chassis, independent front suspension and hydraulic brakes, the 328 belonged to a different generation from the SS 100. On an international scale the 328 out-produced and outsold the SS 100 as 464 were made, mostly between 1937 and

Ian Appleyard, here with his Alpine Cup and other trophies after the 1948 Alpine Rally, kept the SS 100 at the forefront of rallying even after World War Two. By then, LNW 100 had been fitted with a post-war type "Jaguar" radiator badge. (JDHT)

This one-off SS 100 coupé was on the SS Jaguar stand at the last pre-war Motor Show, held at Earls Court in 1938. This car may have inspired the XK 120 fixed-head coupé more than ten years later. (JDHT)

1939, and 46 of these were exported to Britain.[9] Only two SS 100s made it to Germany when new, and SS exports overall were modest. We may reflect that the BMW 328 in its various guises is likely to have had a strong influence on the next Jaguar sports car, and some well known 328 exponents were to change allegiance after the war – notably Leslie Johnson and "Bira" but also Gilbert Tyrer.

Up to 1940, all engines had been supplied from the Standard Motor Company, if increasingly to Jaguar's own design. Then, during the war, Lyons bought the six-cylinder engine production line from Standard,[10] although even after 1945 Standard continued to supply the four-cylinder 1½-litre engine (actually of 1776cc), until the smallest Jaguar went out of production in 1949. This engine was also used in the post-war Triumph 1800, until replaced by the ubiquitous Standard Vanguard engine around the same time.

If Jaguar could now make its own engines, on the other hand there was a gap opening up in the company's body-building capabilities; ironic perhaps for a company which had started out exclusively in this line of business… While Jaguar was still able to make traditional coachbuilt bodies, the introduction of all-steel saloon bodies in 1937 had famously proved a major headache. Lyons had sought to improve the company's body-making capacity by acquiring the firm Motor Panels in·1939, yet felt obliged to sell this company again to Rubery Owen in 1943.[11] As a consequence, bodies for the early post-war cars, up to and including the Mark V, were made in-house much in the same way as before. For his planned all-new luxury saloon, however, Lyons felt the need to approach the successful specialist maker

The BMW 328 was the most important competitor for the SS Jaguar 100. And it is quite possible that the design of this car had some influence on the post-war Jaguar sports car…

of all-steel bodies, Pressed Steel, whose factory was adjacent to the Morris factory at Cowley outside Oxford (now owned by BMW; today it houses production of the new Mini).

In 1945, the first priority for the newly renamed Jaguar Cars Limited was to re-enter the bread-and-butter saloon car market. Before the year was out, small-scale production of the 1½-litre was under way, followed in 1946 by the six-cylinder cars, which became available with the alternative drophead coupé body style in 1948. Exports had now become a necessity, for Jaguar as for the rest of the British motor industry and, in consequence, for the first time Jaguars became available with left-hand drive. Many new agents were signed up, and after a couple of false starts before the war, Jaguar now entered the US market in earnest.

There was initially little thought of a new sports car. When the saloons were re-introduced in September 1945, it was stated that "the 100 series is temporarily out of production".[12] However, perhaps in part to foster the impression that the Jaguar sports car was far from defunct, a pre-war SS 100 which had been stored at Lyons's home during the war, was exhumed for Ian Appleyard, son of the Leeds distributor, and soon to be Lyons's son-in-law. It was fitted with a 3½-litre engine instead of the original 2½ and, interestingly, now displayed the post-war "Jaguar" radiator badge. As LNW 100, this car became Appleyard's mount for his successful first forays in the Alpine and Tulip rallies.

By 1947, when the design of the XK engine and the proper new post-war chassis were both well advanced, Lyons once again turned to a sports car

Jaguar's original factory in Coventry, at Foleshill. In 1928, the company occupied only one of the small blocks at the top of this aerial view. The final additions were the large bays in the foreground, erected in 1948, and this is where XK 120 production took place. (JDHT)

project. He could well have been influenced by requests from the export markets; MG had just begun its meteoric rise in America. Lyons would have been able to experience this for himself during his first visit to the USA in March 1948, when he met a sales representative for MG.[13] By that time, Jaguar and MG already shared some dealer outlets in the USA. As we shall see, however, already before this visit, a sports car prototype had been built in the Jaguar factory.

It was a combination of factors that finally brought the sports car project to the forefront during 1948. Jaguar had both the new XK engine and the new chassis ready to launch, yet the hoped-for new saloon body had been delayed. What's more, the first postwar Motor Show at Earls Court in London had been fixed for October 1948. As an interim measure, it was

decided to launch the new chassis with the old pushrod engine and a modernised body as the Mark V saloon, and yet Lyons also wanted to show off the twin ohc engine. It would be useful to have a guinea pig in which to try out this revolutionary engine before the company committed to full-scale production for the next saloon, and Lyons realised that a limited-production sports car not only offered this opportunity but would also be an excellent publicity tool. He felt that "such a car with the XK engine could not fail (provided, of course, we made no serious mistake) to become outstanding, as it should easily out-perform everything else on the market by a wide margin, irrespective of price".[14] And so it was decided that Jaguar should introduce a new sports car at Earls Court. The stage was readied for the debut of the XK 120.

1. Walker *A-Z of British Coachbuilders 1919-1960* p11
2. Montagu *Jaguar A Biography* first ed. p11
3. Whyte *Jaguar The History of a Great British Car* first ed. p192
4. *The Motor* 2 Jul 1935
5. *The Autocar* 22 Mar 1935
6. *The Motor* 25 May 1937
7. *The Motor* 12 Jul 1938
8. Sedgwick *Cars of the 1930s* p342
9. Simons *From Roadster to Legend* p261; Jenkinson *From Chain Drive to Turbocharger* pp312-314
10. Porter & Skilleter *Sir William Lyons* p86
11. *Ibid.* pp80-81, 86-87
12. Skilleter *Jaguar Sports Cars* p52
13. Porter & Skilleter pp103-06
14. Skilleter p52

Chapter Two

The XK Engine

The various accounts of the history of Jaguar make it clear that the engine was the starting point of the design of the XK 120. It is therefore useful to re-examine the philosophy behind the engine design and look again at its development history. The drive and ambition that William Lyons brought to Jaguar were clearly expressed when, in 1935, he told his new chief engineer William Heynes that his ultimate aim was to build one of the world's finest luxury cars.[1] From 1931 to 1939, development of the product, from SS1 to the 3½-litre Jaguar, was certainly both rapid and remarkable, and accompanied by solid commercial success. Yet compared with later years the results were in overall terms modest, and there was little in the company's pre-war history to prepare you for what was to come.

The outline specification that Lyons set for his ideal future car was that it should be capable of a top speed of 100mph (161km/h) and have a full-size saloon body.[2] This established the parameters for the engine specification, as a few calculations showed that this would require something like 160bhp at an engine speed of 5000rpm and an engine size between three and four litres, with either six or eight cylinders. For a comparison, it may be noted that of the few four/five-seater saloons previously to achieve a 100mph top speed, the 1930 Bentley required an engine of eight litres, and the same designer's Lagonda V12 of 1936 needed 4.5 litres.

It is a well established part of Jaguar lore that the XK engine was conceived during the war-time nights of fire-watching at the factory, where Lyons would ensure that he, Heynes, Walter Hassan and Claude Baily could get together on the Sunday night shift, relatively undisturbed (except, perhaps, occasionally by the *Luftwaffe*).[3] Of the two other designers, the engine man Baily had joined from Morris Engines in 1940, while Hassan, after a spell at the aircraft maker Bristol, had re-joined SS in 1943 to become the chief development engineer under Heynes.

But when exactly did these sessions take place? In the pre-war years, SS had relied on the Standard company for all its engine requirements. However, as Standard did not expect to re-enter the six-cylinder market after the war, and did not want to continue to make engines for the SS Jaguars, in 1942 John Black of Standard unexpectedly offered to sell the engine plant to Jaguar. Lyons quickly accepted, negotiated a price of £6000 and immediately arranged to move the production machinery to Foleshill.[4] The date of Hassan's return to SS means that the design of the XK engine could only have taken place from 1943 onwards. By then, a determining factor for the design may have been that since Jaguar now had the facility to make six-cylinder engines, the company was probably disposed to continue with this type rather than adding complications by designing a V8 (or straight-eight).

Apart from the targeted power output, there were other requirements for the future Jaguar engine. First, it had to be sufficiently advanced to keep ahead of developments among competitors for what was expected to be a long production life, without the need for re-tooling before the original expenditure had been fully recouped. Then, as Jaguar was still considering the possibility of staying in the market for smaller cars, the firm decided it would be desirable to produce both four- and six-cylinder versions. Finally, there was Lyons's insistence that the engine should not only *be* powerful but also *look* powerful.[5]

The various requirements led to the company adopting the twin overhead camshaft layout which Lyons remembered from the Peugeot and Sunbeam racing cars of his youth. Lyons and Heynes agreed that twin overhead camshafts were desirable, while initially Hassan and Baily were more sceptical,[6] – despite (or perhaps because of!) the fact that both men had experience of ohc engines. Hassan had started out with the original Bentley company and later worked for the Alfa Romeo importers, while Baily was familiar with the single ohc engines which had been widely used by the Morris-MG-Wolseley companies until 1935. It is worth pointing out at this point that there had not previously been a twin ohc engine in true mass production. Among the best-known types were 300-odd Sunbeam 3-litres, a similar number of Stutz DV32s, fewer than 500 Duesenbergs and some 700 Bugatti Type 57s. A generous estimate would be 5000 twin cam Alfa Romeos of all models up to 1950, but at least twice that number of Salmsons, if over a period of some 20 years. The resultant figure of 10,000 was similar to the *annual* production of Jaguar XK engines in the 1950s.

For such a small company as Jaguar to design and produce a successful twin-cam engine was a remarkable pioneering achievement. In the immediate post-war period, even single-ohc engines – relatively common in the 1920s and '30s – were thin on the ground, in Britain only AC, Singer and, from 1948, Wolseley used this principle. Single ohc engines were found in Ferrari, Lancia and Maserati cars, as well as the still-born Isotta-Fraschini Monterosa in Italy, and were a little later re-introduced by Mercedes-Benz. Nevertheless, a few other twin-cam engines were at various stages of development at the same time as Jaguar's. In Britain the Invicta Black Prince was doomed to remain a chimera, and the Bentley-designed Lagonda engine had a protracted birth, although it was eventually adopted for the Aston Martin DB2. Alfa Romeo followed Jaguar with mass-production twin-cam engines for its 1900 saloon of 1950 and later Giuliettas. The exotic Spanish Pegaso joined this select list in 1952, while Ferrari only introduced the twin-cam layout on production road cars in 1966, just one year before Fiat brought out the first popular small family car with a twin-cam engine, the 125.

Together with the twin-cam layout came a cross-flow head with hemispherical combustion chambers

The first prototype twin overhead camshaft engine was called the XF, and was only of 1360cc. (JDHT)

which, according to Heynes, offered a number of distinct advantages. These were principally in areas such as valve-throat flow, controlled turbulence and combustion, and exhaust-valve cooling, but also in terms of ease of machining.[7] A hemispherical combustion chamber, however, could be obtained with other types of valve operation such as the BMW cross pushrod system, the twin high-cam engines of Riley and Lea-Francis, or with a single ohc. While Jaguar began its experiments with a twin-ohc engine, the 1360cc four-cylinder XF-type,[8] it also investigated the BMW system on the 1776cc XG-type, which was otherwise based on the existing Standard-sourced Jaguar 1½-litre engine. This was found to be noisy, and was quickly abandoned in favour of the twin-ohc XJ

This is believed to be the experimental XG engine made by Jaguar – or rather SS Cars: note the SS logo on the oil filler – converted from a 1½-litre engine in circa 1944 to feature the cross-pushrod system and overhead valves placed in a V. (JDHT)

As theses photos were taken in July 1948, they probably show the 3.2-litre XJ engine, rather than the definitive XK engine of 3.4 litres, but it is difficult to tell, and the engine size is not yet cast into the side of the block. (JDHT)

series in both four-cylinder 2-litre and six-cylinder 3.2-litre forms. This latter had a bore and stroke of 83x98mm but was lacking in low-speed torque, a trait remedied by lengthening the stroke to 106mm for a capacity of 3442cc (210cu in). And so the final XK engine was born.

We may suppose that the engine dimensions were fixed before Britain abolished the horsepower tax in 1947, since the bore was still relatively narrow and gave an RAC hp rating of 25.6, compared with the old 3½-litre ohv engine which had an 82mm bore and therefore almost exactly 25 RAC hp. Similarly, the stroke of the XK engine was only 4mm less than that of the ohv unit of the same size. Since the ohv unit developed its maximum of 125bhp at a fairly leisurely 4250rpm and the XK engine yielded its 160bhp at 5000rpm,[9] a price had to be paid in terms of higher peak piston speed, up from 3070ft/min on the ohv engine to 3490ft/min on the XK. While this did not affect the reliability or service life of the XK (which turned out to be excellent – even if oil consumption was often prodigious), nevertheless it is conceivable that the engine might originally have been designed with a shorter stroke and bigger bore, if at the time this had been encouraged by the British taxation system.[10] As it was, the final stroke/bore ratio of 1.28 was considered progressive in the 1940s.

The four-cylinder version of the XK was actually less undersquare, with a bore and stroke of 80.5x98mm (RAC hp rating of 16hp, stroke/bore ratio of 1.22) for 1995cc, and the power output was quoted as 95bhp at 5000rpm. This would probably have given the projected XK 100 sports car a calculated top speed of around 98mph (158km/h), with the quoted 4.09 rear-axle ratio, lower than the 3.643 ratio employed on the XK 120. An interesting statistic is that the four-cylinder engine was only around ½ cwt (25kg) lighter than the six, according to the original published data for the dry weights of

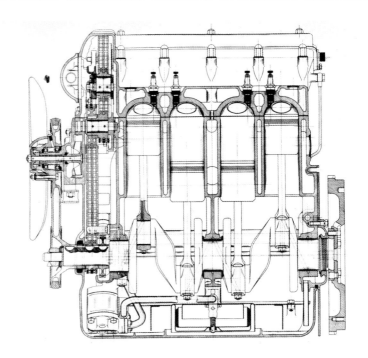

A longitudinal section of the four-cylinder XK engine, probably in its definitive 2-litre form. (JDHT)

This XK 100 engine is clearly the show unit, being prepared for Earls Court in 1948. (JDHT)

complete cars.[11] Arguably, a four-cylinder 2-litre XK 100 could have been competitive on performance with such later cars as the Triumph TR2 and the MGA, but the price – if it had stayed at the same figure as the XK 120, as was originally intended – would have ruled it out of contention. As it was, Jaguar had more than enough orders for the six-cylinder car to abandon the four-cylinder version.

Although some contemporary publications continued to list the planned XK 100 into 1950, after one to two years it was dropped from price lists and data tables. The latest references I have found date to March and October 1950.[12] The model was deleted from Jaguar's own price list in August 1949. The company did, however, allocate chassis numbers to the XK 100, with right-hand-drive cars starting from 460001 and left-hand-drive ones from 470001 (the initial 4 was the only difference from XK 120 chassis numbers).[13] The engine number prefix intended for the XK 100 engine was Y. This makes sense because, once you disregard X (which would not have been used in order to avoid confusion), Y is the next letter after W (the XK 120 engine), and Z was used on the Mark V 3½-litre from May 1950 onwards. The XK 100 bodies may have been expected to share the F body prefix of the XK 120. If so, it is worth pointing out that there is no F number missing in the range for the alloy bodies from F 1001 to F 1240 that could have been used for an early XK 100 prototype. The first steel body number was F 1241 and, in fact, the first F body number not accounted for in the *Car Record Book*[14] is F 1687, a left-hand-drive steel body dating to July 1950.

The idea lingered on and in 1951 the prototype XK 120 fixed-head coupé (chassis number 669001) was fitted with an experimental 2-litre, four-cylinder XK unit of 83x91mm and 1970cc.[15] The engine gave up to 109bhp at 5750rpm, admittedly running without the fan. The test report concluded:
"It will be necessary to carry out development work on the cylinder head, camshafts and induction system before this engine can be considered a satisfactory power unit *and also decide for what purpose the engine is to be used*" [italics added].

Three months before this, a prototype 2½-litre six-cylinder XK engine had already given over 160bhp…[16]

The only experimental XK 100 prototype that we can actually trace is chassis number 470001, which would, in theory, be the first XK 100 open two-seater with left-hand drive. This number appears in the *Car Record Book* with the much later "chassis completion date" of 17 March 1953 and the engine number Y 0502, but no body number is recorded. As Philip

Porter has pointed out, this chassis number also figures on a list of experimental cars dated to August 1953, where it is referred to as "XK 2 Litre No. 1". The August 1953 lists further states that "669001 White Fixed-head Coupé fitted with 2 Litre Engine has been dismantled"[17] (see chapter 8).

Still, in 1953 Heynes could state that the four-cylinder had "not yet been released to the market",[18] implying that the engine might still see use in a production car. He was most likely hinting at the "2-litre saloon" which in the end emerged as the six-cylinder 2.4-litre of 1955. It has been suggested that before the October 1948 announcement Jaguar built around 50 of the four-cylinder engines,[19] and a number are known to be still in preservation. Engine number Y 0502 from the 1953 prototype is in the JDHT Museum, while another is in the Heritage Motor Centre at Gaydon, possibly the one used in Gardner's record car (see below).

The XK engine in detail[20]

While the twin overhead camshafts and the hemispherical combustion chambers were the outstanding features of the XK engine, there were other aspects of interest in the design. The chrome cast iron combined cylinder block and crankcase was as simple as you would expect on an overhead-camshaft engine, reaching precisely to the crankshaft centreline, and was closed by a deep, full-length aluminium alloy sump. There were water passages between all cylinders. The blocks were supplied as raw castings from Leyland Motors and were machined in-house by Jaguar.

The crankshaft was made of EN.16 manganese molybdenum steel. After machining, it was dynamically balanced, and then statically balanced after the flywheel had been fitted. It was fitted in seven main bearings, still quite unusual, and these were of a generous 2.75in (69.85mm) diameter. Big-end journals were of 2.086in (52.98mm) diameter, and their considerable overlap with the mains contributed much to the stiffness of the crankshaft. It was felt that each main bearing could be shorter if seven were employed rather than four, making for a slightly shorter overall engine length. Both the main and the big-end bearings were of Vandervell's thin-wall steel-backed type with bearing shells lined with white metal. To minimise the problem of torsional vibration, which increased with the weight of the crankshaft, the crankshaft was only partly counterbalanced, at the front and rear con rods and on either side of the centre bearing. A crankshaft damper was fitted at the front.

An angled cross shaft, driven from a skew gear at

the front of the crankshaft, drove the distributor and oil pump, the latter being of the conventional gear type. There was an external Tecalemit full-flow oil filter; missing from the earliest engine pictures, which were used by Jaguar as late as 1951.[21] The total oil capacity of the engine was originally quoted as 24 pints (13.6 litres) which, in early 1950, was increased to a recommended 29 pints (16.5 litres).[22] Force-fed full-pressure lubrication was used throughout, with a typical operating pressure of 40-45psi at 2000rpm.

Con rods were also made from EN.16 steel, while the small ends were fitted with bronze bushes and had floating gudgeon pins. The aluminium alloy pistons were long and full-skirted. Two alternative types of pistons were fitted, either Brico with semi-split skirts, or Aerolite with solid skirts. Initially, a choice of two compression ratios was offered, with flat-top pistons for the 7:1 ratio and domed-top for

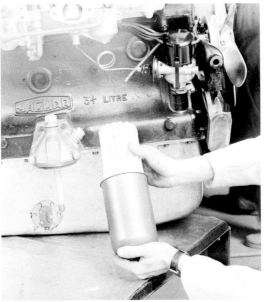

This rendering of the XK engine was used in the 1949 sales catalogue, and for quite some time after, even though it lacked the oil filter which soon became standard. (JDHT)

This photo from April 1949 is the earliest known shot of the Tecalemit oil filter. Below it on the side of the sump is the sender unit for the oil level gauge. (JDHT)

The cylinder head removed from the engine, complete with carburettors, but the camshaft drive sprockets have been detached from the camshafts and have been left attached to the front carrier plate. (JDHT)

the 8:1. The lower ratio was recommended for areas where petrol with an octane rating higher than 72 was not available. It was supposedly for export only but was also found on most of the early home market cars until the low octane Pool petrol was replaced by branded petrol in early 1953 and 80 octane premium-grade petrol became available. At this time, 8:1 became standard in the home market and for designated export markets,[23] and it was always found on cars for the USA. The higher compression needed 80 octane fuel. Later on, there would also be a 9:1 ratio, with higher domes on the pistons, but this was supplied only to special order and required the use of 85-90 octane fuel.[24] In practice, on the XK 120 the 9:1 compression was rarely found.

Bore sizes and pistons were graded by size and matched accordingly, with a letter (F, G, H, J or K) stamped on the crown of the pistons, and on the top face of the block adjacent to the bores. Each grade had a tolerance of 0.3 thou, thus pistons of grade F were for bore sizes from 3.2673in to 3.2676in, G for 3.2677in to 3.2680in, etc. Engines may have different bores of different grades, and were assembled selectively. G and H were probably the most common

sizes. In addition, pistons were available in five over-sizes from five thou to 30 thou.[25]

The cylinder head was cast by either William Mills or West Yorkshire Foundries[26] from DTD 424 or RR50 aluminium alloy and weighed only 50 lb (22.7kg), while a comparable cast iron head would have weighed 120 lb (54.5 kg). Brimol valve seat inserts of high nickel austenitic cast iron were fitted. These had an expansion rate close to that of the aluminium of the head itself. Valve-seat angles were originally 30° for the inlet valves and 45° for the exhaust valves. Valve seats and tappet guides were inserted in the head in one operation at a temperature of 232°C – the valve guides were inserted in a separate operation at 80°C. The inlet valves had heads of 1.75in (44.45mm) diameter and were made from EN.52 silicon chrome steel, while the exhaust valves had heads of 1.4375in (36.51mm) diameter and were made from Fox 1282 austenitic steel. The valve heads were flat. The combustion chambers were almost exactly hemispherical, with the spark plugs mounted vertically, either slightly in front or slightly to the rear of the valves. The plugs were by Champion, with NA8 specified for the 8:1 compression ratio, L10S for the

... as can be seen here where the camshaft chain drive has been laid out, complete with carrier, next to the engine front plate. (JDHT)

7:1. The valves were symmetrically arranged at an included angle of 70°, or each row of valves at 35° from the vertical. The combustion chambers and the inlet ports were designed with the assistance of the cylinder-head specialist Harry Weslake, already familiar to the company as the designer of the 1935 overhead valve cylinder head for the first SS Jaguar.

The camshaft drive was by two-stage duplex chain, driven from a sprocket at the front of the crankshaft, and with a pair of intermediate sprockets on an idler at the top of the cylinder block. Single-chain drive had been tried but was rejected because, according to Heynes, "it produced a high-pitched whine which defied cure".[27] The lower or primary chain had a flat-spring tensioner on the offside, while the secondary top chain had a small idler sprocket mounted on an eccentric spindle so it acted as an adjustable tensioner, fitted at the front of the central valley of the cylinder head.

The inlet camshaft was on the right-hand side (offside) of the engine, the exhaust on the left-hand or nearside. The cast iron camshafts ran in four bearings and operated the valves directly, the cams working on inverted bucket tappets. Valve lift was 0.3125 in (7.94mm), and double valve springs were fitted. Valve clearance adjustment was by hardened shims inserted between the tappet and the top of the valve stem. The shims were available in thicknesses from 85 to 103 thou at one thou intervals, the 19 different sizes distinguished individually by the letters from A to S.

The early cam covers lacked the extra studs at the front. The fan is the original type of cast aluminium, and behind is the water-jacketed inlet manifold. (JDHT)

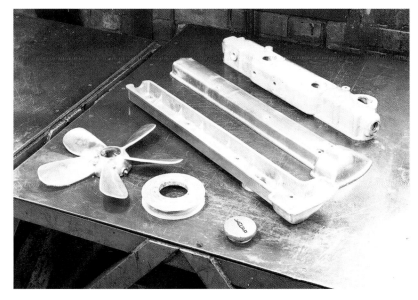

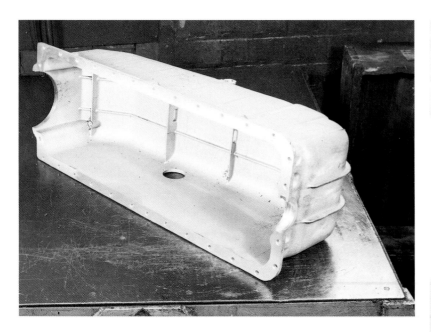

The original type of non-stepped sump, with the hole on the right-hand side (here at the bottom) for the oil level gauge sender unit. (JDHT)

The significance of this photo is that the dismantled engine is the one used in the 1952 Montlhéry record car, LWK 707, here the bores are being checked for wear after the run. (JDHT)

Tappet adjustment necessarily required removal of the camshaft. To assist in this process, or to facilitate the removal of the cylinder head without upsetting the valve timing, the upper drive chain could be left *in situ* on the camshaft sprockets, which were instead detached from the camshafts. A projecting front stud on each sprocket was then moved inwards in a slot on the front carrier plate, and the sprocket secured in a convenient position by fitting a nut to the stud. Another feature which helped to simplify servicing was that the camshaft drive sprockets each incorporated a serrated adjusting plate, which acted as a vernier to allow fine tuning of the valve timing.

There were separate inlet and exhaust ports for all cylinders, and the inlet ports were slightly offset and curved to create a rotational swirl across the spark plug and exhaust valve. Valve timing was originally as follows: Inlet opens 15 degrees before top dead centre and closes 57 degrees after bottom dead centre; exhaust opens 57 degrees before bottom dead centre and closes 15 degrees after top dead centre.

The manifolds were separate castings. The

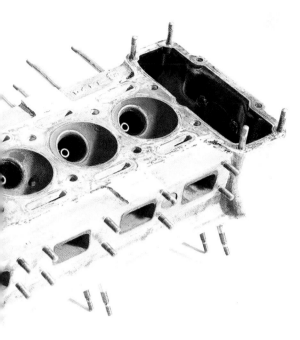

Similarly, here is the cylinder head from LWK 707 laid out for inspection. (JDHT)

fold water jacket before returning to the vertically mounted radiator. A thermostat was incorporated and the system was pressurised at 4psi. The original cast aluminium five-blade fan was replaced by a fabricated six-blade one when some cars were reported to overheat in the USA.

The output of the original XK 120 engine was 160bhp at 5000-5400rpm (depending on which power curve you believe – Jaguar published several slightly different ones!), with torque of 190 (or 195) lb ft at 2500rpm. These figures were obtained with the normal 8:1 compression ratio. With the lower 7:1 ratio, power was 150bhp at 5000rpm. Note that at this time Jaguar measured output by the SAE standard, which gave higher figures than the now-commonly used DIN standard. It has also been suggested that Jaguar measured power output with the engine as "naked" as possible, for instance without a fan. Further development of the engine resulted in substantial power increases, and some figures are mentioned below:

XK 120 engine modified with high-lift camshafts (0.375in or 9.53mm – this necessitated shorter valve guides and tappet guides), lightened flywheel, special crankshaft damper, Champion NA10 plugs, uprated

The crankshaft of the engine from LWK 707 being measured for wear after the record run. (JDHT)

aluminium alloy inlet manifold was water-jacketed to ensure that operating temperature was reached quickly and remained constant. Two SU horizontal carburettors were fitted, type H6 of 1.75in (44.45mm), as well as an auxiliary starting carburettor, which was operated electrically and controlled automatically by a thermostat. This did away with the need for a manual choke control. Broadly speaking, on the alloy-bodied cars into early 1950, the carburettors had dashpots with tall necks while on later cars the dashpots had shorter necks. Two three-branch exhaust manifolds, finished in vitreous enamel were fitted, leading to a two-into-one downpipe.

The dry weight of the complete engine was around 530lb (241kg), but the number of engine ancillaries included in this figure is not specified.[28]

The cooling system was conventional, with the centrifugal water pump mounted on the spindle of the fan, which was driven by belt from the crankshaft pulley. The pump delivered water to a gallery on the left-hand side of the cylinder block from where it passed through the block and head to the inlet mani-

A detail showing the tall carburettors used into the spring of 1950, broadly speaking on the alloy-bodied cars, but also some of the early steel-bodied ones. (JDHT)

This highly-prepared part sectioned engine may have been the engine from the Jaguar stand at the 1948 Motor Show. It has the oil filter, and note that the casting is marked "3½ litre", so it could be a later engine. I believe that this show engine was later updated and featured at several motor shows. (JDHT)

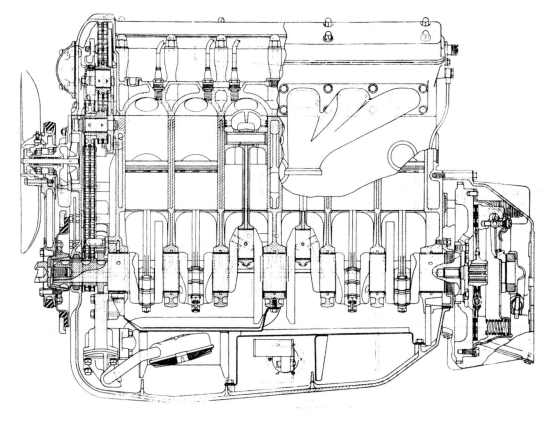

The XK engine in section, an illustration published in the Automobile Engineer, *amongst others. (JDHT)*

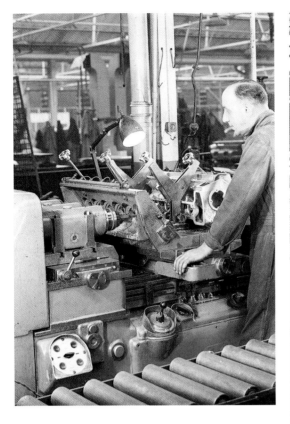

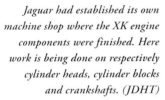

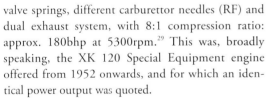

Jaguar had established its own machine shop where the XK engine components were finished. Here work is being done on respectively cylinder heads, cylinder blocks and crankshafts. (JDHT)

valve springs, different carburettor needles (RF) and dual exhaust system, with 8:1 compression ratio: approx. 180bhp at 5300rpm.[29] This was, broadly speaking, the XK 120 Special Equipment engine offered from 1952 onwards, and for which an identical power output was quoted.

Ditto, with 9:1 compression ratio, Champion NA12 plugs and RB carburettor needles: 190bhp at 5400rpm.[30]

XK 120 C (C-type), 1951 works racing car and 1952 production cars: fitted with high-lift camshafts and other modifications as described above, also larger inlet valves (1.875in or 47.625mm), larger exhaust valves (1.5 or 1.625in, resp. 38.1 or 41.28mm), exhaust ports increased in size from 1.25in (31.75mm) to 1.375in (34.93mm), and later fitted with 2in (50.8mm) SU carburettors. With 9:1 compression, 210bhp at 5800rpm or 204bhp at 5500rpm; with 8:1 compression, 194-200bhp.[31]

1953 works racing C-type: as above but now

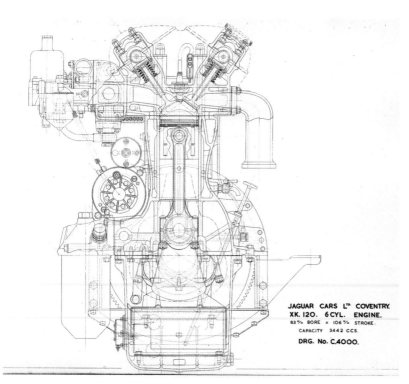

JAGUAR CARS Lᵗᵈ. COVENTRY.
XK. 120. 6 CYL. ENGINE.
83¾ BORE x 106½ STROKE.
CAPACITY 3442 CCS.

DRG. No. C.4000.

fitted with three twin-choke Weber carburettors: 220bhp at 5200rpm.[32]

Even in its standard form the XK engine was among the most powerful in the world in terms of actual as well as specific output as will be clear from the following table, which includes a representative selection of the more powerful engines in production in 1952. Since the figures are sourced from the Swiss annual publication *Automobil Revue – Katalognummer*,[33] all power outputs are quoted in the metric PS rather than in bhp. Bear in mind that the power outputs quoted for British and American engines were probably measured by the SAE standard which gives higher figures than the DIN or CUNA standards used for most Continental cars. The table includes all engines with a quoted output of 150PS or over, and selected engines with less than 150PS but with high specific outputs. Bentley, Pegaso and Rolls-Royce, which did not disclose power outputs, have had to be omitted.

The cross-section is not of the earliest type of XK 120 engine as it shows the carburettors introduced in 1950. (JDHT)

1952 ENGINES, IN ORDER OF SPECIFIC OUTPUT

Make, model	Country of origin	Engine type	Capacity	Compression ratio	Power output in PS	Specific output in PS/litre
Ferrari 212 Export	Italy	V12, 2xsohc	2563cc	8.4:1	170	66.3
Frazer Nash Mille Miglia	Britain	In-line 6, ohv	1971cc	8.5:1	126	63.9
Jaguar C-type (9:1 CR)	Britain	In-line 6, dohc	3442cc	9:1	213	61.9
Jaguar C-type (8:1 CR)	Britain	In-line 6, dohc	3442cc	8:1	203	59.0
Bugatti 101 C (supercharged)	France	In-line 8, dohc	3257cc	6.5:1	190	58.3
Ferrari 340 America	Italy	V12, 2xsohc	4102cc	8:1	220	53.6
Alfa Romeo 1900 C	Italy	In-line 4, dohc	1884cc	7.75:1	100	53.1
Maserati A6G 2000	Italy	In-line 6, sohc	1954cc	7.8:1	100	51.1
Mercedes-Benz 300 S	Germany	In-line 6, sohc	2996cc	7.5:1	150	50.1
Jaguar XK120, Mark VII	Britain	In-line 6, dohc	3442cc	8:1	162	47.1
Healey 2.4 (Riley engine)	Britain	In-line 4, ohv	2443cc	6.9:1	107	43.8
Talbot Lago Grand Sport	France	In-line 6, ohv	4482cc	7.5:1	195	43.5
Delahaye 235	France	In-line 6, ohv	3557cc	8:1	152	42.7
Aston Martin DB2	Britain	In-line 6, dohc	2580cc	6.5:1	108	41.9
Bugatti 101	France	In-line 8, dohc	3257cc	6.8:1	135	41.4
De Soto Fire Dome Eight	USA	V8, ohv	4254cc	7:1	162	35.8
Cadillac Series 62 (US model)	USA	V8, ohv	5424cc	7.5:1	193	35.6
Chrysler Saratoga/New Yorker	USA	V8, ohv	5426cc	7.5:1	183	33.7
Buick Roadmaster	USA	In-line 8, ohv	5249cc	7.5:1	172	32.7
Oldsmobile 88, 98 (US model)	USA	V8, ohv	4974cc	7.5:1	162	32.6
Lincoln	USA	V8, ohv	5203cc	7.5:1	162	31.1
Packard Patrician	USA	In-line 8, sv	5358cc	7.8:1	157	29.3
Daimler DE36	Britain	In-line 8, ohv	5460cc	6.3:1	152	27.8

What would an XK parts supplier not give for this array to-day? The engine store at Browns Lane, these are later engines with the stepped sump and the fabricated steel fan, and many are likely to be for Mark VII saloons. (JDHT)

It will incidentally be noticed that of saloon cars, the Jaguar Mark VII had the engine with the highest specific power output. One reason why Jaguar occupied such a favourable position in 1952 was that the American horsepower race had barely got underway. While there are five new American ohv V8 engines listed in the table, this type of engine would only later prove to be able to deliver much higher power outputs. The specific outputs of engines of this type were soon raised as the increasing availability of high-octane petrol in the USA allowed the use of higher compression ratios than those employed by American manufacturers in 1952. Similarly, of course, the XK engine proved to be capable of further development and with the XK 150 3.8 "S" model of 1959, became regularly available with a 9:1 compression ratio and a claimed specific output of 70bhp/litre based on Jaguar's quoted power output of 265bhp (which was questionable!).

The first public acknowledgement that a new Jaguar engine was under development came in September 1948 when Lt Col A T Goldie Gardner took his pre-war MG EX.135 record car out to Belgium, fitted with a prototype XK (or XJ?) four-cylinder engine, and set a number of new records in the 2-litre class.[34] Gardner felt that he could improve

An XK engine on test at Foleshill in November 1951. The rev. counter on the dynamometer reads 4000rpm, and note the starting handle! – which was only supplied with the very early cars. (JDHT)

the flying mile and for five kilometres. As used in Gardner's car, the engine had a capacity of 1970cc, a 12:1 compression ratio and developed 146bhp at 6000rpm.[35]

Although the record speeds were significantly lower than the 200-plus mph achieved by Gardner in the same car with a supercharged 1100cc MG engine in 1939, his new exploit was given wide coverage in the British press and obviously led to speculation that Jaguar was about to re-enter the 100mph class. In a speech on 30 September at the press launch of the Mark V model, Lyons himself was quoted in *The Motor* as saying that the engine lent to Gardner was "a perfectly standard engine as will be fitted to the new sports car which will be announced in the near future".[36] Presumably the general public had no idea of the new car, and even those in the industry or the press would, on the basis of the Gardner records, perhaps have expected just a four-cylinder car. Above all, few anticipated that the new model would be launched as early as the eve of the Motor Show.

The Jaguar-powered Gardner Special, better known as the MG EX.135, during its run at Jabbeke in 1948. (JDHT)

on the existing Class E records but found that no suitable engine was available from MG or within the Nuffield organisation. In early 1948, he had seen the engine in Harry Weslake's laboratory, and had learnt that this was a new Jaguar unit. He approached Lyons, who readily agreed to lend Gardner an engine and promised a power output of 140bhp – a promise which he kept, despite the figures quoted above. The engine was delivered and installed in the car by early September, and Gardner's party, including "Wally" Hassan from Jaguar, went across to Belgium in readiness for the run, scheduled for 14 September, on a closed stretch of the Jabbeke-Aeltre motorway just inland from Ostend. That afternoon, Gardner set new class records at 176.694mph (more than 284km/h) for the flying kilometre, and at slightly lower speeds for

When Jaguar released details of the XK Super Sports with either the 2-litre or the 3½-litre engine at the end of October it seems to have come as a genuine surprise to most observers, judging by the press coverage. And that was due in no small measure to the fact that so many other features of the car matched the exciting engine. Even so, in the words of *The Motor* on the launch of the new car, looking back on events of the previous weeks:

"...the knowing ones wagged their heads and said that it would not be long before the Jaguar concern would supplement its range with a model to take the place of the famous Jaguar '100' of pre-war days."[37]

Hassan and Gardner (typically with fag in mouth!) pose with the record car after the run. (JDHT)

An historic occasion. The Mark V convention on 30 September 1948, when Lyons first announced Jaguar's intention to make a sports car. (JDHT)

1. Paper by WM Heynes published in 1960, quoted in Porter & Skilleter *Sir William Lyons*, p55

2. WM Heynes "The Jaguar Engine", published in *The Autocar* 24 Apr 1953, *The Motor* 15 and 22 Apr 1953

3. Porter & Skilleter p87

4. SS Cars Ltd board minutes 1 Oct 1942; letter from Lyons to Skilleter, 1974, quoted in Skilleter *Jaguar Sports Cars* p50, and Porter & Skilleter p86

5. In part from Heynes's 1953 paper, also Hassan *Climax in Coventry*, p61

6. Porter & Skilleter p88

7. Heynes's 1953 paper

8. Types XA to XE were only designed on paper and were not built; Hassan p62

9. With the 8:1 compression ratio, cf. below

10. Until 1947, taxation was based on the RAC hp rating which was calculated using only the bore and the number of cylinders

11. For instance *The Motor*, 27 Oct 1948; these weights, claimed by Jaguar, 21½ cwt for the XK 100 and 22 cwt for the XK 120 were, however, unrealistically low

12. The Swiss *Automobil Revue Katalognummer* (annual catalogue issue), Mar 1950; *The Motor* 4 Oct 1950, weekly price list of British cars.

13. Jaguar Cars *Service Bulletin* no.30 issued 30 Dec 1948.

14. JDHT archive

15. Experimental Department Test Report by J Emerson, 22 Dec 1952, "Proving Tests with Equipment as Used in White Coupé", referring to this engine as "No. 1", JDHT archive

16. Experimental Department Power Unit Research Report No. EXP/1140/JE 22 Sep 1952, "XK 2½ litre Prototype 6 Cylinder Engine", JDHT archive

17. Porter *The Jaguar Scrapbook*, and in *XK Gazette* no.10 Jul 1998; Porter draws the conclusion that with the XK 100 470001, there were 241 rather than 240 alloy bodied cars, which I believe to be wrong; see also *Australian Jaguar Magazine* no.108, 2003

18. Heynes's 1953 paper

19. Skilleter p55

20. The following section is based on the article "The Jaguar XK 120" in *Automobile Engineer* Jul 1950; also Newcomb & Spurr "Jaguar XK 120" *Proceedings of the Institution of Mechanical Engineers* vol.202 no.D3 1988

21. *The Autocar* 20 Oct 1950, feature on the Mark VII; *Motor Sport* Feb and Apr 1951, Mark VII advertisement

22. Jaguar Cars *Service Bulletin* no.59, Jan 1950; cp. Jaguar Cars *Jaguar XK 120 Service Manual* pA.25

23. Jaguar Cars *Service Bulletin* no.119, Feb 1953, covering modifications that might be made to earlier engines to benefit from high-octane Premium Grade petrol, including the fitting of 8:1 pistons etc.

24. Jaguar Cars *Service Bulletin* no.95, "Tuning Modification on XK120 Cars for Competition Purposes" Jun 1951, quoted in *The Motor* 4 Jul 1951, *The Autocar*, 17 Aug 1951

25. *Service Manual* pB.38

26. Schmid *Jaguar XK 120* p73

27. Heynes's 1953 paper

28. *Automobile Engineer* Jul 1950: "The dry weight of engine and gearbox is 640 lb, of which the gearbox accounts for 110 lb."

29. Heynes's 1953 paper, also "Tuning Modifications…" in *Service Bulletin* no.95

30. "Tuning Modifications…" *Service Bulletin* no.95

31. The higher power output figures from *The Autocar* 13 Jul 1951 p822 and *The Motor* 18 Jul 1951, the lower figures from Skilleter p117. The larger inlet valves and the 1½in size for exhaust valves are quoted in Heynes's 1953 paper

32. Skilleter p131

33. 1952 issue, published 20 Mar 1952

34. Gardner *Magic M.P.H.* pp110-17; Hassan p64

35. Hassan p64; Skilleter p55; *The Autocar* for 29 Oct 1948 quoted lower figures, of 10:1 and "over 140bhp"

36. *The Motor* 6 Oct 1948

37. *The Motor* 27 Oct 1948

Chapter Three

Designing the XK 120

*A rare photo of a complete
XK 120 chassis on its trolley
on the assembly line at
Foleshill in November 1951,
almost ready for having the
body in the background
mounted. (JDHT)*

The XK engine, discussed in chapter 2, was the key element of Jaguar's plans for new post-war cars. As we have seen, initially the company's efforts were directed towards a high-performance luxury saloon, while a sports car was a lower priority.

To go with the new engine, a new chassis was clearly required as well. As with the engine, the early work was undertaken for the saloon, and its subsequent modification to serve as the basis for a sports car was an afterthought. The germ of the new post-war Jaguar chassis went back to experiments carried out by William Heynes and Walter Hassan (who joined as

Chief Experimental Engineer in September 1938[1]) before the war. At that time, SS Cars Limited was not exactly at the forefront of chassis design, even by the undemanding standards prevailing in the Britain of the 1930s.

The basic design of the pre-war SS Jaguar chassis frame could be traced back to the revised SS1 chassis introduced for the 1933 model year, on which, for the first time, the chassis side members were carried below the rear axle. This feature was undoubtedly inspired by Lyons's desire for building his cars as low as possible, and was retained until 1948. Otherwise, the SS Jaguar chassis and its associated parts were completely conventional, with the rigid axles carried on semi-elliptic springs, centre-lock wire wheels, mechanical brakes, and steering with worm gear. It was typical of British pre-war practice in general. It has often been stated that the excellent road surfaces prevailing in Britain, coupled with the low speeds at which most British motorists drove, delayed the introduction of modern chassis design in this country. More modern features, however, such as hydraulic brakes and independent front suspension, were slowly gaining ground in the 1930s.

Some of the more advanced Continental designs of the 1930s were admired by British engineers, and would in many ways contribute to post-World War II developments. The most influential design was the front-wheel-drive Citroën introduced in 1934. Since this car was built in Britain, of all the modern Continental designs it was most likely to have been the one sold here in largest numbers. Apart from its front-wheel drive, the Citroën incorporated such features as

unitary body construction, torsion bar suspension (independent at the front), hydraulic brakes and rack-and-pinion steering. Among post-war British designs, those which paid homage to the French car included the Jowett Javelin by Gerald Palmer, the Lagonda by WO Bentley, the Morris Minor (and other Morris cars) by Alec Issigonis, and the Riley RM by Harry Rush – as well as the Jaguar Mark V and XK 120 by Lyons, Heynes and Hassan. Most notably, all of these cars featured independent front suspension with torsion bars.

It was during the 1920s that independent front suspension was recognised as the way forward, when the introduction of front brakes and low pressure tyres increased unsprung front-axle weight and resulted in "wheel wobble or shimmy, axle tramp, and other evils".[2] It is, perhaps, less obvious why torsion bars should enjoy a vogue from the 1930s onwards. Porsche in Germany was early in this field, and became particularly famous for the system with transverse torsion bars, used on the Auto Union racing cars and later the Volkswagen. The longitudinal torsion bars used on the Citroën may have been adopted for two reasons. First, they had a certain advantage in packaging terms over coil springs on a front-wheel-drive car, and secondly they transferred some of the suspension stresses into the central and strongest area of the unitary body. It may be noted that neither of these factors was strictly speaking relevant to a rear-wheel-drive car with a separate chassis.

William Heynes was, however, an acknowledged admirer of the Citroën, and before the war he and Hassan had designed an experimental short-wishbone torsion bar suspension which was fitted to a Jaguar chassis.[3] Barrie Price has identified this car as chassis number XA 100, registered DKV 120; outwardly it looked like a normal 3½-litre saloon.[4] This was, perhaps, not a completely satisfactory experiment, since the pre-war chassis, in the manner of the period, was somewhat flexible to supplement the hard leaf-spring suspension. Hassan remembered that this first experimental independent suspension was rather hard, too. While further experiments were carried out during and immediately after the war, including a coil-spring suspension with longer wishbones, eventually a return was made to the original idea of short top wishbones with lower arms operating longitudinal torsion bars. The stub axles were carried on ball joints top and bottom, and the front suspension incorporated telescopic shock absorbers. A young engineer called Bob Knight was involved in the development of the new suspension.[5]

The former Rolls-Royce engineer Maurice Olley,

when working for General Motors in the early 1930s, established that a great improvement in ride was achieved if the front suspension was softer than the rear suspension, so reducing pitch, but this necessitated the use of independent front suspension to avoid shimmy and steering problems and to preserve good handling characteristics.[6] It was, however, desirable to "tune" the rear suspension to harmonise with that at the front, which therefore predicated the use also of a softer – possibly independent – rear suspension. Naturally, the use of softer suspension generally pointed towards the introduction of a far more rigid structure, such as the unitary body used by Citroën and a few others before the war.[7]

So, when the design of a proper post-war Jaguar chassis got under way, in order to accommodate not

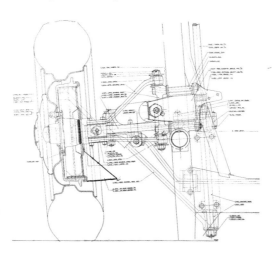

This was Jaguar's first independent front suspension design. The upper wishbone and the shock absorber are prominent in this photo of an early production XK 120. (JDHT)

The front mounting of the torsion bar is at the bottom of this plan view of the suspension layout. (JDHT).

Far right: The cross member also served to support the rear of the gearbox, and the fly-off handbrake lever. (JDHT)

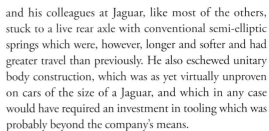

At the rear, the chassis side members rose steeply to clear the rear axle. The rear suspension was of conventional design, but the use of a hypoid bevel final drive was still unusual, note how low the prop shaft is relative to the final drive housing. (JDHT)

only the softer independent front suspension but also a softer rear suspension with greater spring travel, Heynes came up with a far more rigid frame, which was now carried above the rear axle. The underslung type of frame had imposed limitations on suspension movements, and therefore permitted only a fairly hard rear suspension. It also limited ground clearance. Few British manufacturers at the time had the courage to consider independent rear suspension as well, the Bentley-designed Lagonda being the main exception. Heynes

and his colleagues at Jaguar, like most of the others, stuck to a live rear axle with conventional semi-elliptic springs which were, however, longer and softer and had greater travel than previously. He also eschewed unitary body construction, which was as yet virtually unproven on cars of the size of a Jaguar, and which in any case would have required an investment in tooling which was probably beyond the company's means.

As the frame was designed primarily for a large saloon car, the dimensions were generous, and the torsional rigidity was excellent: "For its weight, probably the most rigid frame incorporated in any passenger car".[8] The box section side members were 3½in (88.9mm) wide, and 6½in (165.1mm) deep at their deepest point. On the saloon version, which had a wheelbase of 10ft (3048mm; the same as the pre-war type six-cylinder chassis), the individual side members were virtually straight, but the frame was arranged so that they converged towards the front in plan view. They were horizontal until just in front of the rear axle when they swept abruptly above the rear axle, allowing plenty of room for suspension movement. In the centre of the frame was a substantial x-shaped or cruciform cross member, supplemented by conventional cross members at the front, in front of the rear axle, and at the rear end of the chassis.

In order to adopt this chassis design for a sports car, the wheelbase was shortened to 102in (2591mm), and the width of the chassis was similarly reduced. The big cruciform member was replaced by a single box

section cross member, which incorporated the gearbox mounting and the anchorage points for the front torsion bars, with their adjustment. This shortened XK 120 frame, bereft of the cruciform member, still had torsional rigidity of 1750 lb ft per degree,[9] although it has also been commented that "The frame was very solid but the torsional stiffness of a ladder frame, even with box section members, is nothing remarkable".[10] The after parts of the side members became parallel and were more obviously "sleeved" into the front two-thirds. There was a tubular cross member at the rear, which also provided the rear hanging points for the rear springs.

As regards other features of the chassis design, it should be noted that this was the first Jaguar to use hydraulic brakes. Where the forthcoming Mark V saloon used Girling self-servo brakes with twin leading shoes at the front, for some reason a change was made to Lockheed brakes, again of the 2LS type, on the sports model. Common to both cars was the Burman steering box of the worm and nut type, with re-circulating balls. The transmission comprised a conventional Borg & Beck single dry plate 10in clutch mechanically operated by a lever, and a four-speed gearbox with synchromesh on the upper three ratios, changed by a short remote control lever. The gearbox was a Jaguar design but made by Moss, and used single helical gears; it had already been seen on the post-war so-called "Mark IV" models. Drive was taken by a Hardy-Spicer open prop shaft – two-piece type on the Mark V, single-piece on the XK 120 – to the rear axle, by ENV or later Salisbury, which was of the banjo type. It had hypoid bevel gears for the differential, with semi-floating half shafts. Here Jaguar was a pioneer in Britain, having introduced hypoid bevel differentials already on the first post-war cars in 1945. Wheels were of the five-stud pressed-steel disc type, of 16in diameter with 5in wide rims.

The fact that the XK 120 chassis design was, in effect, a "cut down" saloon chassis was important in determining the car's characteristics. For a sports car of its time, the XK 120 had unheard-of refinement and ride comfort, but the relatively soft suspension which made this possible also meant that the car rolled a great deal on corners. Then the chassis was relatively high off the ground, and since the sports car was built as low as possible, this meant that, despite the overall length of 14ft 5½in (4407mm) there was actually relatively little room in the passenger compartment, and the driving position was awkward. The steering column, lowered and lengthened compared with the saloon, was raked at only 10 degrees from horizontal. At around three turns lock-to-lock,[11] the steering was

The rear mounting points for the torsion bars were on the front of the chassis cross member. (JDHT)

not particularly high-geared by contemporary standards and was not as direct and precise as one could wish for on a high-performance sports car. It would be replaced by rack and pinion on the XK 140. The brakes were not above reproach either. While they were fine for everyday motoring in the early 1950s, it quickly became evident from experiences with the race and rally cars that they were prone to fade, and the linings wore down quickly. Jaguar twice changed the lining material on production cars, and adopted self-

The famous (or infamous?) Moss gearbox, the is the original type fitted to early XK 120s, with bell housing and the characteristic remote control gearlever which was cranked forward. (JDHT)

The steering box and the steering linkage were right at the front of the car. (JDHT)

The "coachbuilder's arrangement" drawing of the XK 120 chassis shows the layout in every detail. (JDHT)

complete car rather than an engine design. On a list compiled in October 1949,[12] some of these cars feature, as XJ no.1, XJ no.3, and XJ no.4, all fitted with 1948 ("Mark IV") saloon bodies, and with 3½-litre pushrod engines. There is also "XJ Mk.5 no.1" with a drophead coupé body, and a 3½-litre saloon with "1948 body" and "1948 frame" with *coil* springs, referred to as Mark 2 no.3. This is all a little confusing, but it is worth quoting the speech that Lyons made at the Mark V convention held on 30 September 1948, where he explained that there had, in effect, been four experimental post-war cars preceding the final Mark V design, and this was the reason why this car was called Mark V.[13]

It had always been the intention that Jaguar's post-war saloon should have a modern, full-width body, the design that was later developed to become the Mark VII. However, there were delays before the Pressed Steel Company at Cowley could tool up and begin manufacture of this new body, and so it was decided to launch the new chassis with the old pushrod engine and a body built in-house by Jaguar. This became the interim Mark V model, introduced before the 1948 Motor Show, with a modernised version of the traditional pre-war Jaguar style.

By the 1930s, it was commonly acknowledged that

adjusting brakes, while the later availability of wire wheels helped to keep the brakes cool. Ultimately, these problems led to the adoption of disc brakes on the XK 150.

During the gestation period of the new chassis design in the immediate post-war years, a number of experimental cars were built, referred to, interestingly enough, by the code XJ; the first time in the history of Jaguar that these letters appear as referring to a

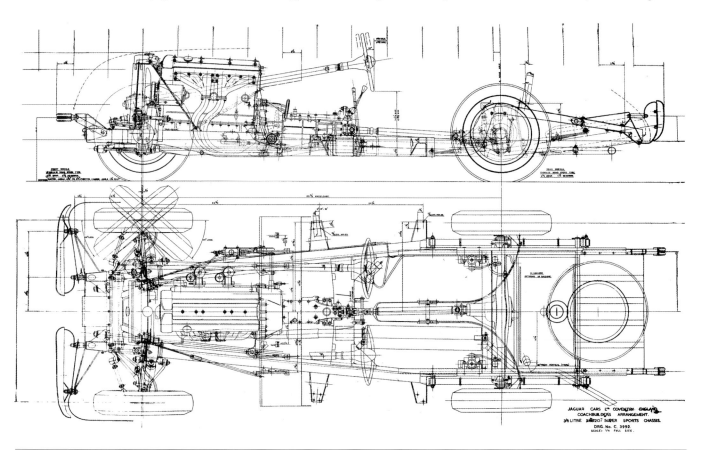

the future belonged to the full width bodied streamlined car. Most of the exploratory work in this field was carried out in Germany; the earliest streamline cars had appeared soon after World War I when the Versailles treaty prevented Germany from continuing in the field of airship and aircraft development, where engineers such as Jaray and Rumpler had been active. They now turned their attention to cars, and their pioneering efforts were followed by other German and central European designers, including Kamm, Ledwinka and Porsche.

Development of aerodynamic cars was accelerated in Germany after 1933 because of two factors, both inspired by the new Nazi regime: the creation of a national network of high speed motorways, the *Auto-bahnen*; and a preoccupation with motor sport. Several streamline designs saw production, while many others were previewed at the Berlin Motor Show, or were built exclusively for racing.

Where streamline cars appeared in other countries, including Britain, they were either closely based on German designs or were somewhat amateurish, showing no real understanding of aerodynamics, but simply following a prevailing fashion. A good example of this trend was the SS Airline saloon of 1935. In 1938, however, Reid Railton designed a superb streamline body for Gardner's MG record car, a design which was probably inspired by the Auto Union streamliners, and which attracted notice even in Germany.

Another aircraft designer who turned to cars in the 1920s was the Frenchman Gabriel Voisin, who produced small numbers of the *Laboratoire* racing cars, while around the same time some racing Bugattis were fitted with the "tank" full-width bodywork. Other French sports cars experimented with similar bodies, including Chenard et Walcker, Aries and Tracta. The intention behind these designs was to improve the speed of racing cars with modest power, particularly on the Le Mans 24-hour circuit with its famous Mulsanne straight. Some years later, the Bugatti type 57 was fitted with an updated "tank" body to become a highly efficient sports-racing car which twice conquered at Le Mans, in 1937 and 1939.

A similar conclusion was drawn by the few German sports car makers who ventured to Le Mans. From

Lyons's discarded toys, redundant prototypes for scrapping. These may be the "Mark I" to "Mark IV" models. The most complete car would appear to be similar to the Mark V but fitted with a radiator grille in the style of the XK 120. (JDHT)

The 1923 Voisin Laboratoire *was a very early experiment in "streamlining" a racing car.*

Even more advanced was the early Bugatti "tank" of 1923.

Tracta was one of several French manufacturers who ran a streamlined car at Le Mans, here in 1929.

1937 to 1939, Adler raced some efficient lightweight aerodynamic coupés, and their example was followed by BMW in 1939. BMW's production model 328 was a semi-streamlined design. The higher speed of an aerodynamic car would also improve the odds in the Italian Mille Miglia road race. Some streamlined Alfa Romeos and Lancias appeared, while a Le Mans-type BMW was the winner of the last pre-war race, held in 1940.

The problem with many early aerodynamic racers was that their bodywork was ill-matched to contemporary conventional sports car chassis which, right through the 1930s, often remained of the vintage type discussed previously – flexible chassis combined with hard suspension. Streamline bodies were bulky, and in order to save weight, some were of rather fragile construction, which aggravated the

The Bugatti 57 "tank" won at Le Mans in 1937 and 1939, this is the 1937 winner of Wimille and Benoist.

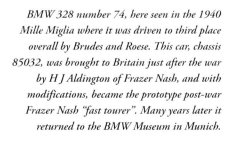

The Jaray-influenced Adler Rennlimousine, an early example of a closed racing car, which appeared at Le Mans in 1937-39.

Full-width bodied streamlined sports cars also emerged from Italy, here is a Lancia Aprilia. Streamlined Aprilias ran in the Mille Miglia and other events, including the 1938 TT.

BMW 328 number 74, here seen in the 1940 Mille Miglia where it was driven to third place overall by Brudes and Roese. This car, chassis 85032, was brought to Britain just after the war by H J Aldington of Frazer Nash, and with modifications, became the prototype post-war Frazer Nash "fast tourer". Many years later it returned to the BMW Museum in Munich.

Brave but misguided effort – the post-war HRG "Aerodynamic". Here two roadsters and a coupé await scrutineering before the 1949 Le Mans.

problem. Only a few designers had begun to appreciate the advantage of rigid chassis construction in combination with softer suspension, although some had this solution forced upon them as they began to investigate unitary body construction. The unitary principle in itself encouraged new departures in styling, with wings becoming more integrated into the overall shape of the car.

Not until after World War II were these lessons fully learnt in Britain. Here again, most of the pioneers were sports car makers. In a classic example of "technology transfer" – or perhaps plunder – the Aldington brothers of Frazer Nash brought a 1940 BMW 328 Mille Miglia roadster back to Britain,

An SS 100 was re-bodied post-war as the Pycroft Special, and was given some publicity at the time, but this half-hearted effort is unlikely to have had any direct influence on Jaguar's own sports car project.

fitted it with a different radiator grille and presented it as their post-war model. (This car eventually went home to the BMW Museum in Munich in the 1970s and was then fitted with a BMW-style grille again![14]) HRG gamely offered the Aerodynamic on their traditional 1500 chassis, but this was a classic mistake as the body shook itself to pieces and most were re-bodied in the conventional style. A similar experiment was the one-off Pycroft Jaguar, a privately built special with a modern body fitted on an SS 100 chassis.[15] Vanden Plas in Belgium similarly re-bodied an SS 100 in a transitional style. Much more important was the first Healey of 1946, combining an advanced post-war chassis with streamlined bodywork, and fitted with a 2.4-litre Riley engine which was powerful enough to make this Britain's fastest production car before the XK 120.[16]

Meanwhile, the styling revolution had begun on two fronts; in Italy with Pininfarina's Cisitalia coupé, and in the USA with Darrin's Kaiser and Loewy's Studebaker. These cars all featured full-width bodies with fully integrated wings, and became the models for numerous imitators. Indeed, most of the first post-war generation of British saloons took their inspiration directly from Detroit, with results that were not always harmonious.

At Jaguar, William Lyons was effectively the chief stylist. There are two points about Lyons as a stylist that are worth bearing in mind. First, his readiness to learn and to seek inspiration from other cars that he saw at *concours d'élégance*, at motor shows, or in motoring magazines.[17] Secondly, his awareness of the post-war styling trends, which he had seen for himself at the Paris Motor Show in 1946.[18] It cannot be doubted that Lyons also knew of cars such as the Le Mans Bugatti and the BMW, and most likely drew some inspiration from them. Even the normal production BMW 328 might have been an inspiration; it is known that Jaguar looked closely at such a car, owned by Leslie Johnson.[19] Certainly the profile of the 328 is not dissimilar to the XK 120. The company had actually bought a BMW saloon before the war, for the use of the development department, and still owned it in 1949, although Lyons then asked Heynes to reduce his fleet![20]

There is good evidence that, in the early post-war period, Lyons drew on inspiration from some of the new Italian designs. In 1947, he asked John Dugdale, then with *The Autocar*, for further information and photos of Italian designs which had been featured in a series of articles in that magazine[21] – while in 2005 I discovered further photos of Italian coachwork in the JDHT archive, filed away in July 1948, one of them is reproduced here. When, on 26 January 1948, Dugdale visited Jaguar in preparation for writing the

John Dugdale of The Autocar *sent William Lyons some photos of contemporary Italian coachwork design in August 1947, however this Pinin Farina bodied Alfa Romeo was filed away in the photographic archive in July 1948. Is there a hint here of the grille and wing line adopted for the XK 120? (JDHT)*

This is the pre-XK prototype which was photographed in June 1948. There are clearly some XK elements, but the grille and windscreen are rather awkward. (JDHT)

In the rear three-quarter view, we can also see the dashboard fitted with a full set of instruments, of a type not seen on any other Jaguar. (JDHT)

article about the company "For Export Only",[22] Lyons personally showed him two mock-ups in the experimental workshop. One was the precursor of the later Mark VII saloon. The other was a sports car, and Dugdale made sketches of both, with notes detailing their specification.[23] Luckily, photos were taken for the record of this XK 120 in embryo. It must also be this car that was listed on the inventory of development department cars in late 1949 as "1½L. [litre] XK No. 1, 2-str. [seater] Special Body Gunmetal (engine) XK 1½L. 4-cyl (chassis) XL No.1 Mark 1".[24]

Its proportions suggested that it used a shorter chassis than the pre-war SS 100, and indeed Lyons confessed to Dugdale that "it needed 6in more chassis or was too wide". Dugdale found the car "rather bulbous… The rear was all enclosed and reminiscent of the Riley Sprite. The front was an unsuccessful Healey-like Italian". He noted on his sketch, "car appears too stubby – tail good – wings good – rad [radiator grille] bad". The grille in Dugdale's sketch had vertical bars and was very XK 120-like but the photos show an inelegant arrangement of horizontal bars. His sketch shows no rear wheel spats, but they were clearly experimented with as they are also seen in the photos. The body was made of alloy, "of very strong construction weighing less than 200 lb". The

cockpit, containing two bucket seats and "lots of gearbox", was "unprotected" except by an awkward three-piece windscreen.

At this time, the new sports car was intended to be fitted with the 2-litre twin overhead camshaft engine, but Dugdale noted less about the technical specification of the car. His note that it was a "development of SS 100" may suggest that it did *not* have the independent front suspension that he observed on the saloon prototype at the same time, but he did note the disc wheels.

Some time between Dugdale's visit in January and the unveiling of the XK 120 almost exactly nine months later, a transformation took place, and the ugly duckling became the swan. Lyons was undoubtedly helped by Fred Gardner, who nominally ran the sawmill, but who was also Lyons's co-conspirator when it came to new styling projects.[25] Lyons himself has stated unequivocally that the XK 120 design was "done more quickly than anything [I had] done before or since … it was not altered from the first attempt".[26] In fact, the design of the final body shape is supposed to have taken two weeks, while the actual construction of the first complete prototype took another six weeks. This is such a well-established legend in Jaguar history that it is almost a pity to try to challenge it, although

The side view clearly shows the family relationship with the XK which was soon to be developed from this prototype. (JDHT)

The original XK 120 mock-up, with wooden supports under the sill and the rear end, photographed outside the Foleshill factory, probably in September 1948. As yet it lacks bumpers and the air vents in the front valance. The front number plate mounting is improvised. The side lamps appear slightly smaller than the later production type. The windscreen frame is topless, and neither centre nor side pillars are as adopted for production. The "seat" is a simple wooden board. A re-touched version of this photo was used in The Motor *for 27 October 1948. (Paul Skilleter/Jaguar)*

... and this is the version that was published in The Motor. *(JDHT)*

some of Lyons's colleagues have done so. But as Heynes later said, tongue firmly in cheek: "I would not like to contradict my managing director."[27] We may also reflect that Lyons still had enough time to have several different radiator grilles made to experiment with on the prototype.[28] Indeed, one of the photos of the prototype reproduced here shows a non-standard eleven-bar grille.

If the XK 120 design was completed as quickly as

Lyons claimed, the explanation must be that the original sports car prototype of 1947-48 had bequeathed the fundamentals of its design to its successor. There were similarities, including the wing lines and overall shape, the use of disc wheels, with spats for the rear wheels, and the suggestion of an alligator bonnet incorporating a grille of similar shape. Even the door shutlines and the shape of the cockpit foreshadowed the XK 120 to come. Nevertheless, apart from the

gawky grille with horizontal bars, the earlier car had headlamps positioned awkwardly low down in the leading edges of the front wings. The three-piece windscreen was ugly, and perhaps most importantly, the rear end was too short and the rear wings were not yet fully integrated into the main shape.

By contrast, the rear end of the XK 120 was lengthened, producing a more elegantly flowing line to the tail, and the rear wings were almost completely integrated. The pronounced inward sweep of the rear wings behind the wheel arch ensured that in front three-quarter view the XK 120 shrank, and from this angle the rear wings appeared almost concentric with the wheel arches. The longer tail was added not only for aesthetic reasons but also, more prosaically, to house the concealed spare wheel and fuel tank while still allowing the car to offer a reasonable amount of luggage space. The basic proportions of the XK 120 – short front overhang, long bonnet and the windscreen midway between the axles – were still classic, and

fundamentally those of a pre-war car. Compared with the SS 100, the XK had a wheelbase 2in (51mm) shorter, but was 20in (508mm) longer overall, thanks to its rear overhang.

Although the XK 120 is commonly held to consist of curved lines, there are three key straight lines which define the side view – the bonnet line, the sloping front wing line, and the lower body line. The bonnet and wing lines are tangents to the front wheel, which dominates the profile as the rear wheel is modestly hiding behind its spat. Curiously, a wire-wheeled XK 120 which lacks spats is somehow aesthetically less satisfying and, in any case, the disc wheels suit the style of the car far better. The front of the front wing forms a circle concentric with the wheel and the perfectly circular wheelarch, while the bonnet line and the lower body line are virtually parallel, exaggerating the length of the car. The bonnet line continues rearwards in the gently falling curve of the tail, and the point where the curve of the tail meets the lower body

In the rear three quarter view of the mock up, it can be seen that the dashboard is plain, there are no rear lamps at all, and the rear number plate mounting is also improvised. (JDHT)

By mid-October the real car was completed, and this is without doubt chassis 660001, HKV 455, the 1948 Motor Show car. It has now got the definitive windscreen, but of course with straight side pillars. It has acquired rear lamps, but not as yet bumpers. It has a proper seat, and even side screens. (Paul Skilleter/Jaguar)

line is also almost where an imaginary continuation of the front wing line would intersect with the two.

As with other great Jaguar designs, the final XK 120 was a classic example of "less is more" – it was utterly simple and wonderfully free of ornamentation; even the headlamp and side lamp nacelles barely disturbed the clean outline. At the rear, of course, allowances

had to be made for lamps, the number plate and a boot handle, but the fuel filler was hidden, first in the boot, then under a separate flap. The two-seater had no external door handles, and originally no visible locks for the rear wheel spats. As first conceived, the car had no bumpers at all, as seen on the mock-up which was featured in some contemporary press illus-

The interior of the same car, the dashboard is complete more or less as production cars, but there is no grab handle for the passenger, nor a mirror. A few minor controls were later re-arranged. Not only the steering wheel is light in colour, but so are the column shroud, and the unusual cover for the column adjustment. The odometer reads 1 mile! (Paul Skilleter/Jaguar)

With the background removed, this photo was published in The Autocar for 29 October 1948. Still no bumpers, but note the plinth or brackets for the front number plate. The street setting is unusual, but probably the photo was taken at the end of the press preview of the car at Grosvenor House Hotel in Park Lane on 22 October 1948. Looks like an obliging transport driver has been roped in to hold the background sheet. (Paul Skilleter)

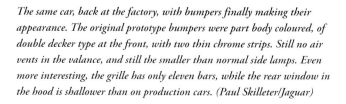

The same car, back at the factory, with bumpers finally making their appearance. The original prototype bumpers were part body coloured, of double decker type at the front, with two thin chrome strips. Still no air vents in the valance, and still the smaller than normal side lamps. Even more interesting, the grille has only eleven bars, while the rear window in the hood is shallower than on production cars. (Paul Skilleter/Jaguar)

The rear view of the prototype shows the slim rear bumper – or rubbing strip – attached to the boot lid. The rear lamps are lower down and have smaller housings than normal. The rear number plate is mounted directly on the boot lid, which is closed with an under sill catch. There is a bracket for the mirror, but the mirror itself has yet to be fitted. There is no external fuel filler, as this was in the boot. (Paul Skilleter/Jaguar)

trations provided by the company. Then the 1948 Motor Show car appeared with slim half bumpers at the front and a rubbing strip on the lower edge of the boot lid, while production models acquired vertical overriders at the rear. The radiator grille that Lyons took such pains over ended up with 13 slim, vertical bars, delicately curved in side view to match the curve of the front wing and bonnet. As first seen, the windscreen side pillars were vertical when viewed from the front, but these straight pillars clearly jarred and they were soon curved inwards.

The uncluttered, harmonious design of the XK 120 offered a remarkable contrast to some other British cars of the same period which arguably shared basic design principles with the Jaguar. The same Earls Court Show that saw the XK's debut also witnessed the launch of the Austin A90 Atlantic, a dumpy and over-fussy interpretation of the streamline theme, and its amazingly similar but grossly oversized counterpart in the shape of a Hooper drophead coupé body on the

Daimler Straight-Eight chassis. Aston Martin and Frazer Nash both tried hard with the modern idiom but neither achieved the purity of line of the XK 120. The Bristol 401 was, perhaps, the most elegant of other contemporary British cars and, like the Jaguar, had been influenced by Continental designs, in this case particularly those of Touring in Italy. This was appropriate because, at this time in Europe, only the Italians had so far completely mastered the new style; Pinin Farina with the Cisitalia and later the Lancia Aurelia GT, and Touring with the starkly functional *Barchetta* ("little boat") for Ferrrari.

Not surprisingly, the XK 120 became the inspiration for the next generation of British sports cars. Its influence was most clearly seen in the Austin-Healey 100 of 1952 and the MGA of 1955. The XK 120 design was also successfully adapted to other body styles on the same chassis, the fixed-head and drophead coupés. By contrast, Jaguar lost the plot slightly with the later updates of the XK shape. The XK 140

THE JAGUAR XK SUPER SPORTS TWO-SEATER

The famous publicity photograph which was a blanked-out and retouched version of the photo taken at the show. Here the car still has the straight windscreen pillars; in later versions of this photo, the retoucher put in curved pillars. (JDHT)

… and this is the artist's rendering based on the same photo, as used in the first full XK 120 catalogue in 1949. (Jaguar)

Since we do not know the exact date of this photo, it is not conclusive proof that HKV 455 was fitted with the six cylinder engine at the 1948 Motor Show, but this photo was taken either just before, or soon after the show. While there is no chassis plate visible, the dual fuel pumps, the sloping bulkhead and the apertures in the inner wing valance are all believed to be unique to HKV 455. The cooling system is unpressurised, and the sorbo rubber strip on the header tank is unusual. (Paul Skilleter/Jaguar)

was marred by its bigger bumpers – however necessary they were for the American market – and coarser radiator grille. The more extensively modernised XK 150, while still handsome, lacked the appealing simplicity of the original. In any case, 10 years later the basic shape was beginning to look a little out of date.

The decision to make the original XK 120 body in aluminium was taken at an early stage, before the body shape had been finalised; Dugdale's notes from January 1948, quoted above, quite specifically refer to the "alloy" body of the sports car that he saw.[29] There were a number of reasons why aluminium was chosen. First and foremost, at this time steel for car manufacture was rationed, and could only be obtained with a government permit. The issue of permits favoured manufacturers or products with proven or expected export success. The XK 120 was a new product, for which Jaguar did not have great expectations, since little more than 300 SS 100s had been made before the war. Similarly, Rover chose aluminium over steel for its leap into the unknown with the Land Rover. Secondly, as the XK 120 was expected to be a limited production model, it was sensible to avoid the high

tooling costs associated with an all-steel body, and make the bodies by hand using traditional coachbuilding techniques involving aluminium panels over an ash frame. Thirdly, although the body shop at Foleshill had switched from aluminium to steel for the SS1 in 1932, and had gone over to all-steel bodywork with the second-generation Jaguar saloon in 1937, there must still have been a resource base of the requisite skills available within the company.

The construction of the body actually employed a mixture of materials. Aluminium was used for all the exterior panels. The largest sub-assembly consisted of the front wings welded together with the scuttle. Steel was used for the front bulkhead, front inner wheelarches, and the integral "boot box", which combined the rear bulkhead and rear inner wings. The main ash frame was under the aluminium skin of the rear tonneau panel. The alligator bonnet was of all-aluminium construction and incorporated the radiator grille, while the doors and the boot lid were skinned in aluminium over ash frames. The exterior aluminium panels were supplied by the local Coventry firm Abbey Panels.[30] The ash frame and fabricated

The final result, an early alloy-bodied open two-seater with right-hand drive. (JDHT)

The spats on disc-wheeled cars soon acquired a budget lock at the top, and were fitted over small pegs front and rear at the bottom. (JDHT)

An interesting series of photos of the body construction was taken in March 1951 as an aid to the CKD breakdown and assembly of the XK 120. Here is the fabricated firewall and front bulkhead assembly, with the rear section in the background. The underside of the rear assembly, with the spare wheel tray on the left and the battery boxes on the right. Here is the boot area of the body roughly assembled on its trolley. The fixed-head coupé bodies in the background must be the first batch of this type. (JDHT)

steel sections were made in house, and the final bodies were assembled on a jig in a corner of the Jaguar factory.

The car was completed with a well-trimmed cockpit, incorporating two separate seats of the split-bench type trimmed in hide, often in two-tone schemes with different colours for the outer bolsters and the inner, fluted panels. There was ample width across the car, but legroom was limited, and occupants sat more or less on the floor with legs stretched out horizontally. The steering wheel was set very close to the driver and too near the vertical for the liking of some contemporary commentators. It was a four-spoke Bluemels steering wheel of 18in (457mm) diameter, with telescopic adjustment on the column.

This shot clearly shows the original seats, with the characteristic curved shape to the backrest. (JDHT)

The hood was fixed to the top frame of the windscreen with this central catch, and to the hooks at the top of each side pillar. This is a very early right-hand drive alloy-bodied car with a light-coloured steering wheel, possibly 660002, as the photo was taken in July 1949. (JDHT)

…but this is where you would normally keep the hood of your XK 120: Stowed behind the seats! (JDHT)

It featured a prominent bullet-shaped horn push with the motif of a jaguar's head in profile, operating twin windtone low- and high-note horns. The layout of the leather-covered dashboard had been familiar from Jaguar saloons since 1937, with a central instrument panel where the two large instruments – rev counter with inset clock on the left, speedometer on the right – flanked three smaller gauges and the switches. The instruments had black faces with white needles and printing, and the rev counter needle swept the dial anti-clockwise. The passenger had a grab handle, and stowage was provided for by pockets in the door trims. The floor was fully carpeted, with heelmats in both footwells, while the remote control gear lever was mounted on the transmission tunnel, with a chrome-plated fly-off handbrake on the side of the tunnel furthest from the driver.

The twin-pane V-shape windscreen was fitted in a simple chrome-plated frame. Triplex laminated glass was used on many export cars, particularly for the USA, and toughened glass on others. The hood frame was attached inside the car, on either side behind the doors, and could be quickly removed by undoing two nuts. The mohair hood was available in five standard colours. The frame was originally chrome-plated but later painted, and there was a shallow Perspex rear window in its own chrome-plated frame. When folded, the hood disappeared completely behind the seats, resting on a shelf which also formed a lid over the battery boxes. There were two six-volt batteries, one either side of the propshaft tunnel. The hood was supplemented by loose side screens, with a flap for hand signalling or for getting at the internal door

release cord (there were no external door handles). When not in use, the screens were stored in a tray under the rear tonneau panel. All cars were supplied with a tonneau cover, in mohair to match the hood. In the boot, luggage was carried on a "false floor" made from plywood and carpeted, below which was a separate compartment for the spare wheel, and in front of this was the 15-gallon (68 litres) petrol tank. The filler cap was under a lockable flap at the front left-hand corner of the boot lid (except the very first car, 660001, which had the filler in the boot). A complete set of tools was provided, with smaller items stored in a canvas roll, larger ones fitted in clips.

Electrical equipment was by Lucas. The headlamps were the distinctive PF 770 type, with a separate reflector mounted on a tripod, and flat glass. Cars destined for the USA, however, where sealed beam headlamps were mandatory, were shipped with empty headlamp bowls taped over, and sealed beam units installed after arrival. It appears that the PF 770 headlamps were sometimes shipped loose with the cars, and often fitted by American owners after they had taken delivery! There were short "spears" on top of the headlamp nacelles. The side lamps and tail lamps were standard Lucas items, side lamps being fitted originally in separate chrome-plated housings. Later, a change was made to a larger side lamp which, on export cars, had double filament bulbs so that it could act as a flashing indicator. These lamps were then fitted in painted housings integral with the wing. Rear lamps were mounted in chrome plated cast alloy housings, while the number plate lamp and reversing lamp were combined in a single central chrome-plated unit

The open two-seater still looked good with the hood up and the side screens in place. This photo of a steel-bodied car was taken outside the service department at Foleshill. (JDHT)

that was a standard Lucas design.

The radiator grille was flanked by the two slim chrome-plated half bumpers, and below them was a backing plate for the front number plate. Below and behind each bumper was a shallow slot shaped as a horizontal D in the front valance, to duct air on to the front brake drums. The rear number plate sat on a flat backing plate, mounted on the boot lid. Below it was a lockable boot handle. On either side of the boot lid was a vertical chrome-plated overrider. A bronze and cream circular badge with a head-on view of a jaguar's face – the so called "growler" – surrounded by the legend "Jaguar Cars Ltd Coventry" was fitted on the bonnet directly above and behind the radiator grille. The name Jaguar was also found in hexagonal badges on the hub caps, which were part chrome, part painted body colour to match the wheels. Similarly, later wire-wheeled cars had the word Jaguar on the twin-eared spinners. But you would look in vain for the type designation on the car itself!

One final fitting should be mentioned. After the 1949 Jabbeke run, XK 120 cars with the higher-compression engines for export markets were fitted

CERTIFIED
THAT THIS JAGUAR CAR IS AN
EXACT REPLICA
OF THE RECORD-BREAKING CAR
WHICH ACHIEVED THE SPEED OF
132.6 M.P.H.
AT JABBEKE, BELGIUM, 30 MAY, 1949
CERTIFIED BY

CHIEF ENGINEER
JAGUAR CARS LTD., COVENTRY ENGLAND

with the so-called "replica" plate on the dashboard, in front of the passenger. Over the engraved signature of William Heynes, this stated that the car was an "exact replica" of the car that had been timed at Jabbeke at 132.6 mph.[31]

The Jabbeke "replica" plate as fitted to the earlier cars, quoting the speed of 132.6mph. (JDHT)

1. Hassan *Climax in Coventry* p50
2. For this and following, cf. Newcomb and Spurr *A Technical History of the Motor Car* p293ff
3. Hassan p50; Whyte *Jaguar The History of a Great British Car* pp130-31; Skilleter *Jaguar Saloon Cars* pp133-35
4. Price *The Rise of Jaguar* pp103, 109
5. Hassan p61; Knight in *XK Gazette* no.10 Jul 1998
6. Newcomb and Spurr p295
7. In Britain, the only examples were relatively small cars by Vauxhall, Morris and Hillman
8. Heynes in 1949 Jaguar catalogue discussing the Mark V frame
9. Knight in *XK Gazette* no.10 Jul 1998
10. Newcomb and Spurr "Jaguar XK 120", *Proceedings of Institution of Mechanical Engineers* vol.202 no.D3, 1988
11. Different sources quote slightly varying figures
12. List of Development Department cars, 28 Oct/1 Nov 1949, Lyons files, JDHT archive
13. Lyons files, JDHT archive
14. This particular car was at one time owned by Gilbert Tyrer who later bought an XK 120
15. *The Motor* 12 Nov 1947
16. A saloon was road tested by *The Motor* (4 Dec 1946). They measured an average top speed of 106.56mph (171.5km/h); another was timed on the Jabbeke motorway in 1947 at 110mph (177km/h)
17. Cyril Holland's reminiscences in interview with Gilbert Mond 1981, quoted in Porter & Skilleter *Sir William Lyons* p59
18. Dugdale *Jaguar in America*, p5, Porter & Skilleter p99
19. Skilleter *Jaguar Sports Cars* p48
20. Price pp106-07; List of Development Department cars, 28 Oct/1 Nov 1949, Lyons files, JDHT archive
21. Dugdale p7
22. *The Autocar* 27 Feb 1948
23. For this and following, Dugdale pp7-9; also Dugdale in *Jaguar Quarterly* winter 1988/89
24. List of Development Department cars, 28 Oct/1 Nov 1949, Lyons files, JDHT archive. This list has been interpreted to suggest that originally, the sports car project was coded XL, confirmed by Bob Knight in *XK Gazette* no.10 Jul 1998.
25. Knight in *XK Gazette* no.10 Jul 1998, and other sources
26. Letter from Lyons to Skilleter, Skilleter p54, Porter & Skilleter p107
27. Knight in *XK Gazette* no.10 Jul 1998; Heynes quoted in *Jaguar World* Oct 1998
28. Alan Docking's reminiscences, quoted in Porter & Skilleter p107
29. Dugdale p7
30. Schmid *Jaguar XK120* p195, confirmed by Paul Skilleter
31. Schmid p53

Chapter Four

No Other Car in the World Like It

The XK 120 "Super Sports" was previewed by the press at Grosvenor House in Park Lane on Friday 22 October 1948, and made its public debut at the Earls Court Motor Show, which opened on the following Wednesday 27 October.[1] The reception was everything that Jaguar could have wished for, and simply confirmed that there was no other car in the world like it.

One piece in the daily press, probably quite typical, ran as follows:

"My prediction is that the car will be the sensation of the Show for three reasons:

(a) Its beauty. Superior to the latest Alfa Romeo and Maserati exhibits at recent Continental shows, the car remains distinctly British.

(b) Its performance. Powered by an entirely new engine, the car will exceed 120mph on the road.

(c) Its price. At £988 the car costs less than half that of models within measurable distance of the Jaguar specification."[2]

This combination of features ensured that the new model had an unheard-of impact on the media and public alike. Even at this most remarkable of all British Motor Shows ever held, with its cornucopia of new post-war cars, the XK 120 stood out. The reports in the motoring journals were a testimonial to this, to the extent that, according to Bill Boddy, in *Motor Sport* "Without a doubt, the entirely new 3½-litre XK 120 Jaguar sports two-seater stole the show".[3]

The Motor gave the new car three pages on the opening day of the show, while its rival *The Autocar*, published two days later, only devoted a single page but followed this up with a more detailed article some weeks later.[4] In addition, both magazines gave further mention to the new Jaguar in their show reports. For instance, Montague Tombs in his article "Keeping up Appearances" reviewing the Show in *The Autocar*, wrote of Lyons and the looks of the XK 120:

"One man is particular in this show and has got sports appearance absolutely taped for a start, and I never saw a more beautifully proportioned car and if I mention his name he will blush… but everybody will know it, all the same. But that is a lovely car – not a curve wrong, not a proportion out of balance, seen from any angle. America and the Continent can't teach him anything. That gold car expresses so much of what I feel – about correct form, balance, harmony of line, with no need of trimmings…"[5]

On the question of the price announced for the new car, commentators were astonished, if not quite disbelieving: "The most surprising matter is the relatively low price" and "relatively a very modest price"[6] were typical comments. As regards the performance, and bearing in mind that nobody outside the company had yet driven the car, there was a slightly more "wait and see" attitude: "…the figures [100 or 120] representing a close approximation to the maximum speeds of which the cars are claimed to be capable" and "a top speed which is likely to be well over 100mph".[7] Similarly, "Speeds of well over 100mph are anticipated from the 3½-litre… Over 80mph should be possible in third gear, and 80mph cruising a normal accomplishment."[8] None of these comments amounted to out-and-out disbelief, but simply represented a careful withholding of final judgement on a promising, but as yet untried, car.

A general shot of the Jaguar stand at the 1948 Earls Court Motor Show where the XK 120 made its debut. (JDHT)

That there was some scepticism in the early days was reflected on by Bill Boddy a few months later: "It was even rumoured by sceptical persons that the 'XK' was too good to be true and must just be a publicity move, that Jaguar's [*sic*] would never put it into series-production, at all events at the original price."[9] Any such scepticism does not, however, seem to have found much of an outlet in the correspondence columns of the motoring journals.

Whatever scoffing may have been heard in the nation's saloon bars was effectively silenced when

Jaguar invited the press to Belgium to witness the demonstration run on 30 May 1949, when Ron Sutton was timed in HKV 500 at an average two-way speed of 132.6mph (213.4km/h), an event discussed in detail in chapter 8. This was followed by the victory of the XK 120 in the Silverstone race in August 1949. Oddly, these performances did spark off some correspondence where writers tried to argue that an XK 120 was not really any faster than an ERA or a Bugatti Type 57 SC. Coming down on the side of the Jaguar was a certain Alan Clark – presumably *the* Alan Clark

Overleaf: Jaguar never bothered much about advertising the XK 120 in the home market – presumably they did not need to; but they took out this double-page spread in the show issue of The Motor *in October 1952, showing both their models. (JDHT)*

Marking another year of

JAG

Grace, Space

Throughout the world the inimitable Jaguar Mark VII Saloon continues to enhance the prestige of the British Motor Industry and, indeed, in every country where it is sold it is clearly the most desired imported car. The equally famous XK120 has ended yet another year of outstanding success in the field of international competitions—

World-wide achievement

JAGUAR CARS LTD.
COVENTRY

U A R

and Pace

while together, all Jaguar models have, during 1952, brought to Britain no less than ten million dollars as part of their great export earnings. A measure of Jaguar's universal appeal is the fact that over 83% of total production is sold overseas and the demand far exceeds supply. With the advent of another Motor Show—marking yet another year of Jaguar achievement—the Jaguar range is once again proudly presented from Earls Court to the World.

The impact of the XK 120 was also felt abroad. Here an example is given pride of place on the Jaguar stand at the 1950 Paris show. (JDHT)

Later, an XK 120 was featured on the front cover of the French magazine L'Automobile – *although it was not the only attraction! (JDHT)*

who bought his XK 120 in 1951 and kept it until his death. As a young Oxford undergraduate, he wrote *inter alia*:

"The Jaguar is fundamentally a parvenu in the world of motor sport; in addition, it is an English parvenu and a highly successful one. For years a section of enthusiasts have tried with increasing feebleness to wave these remarkable motorcars aside, and now, confronted with Jaguars… making the fastest production car in the world, they are forced to fall back on increasingly vague and improbable suggestions."[10]

There would be no better end to the argument than for the car's performance to be independently assessed, but it still took some time before Jaguar released a car for road test, in the first instance to *The Motor* in the autumn of 1949. They were lent the original year-old show and racing car, now registered HKV 455.[11] The test was carried out by Harold Hastings and Joe Lowrey, who were accompanied by "Wally" Hassan from Jaguar. An initial attempt at timing the maximum speed at the Montlhéry race track near Paris gave a figure of 117.7mph (189.4km/h), but then a rear tyre blew out under the extra load endured on the banking. The party then moved to the same stretch of motorway near Jabbeke in Belgium that had been used the previous spring, and duly measured a mean top speed of 124.6mph (200.5km/h) with the hood and sidescreens in place. We now know that HKV 455 was lighter than the standard alloy cars, with 18-gauge skin for the body (cp. chapters 5 and 8).

As well as the road test report, in the same issue *The Motor* printed a leading article headed "An Astonishing Performance" in which it referred to the Jabbeke demonstration run and the win at Silverstone: "Despite these performances, there may have been many who reserved their judgement until figures could be given for a car capable of running on British Pool petrol, and equipped with full-width screen and touring equipment. We are proud that 'The Motor' became the first instrument whereby such impartial figures could be attained… Not only was the 120mph mark exceeded, but it was possible to start the car on top gear, and to accelerate from rest more quickly than any other car so far tested… To have achieved these results with a car offering comfortable springing, smooth and quiet running, tractability and a factory cost of under £1000 is a signal achievement…"

The road test report included the actual figure for acceleration from 0 to 100mph on *top gear* of 44.6 seconds, which, if all the gears were used, dropped to 27.3 seconds. The report was glowing, but the comment that the XK 120 was a "fast touring car with

NO OTHER CAR IN THE WORLD LIKE IT

impeccable handling" rather than "a super-sports model" as claimed by Jaguar, reads like a somewhat back-handed compliment. By way of explanation, they added that "sport… implies deliberate acceptance of… discomfort in the quest for utmost performance or precision… whereas… in the design of [the Jaguar] sacrifice of comfort has certainly not been accepted". The handling, steering and brakes all merited high praise. In fact, the only minor points of criticism concerned aspects of the driving position, and the headlamps, which were found inadequate for speeds higher than 70mph at night. The facia-mounted cigarette lighter was described as "especially useful on an open car", while the absence of an ash tray was considered no great hardship!

The rival weekly magazine *The Autocar* had to wait a little longer but was eventually lent JWK 675, the first steel-bodied left-hand-drive car, in the spring of 1950.[12] The road testers do not appear to have taken their test car across the Channel and, perhaps in consequence, quoted a top speed of 115mph (185km/h). The report mentioned that the car was "the first of the production examples with a steel body. Experience has been had also of one of the earlier aluminium-bodied cars that ran at Silverstone last

The rival magazine **The Autocar** *had to wait a little longer, before they got a car to test. JWK 675 was the first steel-bodied XK 120.*

year… Independent weighing showed, contrary to expectation, the steel-bodied car to be some 40 lb *lighter* than the early example, in the running trim as tested". The weight quoted was just over 26cwt, 2919 lb (1325kg). *The Motor* had measured an unladen kerb weight of 25½cwt (1296kg) for its alloy car, while Jaguar's own figure at launch was an unrealistically low 22cwt (1119kg). Otherwise, there is little point in quoting *The Autocar* in detail as there was broad agree-

This photo of HKV 455, the original show car, was taken when it was being road tested by The Motor *in 1949.*

Sombre black suits the simple lines of the alloy-bodied XK 120 very well, and the foreshortened view emphasizes how the car looks smaller, as the rear overhang disappears in the front three-quarter view.

The rear view of the alloy car, again showing the commendable simplicity and lack of ornament characteristic of the design as a whole. The shape and position of the over riders were probably dictated by the need to have the boot lid continue all the way down, for access to the spare wheel. This view also gives some idea of how much the rear wings curved inwards in plan towards the rear of the car.

The front view is splendid, even if from this low angle you get the impression of the bonnet rising towards the front! The individual elements are superbly balanced. The Lucas P.F.770 headlamps feature the distinctive tripods carrying the reflectors. The elegant grille features thirteen delicate bars. The simple half-bumpers unfortunately barely offered sufficient protection..

The length of the rear overhang is actually considerable! This is how the XK 120 was original conceived, with disc wheels and rear spats, and remains the purest expression of Lyons's styling genius, even with the hood up.

After its first Alpine Rally in 1950, NUB 120 was lent to Montague Tombs of The Autocar *who here seems attired for the vagaries of an English summer. Note there had not yet been an opportunity to repair the cut-away front valance. (Paul Skilleter)*

ment between the two magazines about the characteristics and qualities of the car. The only significant exception was that *The Autocar* found the headlamps adequate up to "90mph on known roads".

A few months later, Montague Tombs, technical editor of *The Autocar*, was also able to try out NUB 120, the Appleyard rally car, soon after its return from victory on the Alpine Rally.[13] He delighted in the dual nature of the car, which could be either a docile touring vehicle or almost a racing car according to the driver's whim, and even after a hard 2000-mile rally found very little wrong with it, other than a recalcitrant first gear and brakes badly in need of adjustment.

Several more months went by before Bill Boddy of *Motor Sport* was lent a test car by Jaguar. This was the factory demonstrator KHP 30, chassis number 660228 built in October 1950.[14] He provided a very detailed assessment in typical Boddy style, including the oft-quoted description that the XK engine "like a bank clerk, is quite devoid of temperament", and he

summed up the XK 120 as "one of the highest pinnacles of modern motoring". Boddy invariably wrote positively about Jaguar and the XK, but he did not shy away from discussing the car's tendency to roll when cornering hard, often accompanied by undignified tyre noise, although he clearly found that this did not detract from the handling. More seriously, after a brake test he suffered immediate and total brake fade; the first time this deficiency had been experienced, or at least mentioned, by a road tester. The brakes recovered of their own accord after a stop, but Boddy felt that he could "now sympathise with XK 120 drivers who have slapped the straw during a sports car race or come down an Alp a thought too quickly". The drivers of the works cars had already had similar experiences.[15]

During 1951, an XK 120 (LRW 174, chassis 660917, built in September 1951, which later became Bob Berry's racer) was lent to Laurence Pomeroy junior, technical editor of *The Motor*, who published his impressions in his annual overview "Account Rendered".[16] Pomeroy found the car "pre-eminently an excellent and very high-performance two-seater touring car". He felt that the length of bonnet and car was intimidating, and that the low driving position, especially in relation to the pedals, was a handicap. He was also critical of the hood and the lack of direction indicators, but was impressed by the handling and the performance – as was Rudi Uhlenhaut, the Mercedes-Benz engineer, whom he took along for a ride. Pomeroy concluded with the following imaginary dialogue:

"Q: Has the production model Jaguar the performance of a racing car?

A: Yes.

Q: Does it behave like a racing car?

A: No.

Q: Would you, Pomeroy, prefer if it did so behave?

A: Yes.

Q: Would most people prefer if it did so behave?

A: No."

The fixed-head coupé was road tested by *The Autocar*, the car was a left hand drive example (MHP 682, chassis S 679970, built in August 1952) as at this time there were no right hand drive cars available.[17] This also afforded them an opportunity to test the more powerful Special Equipment model with 180bhp and they measured a mean top speed of 120.5mph (193.9km/h); this time they, too, had recourse to the by-now-well-used motorway at Jabbeke. The car "has the very desirable quality of a small amount of understeer"; "The synchromesh is very effective and not easily beaten"; and "The brakes are extremely effective and no noticeable fade was experienced…" were among their paeans of praise. Indeed, the most serious criticism was reserved for the driving position.

The final important road test carried out by a British magazine was by John Bolster in *Autosport*, and this was also the only test of the drophead coupé.[18] The car was OHP 503, chassis 667033, a standard model that was the Jaguar demonstrator and was built in September 1953. Bolster's top speed was 119.5mph (192.3km/h), with acceleration through the gears to 100mph of 31 seconds. His comments generally echo those made by other testers, but after the car had been on the market for some years, it is illuminating that he should mention that "What I do know, from the experience of several of my friends, is that the XK is one of the hardest-wearing vehicles on the market… The 'Jag' can take it, and in the hands of all sorts of drivers, it has acquired a reputation for toughness that has never been surpassed". He also appreciated the traditional walnut dashboard, the luxuriously appointed interior, and the comfortable seats.

Generally speaking, the coverage in contemporary American magazines mirrored the UK road tests, but, perhaps because slightly different standards prevailed in the USA, one detects a greater readiness to acknowledge the XK 120 as a proper sports car, as opposed to the "fast touring car" that many British commentators classified it as. There is also evidence that under driving conditions more typically experienced in the USA, such as extremes of weather and

This is none other than the Mercedes-Benz engineer Rudi Uhlenhaut, trying out an XK 120 when it was lent to The Motor *in 1951. (JDHT/*The Motor*)*

temperature, or very heavy traffic, the XK 120 displayed shortcomings which had not manifested themselves on British roads.

Road and Track commented that engine torque was low at low engine speeds. It was critical of the driving position (again!), and thought the weather protection was inadequate in heavy rain. But the steering was considered both fast and positive, the brakes were powerful and the magazine believed that fade would only be encountered during racing. The cornering ability was highly praised, with no mention of roll. By American standards, the metallic paint was found unattractive, and the luggage accommodation, which had elicited praise in Britain, was considered small. They would have liked bigger bumpers, and even emergency seats in the rear, and it was noted that driving in traffic brought about a rise in engine temperature. Their staff measured an average top speed of 121.6mph (195.7km/h).[19]

Morris B Carroll writing in *Speed Age* suggested that the steering was too fast if you were used to American cars, and found the brakes too weak for racing but fine for average use. Ride was inferior to American cars at low speed, but excellent at higher speeds. He was impressed by the traction in snow, but found that the car was somewhat prone to skidding in slippery conditions. He was critical of the cooling because the temperature rose to boiling point during summer driving in New York traffic; on the other hand the heater was equally inadequate in winter. He timed a two-way average top speed of 126.47mph (203.5km/h) – possibly the highest top speed quoted in a published road test of any XK 120.[20]

One of the characteristic features of the alloy-bodied cars is the grab handle mounted under the scuttle, rather than on the dashboard. Otherwise the interior is similar to the later steel-bodied version. You normally expect the rev. counter to be on the left on an XK 120, but this alloy car has the speedometer on the left. That this is correct for some of the early cars, is borne out by some contemporary photos.

The foot of the centre windscreen pillar, clearly demonstrating the effort that was put into making every part of the car a visual delight.

Another distinguishing feature of the alloy cars is this thick wedge-shaped rubber pad under the windscreen pillar, just visible to on the right of this photo.

The hood on the open two-seater was unlined, and the hood frame as seen here was chrome-plated until 1951.

In 1953, *Road and Track* had a Special Equipment fixed-head coupé on test which, of course, it referred to as the "XK 120 M". The car was borrowed from a private owner and was finished in "crushed-strawberry paint", possibly the work of the owner who was also having the wire wheels chromed. Or did they just mean red? Interestingly, the magazine felt that the coupé held special appeal for a female audience, and described it as a "jewel box on a sports car chassis" – but they were not in any doubt that this *was* a sports car. The slightly stiffer suspension on the SE model was not considered to be detrimental to comfort, and the performance was as impressive as ever. The top speed was measured as 120.8mph (194.4km/h), the higher engine power of the SE car being presumably offset by the increase in weight of the coupé body.[21]

The similar SE fixed-head tested by *Auto Sport Review* was "a sort of Gantron red"! The report offered a light-hearted approach and the worst criticism was of the near-vertical, too-large steering wheel, while it was only too easy to operate the horn push inadvertently. Since the testers were based in California rather than New York, they considered the heating adequate. They praised the wire wheels for allowing better cooling of the brakes, and did not experience any fade. They loved the note from the twin exhaust and deplored the fact that Jaguar was discontinuing the twin system on SE coupé models. The top speed measured was very similar to that achieved by *Road and Track*, at 120.2mph (193.4km/h).[22]

Possibly a more strenuous ordeal than any road test carried out in the UK or the USA was the drive across the Andes, from Buenos Aires to Santiago and back, which Lucio Bollaert accomplished in his XK 120 SE open two-seater in 1955 (he had previously owned an alloy-bodied car). Having the SE engine with an 8:1 compression ratio inevitably meant "pinking" on most petrol encountered *en route*, which was typically 76 octane or less. But performance was unaffected, and the car behaved impeccably, even at 13,000ft. While the

Except for a few very early cars, the spats found on disc-wheeled cars had an external budget lock or coach lock fitted centrally at the top.

brakes were "boiling" after a particularly steep descent, they continued to function. No mechanical trouble was experienced, and although Mr Bollaert was somewhat unhappy with the rain- and dust-sealing, he considered the car "a good advertisement for Coventry".[23]

While the XK 120 constantly attracted rave reviews from the motoring press and from owners, how did it compare with other cars of the same period, even if the analysis is carried out mainly on the basic attributes of price and performance? Because up until 1954 the British market was closed to imports (even subsequently these were subject to import duty of one-third of value), the best comparisons are obtained by looking at the "neutral" Swiss market, where a wide variety of cars was available, including American models. Only a few XK 120s had reached Switzerland by March 1950, when the annual catalogue issue of *Automobil Revue* described the car as "at this time, probably the fastest series production car in the world" with a top speed estimated as 200km/h (124mph). The price was 18,900 Swiss Francs (Sfr); the same as a Mark V 3½-litre drophead coupé.[24]

In the Swiss market, that sort of money would buy you a mid-range American car; the cheapest models of Buick, Chrysler and Packard were all in the bracket from Sfr18-19,000. This formed an interesting contrast with the USA, where the XK was always substantially more expensive than these domestic products. Of cars more comparable with the XK, the Allards undercut it, as the J-type was Sfr15,000, although its top speed was only 109mph (175km/h).

The two-tone seats were commonest in the early years of open two-seater production. The early chrome-plated type of seat frame is also shown.

The original carburettors with the tall necks to the dashpots were found on the alloy cars and the first few steel-bodied cars. The cam covers are the early type, lacking the extra three studs at the front of each cover, introduced in 1952.

When opened, the alligator-type bonnet took the grille with it. This is already the second type of radiator, which no longer had a hole for the starting handle.

The loose side screens have a flap below the window enabling you to reach the door release cord on the inside. It should be added that it is possible to achieve a better fit between side screen and windscreen frame, respectively hood, than is seen here!

With the door open, we can see the brackets for attaching the side screen, held in place by the knobs, also the release cord and the flap covered door pocket. … while below is the door trim sans side screen, showing the area below floor level closing against the sill which was not trimmed on the early cars.

A similar performance was offered by the Healey Silverstone at Sfr16,500. A Healey saloon had, at that time, been the fastest post-war car tested by *Automobil Revue*, with a top speed of 158km/h (98mph). On the other hand, the Aston Martin 2-litre, which hardly saw production, was listed at Sfr25,500, and the Bristol 400 at Sfr21,600; the 401 was much more expensive, as was the Frazer Nash – a similar position to that in the home market.

Among Jaguar's potential European competitors, none produced a true sports car. The Alfa Romeo 2500, the Delage and the various Delahayes were all more expensive, were not available with two-seater bodywork and were left hopelessly behind in the performance stakes. Only the Talbot Lago Grand Sport would (on paper) match the top speed of the XK, but a chassis cost Sfr26,100 and complete cars would have been around twice the price of the Jaguar. Potentially, some Ferraris and Maseratis offered higher speeds than the XK but were not yet available for sale in Switzerland and were, as yet, hardly credible production cars.

Towards the end of production of the XK 120 in 1954, the Swiss price for the open two-seater had increased modestly to Sfr19,900, with the fixed-head and drophead coupés available, in round figures, at respectively Sfr1000 and 2000 more. By this time, there was at least one comparable car available. The Mercedes-Benz 300 SL, launched at the 1954 New York Motor Show, reached the Swiss market at Sfr33,500, and with a top speed claimed by the factory to be as much as 267km/h (166mph; an unrealistic figure) with a high-ratio rear axle.

Others included the Aston Martin DB2, which had a starting price of Sfr32,500, and the Bristol 404

The Allard J2 was formidably fast when fitted with the Cadillac V8 engine, with quicker acceleration than the XK 120 (0-50mph in less than 6 seconds) although the top speed of around 110mph was less than the Jaguar. In third place, this was the highest-placed British car at Le Mans in 1950.

The Healey Silverstone, here leading a pack of XK 120s, was another car to be reckoned with in sports car racing, but neither this nor the Allard offered the comfort for everyday motoring that the XK 120 did.

The Frazer Nash Le Mans Replica was a remarkable lightweight, and its BMW-derived Bristol engine had amazing performance for a 2-litre car. It often gave the XK 120 a run for its money on the race tracks; one of these cars was third after the two XK 120s at Silverstone in August 1949.

An interesting grid at the American Watkins Glen racetrack in September 1956, mostly XK 120s, but also two Corvettes (the second-generation with the V8 engine), a Ford Thunderbird, and at the front, the ultimate winner, the 300 SL of national champion Paul O'Shea.

Road-going Ferraris in the early 1950s were rare and expensive, but also very fast, and had the measure of the Jaguars in racing. Here is the car that won the 1953 Mille Miglia.

Appearing as a racing car in 1952 and in production form in 1954, the Mercedes-Benz 300 SL was both beautiful and fast. It cost a lot more than any Jaguar XK, but in a way inherited the XK 120's mantle as the "must-have" sports car for the jet-setters and glitterati.

at Sfr29,500. Allards were no longer offered in Switzerland, and while Ferraris began to be imported, prices were not always quoted, although they typically started around the Sfr50,000 mark. *Automobil Revue* had tested two Ferraris; first a 212, which reached 187km/h (115mph) and later a 340 – none other than the car that had won the 1953 Mille Miglia – for which they had measured a top speed of no less than 260km/h (over 160mph). Perhaps surprisingly, the Swiss magazine does not appear to have tested the XK 120.

Another way of comparing the XK with other cars of the period is in terms of engine power output, both overall and specific, and power-to-weight ratio. The following table shows some of the most powerful cars of the early 1950s, with engines of two litres or over, figures again taken largely from *Automobil Revue*:

THE MOST POWERFUL CARS OF THE EARLY 1950S

Make	Model	Capacity	Bhp (PS)	PS/litre	Weight	PS/ton	Est. top speed	Notes
Alfa Romeo	Disco Volante	2995cc	200	66.8	800kg	250	155mph	
Alfa Romeo	Disco Volante	1973cc	125	63.4	700kg	179	137mph	
Allard (Cadillac engine)	JR	5424cc	212/278	39.1/51.2	910kg	233/305	137mph	
Aston Martin	DB2-4	2580cc	127	49.2	1220kg	104	118mph	
Bristol	404 (100 C)	1971cc	127	64.4	1040kg	122	118mph	
Bugatti	101 (C)	3257cc	135/190	41.4/58.3	1750kg	77/108	93mph/ 112mph	1
Buick	Century	5276cc	203	38.5	1752kg	116	100mph	
Cadillac	62	5424cc	233	43	1960kg	119	105mph	
Chrysler	New Yorker	5426cc	238	43.9	1825kg	130	105mph	
Cunningham (Chrysler engine)	C53	5426cc	223	41	1270kg	176	118mph	
Delahaye	235	3557cc	152	42.7	1450kg	105	112mph	
Ferrari	250	2963cc	200	67.5	1350kg	148	130mph	
Ferrari	375	4522cc	300/340	66.3/75.2	1350kg/ 1050kg	222/324	137mph/ 162mph	2
Fiat	8 V	1996cc	105	52.6	930kg	113	112mph	
Frazer Nash	Competition	1971cc	142/152	72/77	635kg	223/239	124mph	3
Healey	Silverstone	2443cc	105	42.9	965kg	109	109mph	
Jaguar	Mark VII	3442cc	162	47.1	1712kg	95	103mph	
Jaguar	XK 120	3442cc	162/190	47.1/55.2	1120kg	145/170	120mph/ 135mph	4
Jaguar	C-type	3442cc	203/213	59/61.9	950kg	214/224	145mph/ 155mph	5
Lancia	Aurelia GT	2451cc	118	48.1	1100kg	107	115mph	
Lincoln	all	5203cc	208	40	1900kg	109	105mph	
Maserati	A6 GCS	1985cc	180	90.7	700kg	257	143mph	
Mercedes-Benz	300 S	2996cc	165	55	1680kg	98	110mph	
Mercedes-Benz	300 SL	2996cc	215	71.7	1310kg	164	160mph	6
Oldsmobile	Super 88	5314cc	187	35.2	1695kg	110	103mph	
Packard	Patrician	5883cc	215	36.5	1900kg	113	100mph	
Talbot Lago	Grand Sport	4482cc	210	46.9	1600kg	131	124mph	

Notes to table:
1. Higher PS figure for engine with supercharger
2. Figures for America, resp. Mille Miglia models
3. PS figures for 8.8:1, resp. 10:1 compression
4. Higher PS figure for SE model with 9:1 compression
5. Higher PS figure for 9:1 compression

6. Fuel injection; figures quoted are from later sources
All weights and top speeds are believed to be estimates by the manufacturers or by *Automobil Revue*, and it should be noted that the power outputs quoted for British and American were measured by the SAE standard which gives higher figures than the DIN or CUNA standards used for most Continental cars.

The bonnet badge featured the first representation of the jaguar's face seen head-on which has since become known as the "growler".

There is a wide variety of cars in this table, from out-and-out racing cars to large saloons, and some of them you could, for practical purposes, hardly buy! What is, however, interesting is that, by 1954, the most powerful American engines (Cadillac, Chrysler) were approaching Jaguar in terms of specific output. Both were short-stroke V8s and, thanks to the ready availability of high-octane petrol in the USA, compression ratios were on the increase, the most powerful Cadillac and Oldsmobile running at 8.25:1 and Packard even posting 8.7:1. Jaguar engines still used 7:1 or 8:1; while 9:1 was available for the XK 120 engine by this time, it was still a rarely seen option. Anything higher was the preserve of racing cars.

While the XK engine was still, five years on, among the most powerful engines in the world, in terms of specific output and power-to-weight ratio Jaguar was now equalled or bested by the Ferraris and (more importantly, from a sales point of view) by the new Mercedes-Benz 300 SL. The Mercedes's limited production (less than 3300 cars from 1954 to 1963) and high price prevented it from becoming a more effective competitor for the XK, and its original swing-axle rear suspension might have given it dubious high-speed handling, but with a Le Mans win to the credit of the 1952 prototype its heritage was impeccable. It certainly had the advanced design, style and performance to take on even the later E-type.

Nevertheless, if price is also included in the equation, the XK 120 continued to be the undisputed leader of the pack. The following tables quote basic prices in the UK, less Purchase Tax, and in Switzerland for three different years during XK production. The rate of exchange was then around Sfr12.25 to the pound.[25]

PRICE COMPARISON, MARCH 1950:

Make	Model	Body	Basic UK price in £	Price in Sfr
Allard	J	Roadster	£999	15,000
Healey	Silverstone	Roadster	£975	16,500
Jaguar	XK 120	OTS	£988	18,900
Bristol	400	Coupé	£1750	21,600
Delahaye	135M/MS	various	n/a	From 22,900
Delage	D6 3 litre	various	n/a	From 23,450
Aston Martin	2-litre	Roadster	£1450	25,500
Talbot Lago	Record	various	n/a	28,500-36,700
Frazer Nash	Le Mans	Roadster	£1750	32,000
Alfa Romeo	6C 2500 S	various	n/a	32,000-41,000
Bristol	401	Saloon	£1925	34,000
Alfa Romeo	6C 2500 SS	various	n/a	42,000

PRICE COMPARISON, MARCH 1952:

Make	Model	Body	Basic UK price in £	Price in Sfr
Jaguar	XK 120	OTS	£1078	19,450
Alvis	3 litre	Roadster	£1250	19,800
Jaguar	XK 120	FHC	£1088	20,250
Talbot Lago	Grand Sport	Chassis	n/a	27,450
Bristol	401	Saloon	£2270	28,500
Aston Martin	DB2	Coupé	£1750	30,200
Lancia	Aurelia GT B20	Coupé	n/a	31,000
Delahaye	135M/MS	various	n/a	34,750-42,550
Frazer Nash	Le Mans replica	Roadster	£1975	35,000
Alfa Romeo	2500 GT	Cabriolet	n/a	38,500
Delahaye	235	Saloon	n/a	43,000
Alfa Romeo	2500 SS	Coupé	n/a	43,700
Ferrari	212 Inter	Coupé	n/a	48,000
Mercedes-Benz	300S	Cabriolet	n/a	49,600
Ferrari	340 America	Coupé	n/a	62,000

PRICE COMPARISON, MARCH 1954:

Make	Model	Body	Basic UK price in £	Price in Sfr
Austin-Healey	100	Roadster	£750	14,500
AC	Ace	Roadster	£915	n/a
Porsche	1500/1500 Super	various	£1367-£1524*	15,950-19,750
Mercedes-Benz	190 SL	Roadster	£1850**	19,500**
Jaguar	XK 120	OTS	£1130	19,900
Jaguar	XK 120	FHC	£1140	20,750
Healey	2.4 litre	various	£1218-£1268	21,250-22,120
Jaguar	XK 120	DHC	£1160	21,800
Daimler	Conquest	Roadster	£1180	23,000
Salmson	2300 Sport	Coupé	n/a	24,000
Alfa Romeo	1900 C	various	n/a	25,500-25,850
Lancia	Aurelia GT B20	Coupé	n/a	27,900
Bristol	403	Saloon	£2100	28,500
Alvis	3 litre TA/TC 21	various	£1250-£1325	28,500-29,700
Healey	3 litre (Alvis)	Roadster	£1250	n/a
Nash-Healey		various	n/a	28,700-31,000
Frazer Nash	various	various	From £1950	n/a
Bristol	404	Coupé	£2500	29,500
Delahaye	135M	Cabriolet	£1750*	32,000-37,300
Aston Martin	DB 2/4	various	£1850-£1950	32,500-34,000
Mercedes-Benz	300 SL	Coupé	£3100**	33,500**
Talbot Lago	Grand Sport	Coupé	n/a	35,500
Delahaye	235	Saloon	£2260*	38,750
Mercedes-Benz	300 S	various	£3902*	43,300
Ferrari	250 Europa	Coupé	n/a	52,000**

*Including import duty   **Prices quoted are from 1955-56

A much more civilised Italian contender was the Lancia Aurelia GT with its beautiful Farina styling. Performance was excellent, but this closed two-plus-two GT car cost a great deal more than an XK 120.

The AC Ace, based on a Tojeiro design, was an advanced car for its day, but was handicapped by using the venerable AC engine

The closest British equivalent of the Lancia, in terms of price and performance, was the Aston Martin DB2, this is one of the early works racers. Again, the price difference put this car upmarket from the XK 120.

There is a nugget of popular wisdom that maintains you can have good, cheap or quick, but only two of the three at the same time. This formula was confounded by the XK 120, which offered remarkable performance at a more-than-reasonable price, and had so many other outstanding qualities. Whether or not the XK 120 really had any competitors depends on your point of view and what you wanted a car for. It is true that such cars as the Allard J-type, the Frazer Nash Le Mans replica and the Healey Silverstone offered performance approaching that of the XK 120 at similar prices, and sometimes got the better of the XK on the race track, but none was as accomplished as a road car for everyday motoring. They were also all products of tiny concerns which lacked the production facilities and sales organisation of Jaguar, so their production was minuscule, and, in consequence, none had the impact of the XK.

Only later did cars with similar attributes begin to appear, and these were perhaps more comparable. While the Austin-Healey 100 of 1953 had a top speed of around 105mph (169km/h) in its original form, it also cost a lot less than an XK, and the Triumph TR2 was billed as the cheapest 100mph production car at only £595 basic. Both were produced and marketed by large organisations and reached substantial production figures, and enjoyed large sales in the USA. These two cars were to fill the gap in the marketplace between the MG and the Jaguar. The original AC Ace launched in 1953 sat uneasily half-way between the Austin-Healey and the Jaguar in terms of price, but despite having an extremely advanced chassis design, the old AC engine limited its top speed to 103mph (166km/h). It was a good car in search of a better engine. Later examples fitted with Bristol – or Ford Zephyr engines – were appreciably faster, and the basic design would a decade later be transmuted into the legendary Cobra.

In Germany, at the end of the production life of the XK 120, Mercedes-Benz brought out the 300 SL – a car that would certainly beat an XK 120 on performance but also cost more than half as much again. The firm's 190 SL, comparable on price in open markets, had performance more in line with the Austin-Healey and Triumph. Similarly, the early Chevrolet Corvette could compete with the Jaguar on price, but not yet on performance. The best of the rest were the Aston Martin DB2 and the Lancia Aurelia GT, both

The Triumph TR2 was the cheapest 100mph car available in Britain and had excellent performance for its size and price.

outstanding cars with performance close to an XK 120, but inevitably more expensive, with their closed GT bodywork. The conclusion must be that the XK 120 was indeed unique.

The first serious attempt at a sports car from a large American manufacturer, the 1953 Chevrolet Corvette had a fibreglass body but performance from its six cylinder engine was limited. However, undoubtedly it beat all British sports cars when it came to luggage space!

1. Dugdale *Jaguar in America* p16
2. *News Chronicle* 25 Oct 1948, subsequently quoted in Jaguar advertisements
3. *Motor Sport* Dec 1948
4. *The Motor* 27 Oct 1948; *The Autocar* 29 Oct and 17 Dec 1948
5. *The Autocar* 5 Nov 1948
6. *The Autocar* 29 Oct and 17 Dec 1948
7. *The Motor* 27 Oct 1948 written *very* carefully by a sceptical Harold Hastings, cp. note 11, and 3 Nov 1948
8. *Motor Sport* Dec 1948
9. *Motor Sport* Jul 1949
10. *The Motor* 12 Oct 1949; letters from Clark on the XK 120 *v.* Allard and Frazer Nash may also be found in *Motor Sport* Mar 1951, Aug 1951
11. *The Motor* 16 Nov 1949; Harold Hastings in *Collector's Car* Jan 1981
12. *The Autocar* 14 Apr 1950
13. *The Autocar* 1 Sep 1950
14. *Motor Sport* Apr 1951; Boddy in *Jaguar World* Jan/Feb 1998
15. Letter from LH Haines to William Heynes 21 Jul 1950, England's Competition File, JDHT archive
16. *The Motor* 2 Jan 1952
17. *The Autocar* 17 Oct 1952
18. *Autosport* 14 May 1954
19. *Road and Track* May 1951
20. *Speed Age* Dec 1952
21. *Road and Track* May 1953
22. *Auto Sport Review* Jun 1953
23. *The Autocar* 5 Aug 1955
24. *Automobil Revue – Katalognummer* published 15 Mar 1950, prices as at 28 Feb 1950
25. Rate quoted from *The Economist*, 22 Dec 1951

Chapter Five

Evolution and Production Changes

Of all the XK 120s, it was the fixed-head coupe which most clearly showed the resemblance to other Jaguars, thanks to its characteristic roof line and rear three-quarter window.

All cars develop during their production period, and in the case of the XK 120, apart from the inevitable detail modifications, there were four major evolutionary steps that merit special attention. These were: the change from alloy to steel bodywork in April 1950; the introduction of the fixed-head coupé model in 1951; the introduction of the Special Equipment version in 1952; and the introduction of the drophead coupé model in 1953.

The change from alloy to steel bodywork went largely unheralded at the time, except for the road test in *The Autocar* of the first steel-bodied car, where it was specifically mentioned.[1] It is usually stated that the decision to change from aluminium to steel was made almost immediately after the launch of the car at the 1948 Motor Show, when it became clear that orders were pouring in at such a rate that the planned production run of 200-odd cars was never going to

satisfy demand. Jaguar was already then in negotiation with the Pressed Steel Company at Cowley over the supply of a new saloon body for the future Mark VII model. According to Bob Knight, during the Show PSC approached Lyons and made him the proverbial offer that he could not refuse: they would supply pressed-steel panels for the XK 120 body without a large up-front payment for tooling (which was a sticking point in the negotiations for the Mark VII body).[2]

The change meant that the body had to be totally

re-engineered, and although the cars looked just the same, the bodies were completely different. On the steel cars, the bonnet, doors and boot lid were still skinned in aluminium, but even they were changed; the bonnet was strengthened, and wood frames were eliminated from the doors, although not from the boot lid. A major benefit was that the ash framework of the rear tonneau panel completely disappeared, together with the structural wood in the door hinge posts and the sills. And with that particular bottleneck in production out of the way it became easier to build

Even the shape of the fixed-head coupe rear window echoed contemporary saloon models, but the glass was fitted particularly neatly without any visible rubber strip or finisher.

Except in detail photos it can be difficult to spot the small differences between an alloy-bodied car and a steel-bodied car. On the alloy-bodied car (the car facing right), the windscreen pillar rubbers are thick, the grab handle is fitted under the scuttle, the fuel filler lock is on the tonneau panel and there are four visible screws in the corners of the rear number plate backing plate. All of these changed on the steel-bodied car (the car facing left). In addition, this late steel-bodied car has the air vents in the front wings and the body-colour side lamp housings, and is probably a 1953 car. (JDHT)

the car in larger numbers. Bodies were still assembled in the Jaguar factory.

The casual observer who wishes to establish whether an XK 120 has an alloy or steel body should look for details such as the rubbers under the windscreen pillars; a thick wedge on the alloy car, but a thin gasket on the steel car. The passenger grab handle on the alloy car was fitted on the underside of the scuttle, but on the steel car it was fitted to the dashboard panel. On the alloy cars, the lock for the fuel filler cover was on the tonneau panel while on the steel cars it was on the cover itself. On alloy cars, the backing plate for the rear number plate had screws with heads visible from the outside, but these were hidden on steel models. To distinguish other features you almost need to have two cars side by side;

These three photos of the engine, interior, and the boot, are all of the first steel-bodied car, chassis 670172 JWK 675, which was the road test car for **The Autocar** *and was later converted to right-hand drive and raced. It will be noted that this car still had the tall carburettors.*

they include longer and less barrel-shaped headlamp nacelles on the steel cars. In addition, the corner of the lower edge of the front wing to the wheelarch formed a right-angle in side view on alloy versions, but was radiused on steel cars.[3]

It is not quite certain how much the change affected the weight of the XK 120. At the time, *The Autocar* claimed that the steel car was *lighter* than the

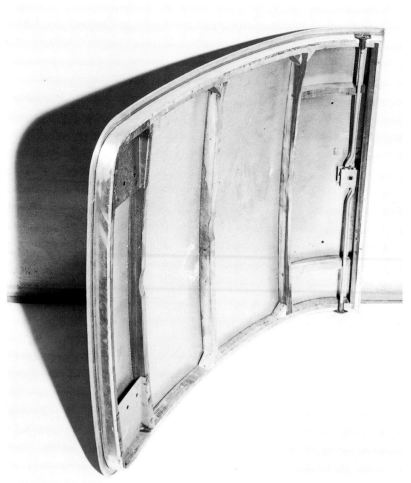

Even on the steel-bodied cars, some panels were still made of aluminium, including the bonnet, the doors and the boot lid. This is the earlier type of bonnet for a steel car, lacking the front cross brace. (JDHT)

alloy car, but this was contradicted by the kerb weight that the magazine quoted, which was more than that quoted by *The Motor* in its earlier test of an alloy car.[4] For public consumption, Jaguar originally quoted weights for the XK 120 that were far too low, such as 22cwt (1119kg).[5] They were actually concerned about the weight of the car, and internal documents show that the prototypes weighed around 23-24cwt (1170-1220kg), depending on whether the body was in 16-gauge aluminium (on 670002, HKV 500) or the thinner 18-gauge aluminium (on 660001, HKV 455, and 670001). A production alloy car weighed 25cwt (1271kg).[6] Jaguar later quoted 24½cwt (1245kg) for a steel-bodied car[7] but in 1953, Jaguar's experimental department weighed a standard production car and recorded a figure of 25¾cwt (1309kg).[8] Most independent experts have since quoted similar weights, such as 25cwt 20 lb (1280kg) for an alloy car and 25cwt 75 lb (1305kg) for a steel car, and agree that

the steel car was at least around ½cwt (25kg) heavier.[9]

This may have affected performance slightly. As discussed in the previous chapter, the highest-ever reliably recorded top speed for an XK 120 on independent road test in the UK was the 124.6mph achieved by *The Motor* in 1949.[10] The test car on that occasion, however, was not only an alloy-bodied model but a car that, as explained above, had a body of thinner-gauge material than normal and was lighter than the production alloy cars. It is not, therefore, an appropriate yardstick for performance with which to compare the steel-bodied cars.

The wire wheels were a hallmark of the more powerful Special Equipment model, and chrome wire wheels were available by 1954, whereas the (very useful) external mirror is a later addition.

The Fixed-Head Coupé

Lyons had the idea for a fixed-head coupé version of a sports car before the war, when an SS 100 with this type of body was exhibited on the company's stand at the 1938 Earls Court Motor Show. This was a car of outstanding beauty, and may have been inspired by the "Atalante" coupé body on the contemporary Bugatti type 57 chassis. In turn, it was to exercise considerable influence on the fixed-head version of the XK 120. This was being planned at a very early stage in the development of the car, and a first prototype was photographed outside the Foleshill factory, as

The original fixed-head coupé prototype, here photographed as early as April 1950. It had a vertical pillar for the rear quarterlight, and trafficators in the front wings. This white car was later experimentally fitted with a four cylinder engine. (Paul Skilleter/Jaguar)

The fixed-head windscreen was fitted in a slim chrome-plated finisher.

The later engines had additional studs at the front of the cam covers to prevent oil seepage. Note also the position of the chassis number plate, at rear right in the photo.

The fixed-head door trim with its walnut capping, also showing the front quarterlight and the chrome channel frame for the drop glass.

In this close-up, we see the headlamps with the characteristic spears, the body-colour side lamp housings, the elegant grille, and the front bumper with its brackets.

The nicely finished boot of the fixed-head. Note that this 1954 car, an SE model as it is fitted with wire wheels, but with the single exhaust system, which is correct!

The interior of a fixed-head, with the radio fitted in an additional box below the dashboard, and possibly a modern gearbox. This dashboard has the revised positions for the minor instruments and controls, and the new light switch introduced in March 1954.

*Behind the seats is the
storage box with its
hinged lid, which in turn
folds forward to give
access to the batteries
when both seat backs are
folded forward. Note the
painted seat frames on
this car.*

*The interior of the prototype
fixed-head coupé, with an
unusual seat pattern and
two-tone upholstery.
(JDHT)*

early as April 1950, with a slew of left-hand-drive
Mark V saloons in the background. This car had right-
hand drive and was probably chassis 669001; it had
some unusual features such as a vertical side-window
pillar and trafficators in the front wings. It featured
chrome side lamp housings.[11]

The fixed-head roofline was very similar to that of
the pre-war SS 100 coupé and the Mark VII saloon.
There was a swivelling quarter-light window in the
rear pillar, incorporating the curved shape first seen on
the Mark V and Mark VII, and which became such a
Jaguar hallmark. On the final production version, the
line between door and quarter-light was inclined to
the rear. As on the open two-seater, the doors were
made from aluminium but later reverted to a wood-
frame construction; they had chrome-plated frames
above the waistline, with wind-down windows and
small opening front quarter-lights. There were
external door handles. Internally, the car was finished
to a higher standard than the open two-seater, having
a full-width walnut dashboard and walnut cappings to
the doors. The passenger had a lockable glovebox,
there was a small drawer below the instrument panel,
and even an ash tray on the garnish rail above. If a

*The neat swivelling rear
quarterlight on the fixed-
head, in its half frame.*

The wooden dashboard of the prototype fixed-head coupé was of this simple design. A more sculpted version was adopted for production cars. (JDHT)

A rare contemporary colour shot of what is possibly the first left-hand drive fixed-head coupé, 679001, which was the unusual colour of Twilight Blue, outside the Foleshill factory in 1951. (JDHT)

radio was fitted, the control unit took the place of the drawer. Recessed interior lights appeared in the rear quarter pillars, and behind the seats was an enclosed parcel box with an opening top, the complete box was hinged at the front to allow access to the batteries. The left-hand-drive Geneva show launch car (679002) had a sort of hearse-like "flower rail" on the shelf behind the parcel box, but this rather unnecessary refinement was deleted on production models.[12] The penalty paid for greater weather protection and a more sybaritic interior was an extra 1½cwt (76kg) of weight. It may be noted that some entries in the original factory records refer to the fixed-head as the *XM* model but this designation was never used in public or in print.

The fixed-head coupé was first shown to the world at the Geneva Motor Show in March 1951, less than five months after the Mark VII saloon had been introduced at the Earls Court Show the previous October. It was warmly welcomed as an attractive addition to the growing Jaguar family. Unfortunately, this was an awkward time for Jaguar, as production of left-hand-drive cars had been halted in the winter and spring of 1951, and all production was then stopped by a seven-week strike (see chapter 6). In consequence, it took quite a while for production even of the left hand

The interior of the early left-hand drive fixed-head coupé, showing the "flower rail". (Paul Skilleter/Jaguar)

Again an early left-hand drive fixed-head coupé, possibly 679001 or a show-prepared 679002, photographed with Ernest Rankin who was Jaguar's long-serving head of publicity. (JDHT)

Taken in the winter of 1951, this is probably the second left-hand drive fixed-head coupé, which still sports separate side lamp housings, and the "flower rail" on the shelf behind the seat can just be seen. This was probably the car seen at the Geneva Motor Show, and which now survives in Australia. (Paul Skilleter/Jaguar)

The interior of a production fixed-head coupé, predictably a left-hand drive model. The dashboard offered a glove box on the passenger side and a small drawer below the instrument panel. The seats used on production cars were similar to the open two-seater. (JDHT)

A later Special Equipment fixed-head coupé, awaiting despatch in February 1954. The wire wheels appear to be painted body colour, and the whitewall tyres are still fitted with their protective covers. The car is fitted with a radio. The body store is in the background. (Paul Skilleter/Jaguar)

On the original photo, it can be seen that the label on the windscreen has the chassis number 681385 written on it, and next to it is a chalk mark "Hornb" indicating the destination. Note the radio aerial on the front wing and the rather poor fit of the bonnet! The open two-seater in the background on the right has a windscreen label with its body number F 7335. (Paul Skilleter/Jaguar)

This left-hand drive fixed-head coupé photographed at Browns Lane in the Coronation Year 1953 (note the loyal decorations) sports a baroque chrome-plated roof rack, as well as whitewall tyres. One guesses it was a Personal Export Delivery car for an American customer. It may just be possible to see the correct positioning of the red tell-tales on the side lamp housings, with the gentler slope to the rear and the vertical face to the front. (JDHT)

drive fixed-head to get under way. It finally got going in July, and only one production car had left the factory by the end of that month, bound for Toronto. The right-hand-drive production cars followed 18 months later, the first two such cars being built at the end of December 1952.

Tuning Modifications and Special Equipment Cars

In June 1951 – co-incident with the astonishing victory of the C-type in its debut race at Le Mans – the Jaguar Service and Spares department issued a new *Service Bulletin*, giving details of modifications that could be made to the XK 120 for competition.[13] The main engine modifications were camshafts with 0.375in lift (standard camshafts had 0.3125in lift), to be used with different carburettor needles and sparking plugs, a flywheel lighter by 8lb and a special crankshaft damper. In addition to the stan-

dard pistons with either 7:1 or 8:1 compression ratio, 9:1 pistons with higher-domed crowns were now available, but were only recommended if petrol with a minimum octane rating of 85 was available, or if 10 per cent benzole was added to 80 octane petrol. A change from 7:1 to 8:1, or from either 7:1 or 8:1 to 9:1, would require a change of distributor. Also now on offer were a dual exhaust system, a special racing clutch with a solid centre, stiffer torsion bars and rear springs, and brake shoes with 0.25in lining for long races. For racing, owners were advised to improve brake ventilation and to race only "with the rear wheel spats and wheel nave plates removed".

The choice of rear axle ratios was listed as follows, with an indication of the theoretical top-gear performance at the maximum speed of a modified engine; 5800rpm as opposed to the 5400rpm of a standard engine:

These pictures show the range of Special Tuning "goodies" that Jaguar introduced in 1951, including the lightened flywheel, crankshaft damper, high-lift camshafts, as well as higher compression pistons and associated distributor. The suspension could also be upgraded, with special torsion bars and rear leaf springs.

These were the aero screens which for a time were supplied with all two-seaters to Special Equipment specification. (JDHT)

3.27:1	145mph (233km/h) at 5800rpm
3.64:1	139mph (224km/h) at 5800rpm
(the standard ratio)	
3.92:1	121mph (195km/h) at 5800rpm
4.3:1	112mph (180km/h) at 5800rpm

Finally, bucket seats upholstered in Bedford cord, and racing windscreens with cowling for either right- or left-hand-drive cars were now available.

A price list was published, on which the dual exhaust system was £15, the high-lift camshafts £15 each, a set of 9:1 pistons £3.10.0 and the special distributor £6.10.0. The lightened flywheel was £7.10.0, and the special clutch £9.12.0. The stiffer torsion bars and road springs worked out at £4 each, the racing brake shoes were £13.18.3 for a set of four, while bucket seats or racing windscreens were £7.10.0 a piece.

These developments were greeted with interest by the magazines.[14] They also published specific bhp

This gentleman was at the time the oldest driver in Coventry. He is sitting in an XK 120 which is fitted with the bucket seats that became available in 1951. The photo was taken a little later, as the location is the Browns Lane car park. (JDHT)

Not forgetting that wire wheels also became available, as seen on this two-seater, if at some detriment to the purity of the aesthetics of the original design! (JDHT).

figures and, in the case of *The Autocar*, power curves. While the power output was normally 150bhp with the 7:1 compression and 160bhp with 8:1, the high-lift camshafts and dual exhaust system would boost the latter figure to 181bhp, and if 9:1 pistons were fitted as well, some 190bhp should be available. *The Autocar* worked out that "to 'go the whole hog' would cost about £160".

By contrast, the emergence of the factory-built

Special Equipment model in the summer of 1952, which was also announced in a *Service Bulletin*, does not seem to have caused any editorial interest.[15] On the "SE" cars, as well as the high-lift camshafts, the dual exhaust system and the stiffer road springs, wire wheels (in body colour) were fitted. They had the lighter flywheel and special crankshaft damper. The 8:1 compression ratio was standard (I have found only four SE cars with the 7:1 compression ratio), and a

few cars were fitted with the 9:1 pistons. The dual exhaust system on fixed-heads to SE specification was replaced by the normal single system in early 1953.[16] Dropheads to SE specification had the single system from the start. Two-seaters to SE specification were originally supplied with a racing windscreen and cowling, packed loose in the car, but this practice was discontinued after a year;[17] apparently some dealers abstracted these parts and sold them on separately!

The additional cost of an SE model was £115 in the case of the open two-seater in 1953, and £105 for a fixed-head coupé (with single exhaust). Prices of the SE models were, however, reduced twice in late 1953 and early 1954, so the differential narrowed to £65 for the two-seater and £55 for the coupés.[18] In the USA, the price differential in 1953 was $395 or, in round figures, 10 per cent of the cost of an XK 120.[19] And right from the start the SE version was referred to as the XK 120 "M" in the USA, where "M" stood for modified.

Special Equipment cars were identified by a prefix letter S in front of the chassis number, and a suffix letter S after the engine number. Even so, from the *Car Record Books* it seems there were anomalies, in that some cars with S prefix chassis numbers did not have the S suffix to the engine number. A smaller number of cars without the S chassis prefix still had the engine suffix, and in a few cases it is noted that an otherwise standard car was supplied with the SE engine only, but presumably not with the other SE features. The best production figures that I can provide for SE models, counting those cars that clearly have the S prefix, are as follows:[20]

Open two-seater: RHD 43, LHD 2194 Total 2237
Fixed-head coupé: RHD 57, LHD 751   Total 808
Drophead coupé: RHD 36, LHD 706   Total 742
Grand total: 3787

From the more detailed statistics quoted elsewhere, it is evident that in 1953 and 1954 the SE models were more popular than the standard models in the USA. In addition, there are around 17 or 18 cars in the records which appear to be standard models fitted with the Special Equipment engine. But it may be that any anomalies in the *Car Record Books* were caused by clerical errors as much as anything else! As far as the 9:1 compression ratio is concerned, it appears that there were altogether 32 cars with this, of which five were not to SE specification.

Later on, an even more extensive range of tuning equipment became available for the XK 120. A price list from January 1954, probably aimed at Americans buying Jaguars in England,[21] also contains the following items as well as the SE specification items:
• Wire wheels, chrome spokes and "platinum" rims – £46.5.0 (when fitted to a standard car)

The special equipment fixed-head coupé NHP 533 was a Personal Export Delivery car in February 1954, chassis S 669132, and its owner elected to have the twin exhaust system fitted. PED cars were customarily registered by Jaguar in Coventry before delivery. (JDHT)

• Wire wheels, all chrome – £62.10.0 (ditto) (Painted wire wheels as fitted on SE cars cost £20.0.0 if fitted to a standard car, and the alternative wire-wheel options were £20 cheaper when fitted to an SE model.)
• Racing tyres for SE models – £28.18.9
• XKC-type cylinder head, standard carburettors – £60.0.0
• ditto, with 2in carburettors (sand cast) – £80.0.0

The C-type cylinder head had 1.625in exhaust valves, and enlarged inlet and exhaust ports. It required a special exhaust manifold and, if the bigger carburettors were fitted, a special inlet manifold as well.[22] The *Car Record Books* do not identify any XK 120s as being fitted with the C-type head when they were made.

The Drophead Coupé

The third and final body variation of the XK 120 followed in early 1953, production (again of left-hand-drive cars) began in January and the two first cars were despatched in March to New York, destined for the Motor Show at which the model made its debut. Reviews appeared in the UK magazines – which called it a "convertible" – at the beginning of April.[23] The drophead, with its shorter production

From the front, the drophead coupé can be identified by the body colour windscreen frame. (JDHT)

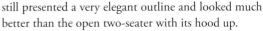

The dashboard of the drophead coupé was very similar to that of the fixed-head , while the wind-down windows had chrome-plated channels fitted to the edge of the drop glasses. (JDHT)

period of only one-and-a-half years, was destined to remain the rarest of the XK 120s (although in right hand drive form it out-produced the fixed-head), but in many ways it represents the most satisfying of the different versions of the XK 120s. It had the more luxurious interior of the fixed-head but offered the option of fresh-air motoring. With the hood raised, it still presented a very elegant outline and looked much better than the open two-seater with its hood up.

Like the fixed-head, the drophead had doors with a wood frame, and while the door skins were originally in aluminium, by the end of 1953 these had been replaced by steel ones. The wind-down windows had slim chrome-plate frames, which were fixed to the drop glasses, and the quarter-lights in the doors were of a different shape from those found on the fixed-head. The windscreen pillars and frame resembled those on the fixed-head, being integral with the body, and painted body colour. External door handles were similar, but not quite the same. The rear tonneau panel was shorter than on the other two cars, and the fuel filler was moved further back. The Mohair hood was well padded and fully lined, its rear window fitted in a zip-out panel. It even incorporated an interior light. When folded, the hood rested on a shelf in the tonneau area, roughly where the sidescreen tray was found on the open two-seater, behind the hinged parcel box familiar from the fixed-head. A cover was supplied to fit over the folded hood.

The weight of the drophead was initially quoted as 26½cwt dry (1347kg) or 27.25cwt (1386kg), a bit more than the fixed-head, and the rear axle ratio was stated to be higher than the other XK 120s, at 3.54:1

The hood of the drophead coupé had this rear window fitted in a zip-out panel. (JDHT)

rather than 3.77:1, although *The Motor* mentioned that three alternative ratios were available. *The Autocar* was very specific in stating that the drophead had a Salisbury axle instead of the ENV used on other models. According to its article, on the Salisbury axle "wire wheels can be fitted without changing the half shafts" while on the ENV "the ratio can be changed without having to remove the complete axle". In fact, it would appear that from March 1953 all cars had the Salisbury 4HA axle with the 3.54:1 ratio as standard. Compare the list of production changes below.

Production changes

This is not a complete list of detail changes but it does highlight some of the more important mechanical and cosmetic revisions to the XK 120 models, here arranged in chronological order. Those in search of greater detail should refer to the *Jaguar XK 120 Spare Parts Catalogue* publication number J.8 (amended edition, June 1954), together with the additional catalogues for the fixed-head and drophead coupé bodies, and the collected *Service Bulletins*. These are all available on CD (PDF format) from the Jaguar Daimler Heritage Trust.

These factory publications have been the basis for information in the followings books: Paul Skilleter *The Jaguar XKs A Collector's Guide* (1981), Bernard

Viart *Jaguar XK Le Grand Livre* (1993), Philip Porter *Original Jaguar XK* (second revised edition, 1998 or later), and Urs Schmid *Jaguar XK 120 Anatomie eines Kultobjekts – Band 1* (2000). These books explain changes in greater detail and include more pictures, even if they do not always agree with each other, or with the original factory publications.

The interior of the drophead coupé again resembled that of the fixed-head model, with walnut cappings and pockets for the door trims (JDHT).

PRODUCTION CHANGES

Oct 1948: First OTS RHD, 660001.

c. Feb 1949: First OTS LHD, 670001.

Jul/Aug 1949: First production cars, 660002 (RHD) 670003 (LHD).

Jan 1950: Starting handle deleted, new radiator, from 660029 (RHD) and 670071 (LHD).

Mar 1950: Last alloy cars, to body no. F 1240: 660058 (RHD) and 670184 (LHD).

Mar/Apr 1950: First steel-bodied cars, from body no. F 1241: 660059 (RHD) and 670185 (LHD), also 670172.

Sep 1950: Introduction of the stepped Mark VII-type oil sump with total engine oil capacity reduced to 24 pints (13.6 litres) from engine number W 2058 (in chassis number 670660 OTS LHD), but the earlier type sump was fitted to a small number of engines right through to W 3971 in November 1951.

Sep 1950: New radiator, from 660215 (RHD) and 670683 (LHD).

Nov 1950: New modified design of cylinder block part no. C 4820 from engine number W 2012 (in chassis number 660279 OTS RHD).

Jan 1951: Mintex M14 brake linings introduced to replace M15 linings, from 660551 (RHD) and 671097 (LHD).

Feb 1951: Air vents added to front wings, from 660675 (RHD), 671097 (LHD), and all FHC except the 1950 RHD prototype 669001.

Feb 1951: Longer hood for OTS, with alterations to frame, and zip-out panel for rear window, from 660729 (RHD) and 671098 (LHD).

c. Feb 1951: First production FHC LHD 679001. Regular production from 679003 in July 1951.

Mar 1951: Wire wheels with 54 spokes, painted body colour, offered as optional extra.[24] This may be questionable, as the Spare Parts Catalogue seems to suggest that wire wheels (a) were only fitted to Special Equipment models which began in mid-1952, and (b) were only compatible with the Salisbury rear axle fitted from January 1952 onwards. In the spring of 1951, a Borrani wire-wheel conversion became available in the US aftermarket.[25]

Sep 1951: Heater fitted as standard on OTS, from 660911 (RHD) and 671493 (LHD). It was optional on previous OTS models, and was fitted to all FHC and DHC models.

In September 1951, this heater mounted under the scuttle became standard equipment on all cars. Its efficiency was disputed! (JDHT)

Sep 1951: Modified cylinder block incorporating a boss allowing fitting of an engine heating element of American manufacture from engine number W 3686 (in chassis number 671587 OTS LHD).

Jan 1952: Salisbury 2HA rear axle with

Stages in folding the drophead hood. After the hood has been folded back, the frame is broken, and the hood lowered on to the shelf behind the seats, with finally the hood cover being fitted over it. (JDHT)

PRODUCTION CHANGES

3.77:1 standard ratio introduced as an alternative to the ENV axle from 660935 (OTS RHD), 671797 (OTS LHD), 669003 (FHC RHD) and 679222 (FHC LHD). At the same time, the JL-type gearbox with a shorter main shaft replaced the JH type – NB on FHC LHD from 679215 – starting with gearbox no. JL 8806, and a longer prop shaft was fitted on cars with the JL gearbox.

Jan 1952: Revised carburettors, from engine number W 4096 (in chassis number 671838 OTS LHD); these carburettors were also fitted to nine earlier engines, from W 3450 onwards.

In January 1952 revised carburettors were introduced. (JDHT)

Mar 1952: Oil filter changed to the shorter Mark VII type, from engine number W 4383 (in chassis number 660286 OTS RHD, an earlier car which had an engine change in the factory).

Mar 1952: Valve guides and tappet guides modified to permit the fitting of the high-lift camshaft (0.375in) from engine number W 4483 (in chassis number 679494 FHC LHD).

Apr 1952: Three extra studs fitted at the front of each cam cover to prevent oil seepage, from engine number W 4691 (in chassis number 679605 FHC LHD).

Apr 1952: Self-adjusting front brakes introduced, together with a tandem master cylinder and a divided supply tank, from 660980 (OTS RHD), 672049 (OTS LHD), 669003 (FHC RHD) and 679622 (FHC LHD), and on DHC models from start of production.

May 1952: New tail pipe for single-exhaust system on OTS model, from 660984 (RHD), 672144 (LHD).

May/Jul 1952: Gradual introduction of the Special Equipment model, with tuned engine and wire wheels etc., from S 660983 (OTS RHD), S 672150 (OTS LHD), S 669003 (FHC RHD) and S 679841 (FHC LHD), with engine numbers starting from W 4856-8S. Porter says that the SE version became available during 1951 at the same time as the fixed-head coupé model – that is, the FHC with left-hand drive.[26] While the individual tuning modifications were available earlier,[27] it is clear from the *Car Record Books* that fully-fledged SE cars were supplied from the factory only from the summer of 1952 onwards (cp. above).

Jul 1952: Revised design of engine mountings, at the front with two separate brackets rather than single front plate, together with changes as required to the chassis frame, from 660994 (OTS RHD), 672482 (OTS LHD), 669003 (FHC RHD) and 679816 (FHC LHD), around engine number W 5335.

Jul 1952: Cast-alloy radiator fan replaced by six-blade fabricated steel fan from engine number W 5465 (in chassis number 672556 OTS LHD).

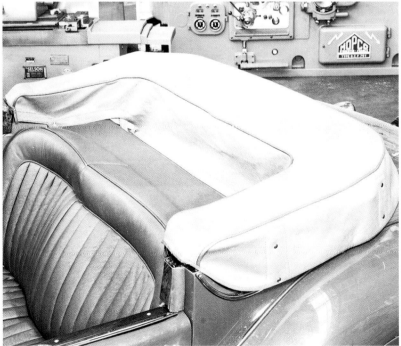

PRODUCTION CHANGES

Sep 1952: Side lamp housings integral with front wings, from 661025 (OTS RHD), 672927 (OTS LHD) and supposedly all FHC, except for the first RHD car and the first few LHD cars. At the same time, flashing indicators were fitted as standard on export cars.

Oct 1952: Instrument panel changes, with conventional petrol gauge (without oil level gauge), new switches, and a rheostat heater switch on OTS models, from 661026 (OTS RHD), 672950 (OTS LHD), 669003 (FHC RHD) and 680116 (FHC LHD). The deletion of the oil level indicator coincided with the deletion of the oil level element in the sump, intermittently from engine number W 6131 (in chassis number 672947 OTS LHD), and on all engines from W 6149 (in chassis number 672951 OTS LHD).

Oct 1952: Demister vents added to the scuttle of the OTS, 661026 (RHD) and 672963 (LHD).

Oct 1952: Windscreen washer fitted as standard, from 661037 (OTS RHD), 673009 (OTS LHD), 669003 (FHC RHD) and 680271 (FHC LHD); also on all DHC models.

Oct/Nov 1952: Type of paint changed from cellulose to synthetic, deletion of metallic paint colours. The first cars with synthetic paint were 661033 with body F 5090 (OTS RHD), 673046 with body F 5082 (OTS LHD), 669003 (FHC RHD), and 680214 with body J 2223 (FHC LHD). All cars were finished in synthetic paint from 661041 with body F 5335 (OTS RHD), 673240 with body F 5282 (OTS LHD), 669003 (FHC RHD) and 680416 with body number J 2421 (FHC LHD). In fact, all bodies from body numbers F 5272 (OTS) and J 2375 (FHC) were finished in synthetic paint, as were all DHC models.

Nov 1952: New type of distributor cap, with leads emerging from the top rather than sideways, and HT leads re-routed, from engine number W 6697 (in chassis 673214 OTS LHD).

Dec 1952: Disc road wheels, rim width increased from 5in to 5½in, from 661042 (OTS RHD), 673298 (OTS LHD), 669003 (FHC RHD), 680477 (FHC LHD), and on DHC from start of production.

Dec 1952: Stiffer rear road springs as fitted to Special Equipment model now standardised on all cars, from 661040 (OTS RHD), 673320 (OTS LHD), 669003 (FHC RHD), 680397 (FHC LHD), and on DHC from start of production.

Dec 1952: First production FHC RHD 669003.

Jan 1953: Improved zip-out panel for rear screen in OTS hood, from 661046 (RHD) and 673396 (LHD).

Jan 1953: First production DHC LHD 677001.

Two slightly different dashboards. The right-hand drive car has the ammeter on the right, the ignition lock at the top and the early light switch, while the left-hand drive car has the ammeter on the left, the ignition lock at the bottom and the later light switch, apart from other differences. This car also has the indicator switch above the steering wheel boss. (JDHT)

PRODUCTION CHANGES

Jan/Feb 1953: FHC models to SE specification now fitted with standard single-exhaust system, from 669005 (RHD) and 680738 (LHD).

Mar 1953: Salisbury 4HA rear axle with standard ratio 3.54:1 now fitted to all cars, from 661054 (OTS RHD), 673695 (OTS LHD), 669007 (FHC RHD), 680880 (FHC LHD), 667002 (DHC RHD) and 677016 (DHC LHD).

Spring 1953: Wire wheels now also available painted silver, fully chromed, or with chrome spokes and "platinum finish" rims.[28]

Apr 1953: Lightened flywheel as found on SE engines now fitted to all engines, from engine number W 8275 (in chassis number 681144 FHC LHD).

June 1953: Mintex M20 brake linings now fitted instead of M14, from 661087 (OTS RHD), 674076 (OTS LHD), 669034 (FHC RHD), 681207 (FHC LHD),

667002 (DHC RHD) and 677492 (DHC LHD).

Jul 1953: First production DHC RHD 667002.

Oct/Nov 1953: Change of engine prefix from W to F, from 661135 (OTS RHD), 674286 (OTS LHD), 669089 (FHC RHD), 681246 (FHC LHD), 667116 (DHC RHD) and 678070 (DHC LHD). The actual first engine number F 1001 was in chassis number 661137 OTS RHD.

Dec 1953: Flatter seat backs on open models, from 661152 (OTS RHD), 674434 (OTS LHD), 667161 (DHC RHD) and 678083 (DHC LHD).

Dec 1953: Door skins of steel instead of aluminium on DHC models, from 667163 (RHD) and 678086 (LHD).

Jan 1954: JL-type gearboxes fitted with close-ratio gear sets are now identified by the letters CR after the gearbox number. I have found only 18 cars thus identified in

the *Car Record Books*. Close-ratio gear sets were available for retro-fit to JH- and JL-type boxes at least from April 1953 onwards.[29]

Mar 1954: Instrument panel changes, with ammeter and petrol gauge changing places, new light switch, and panel light rheostat added, from 661167 (OTS RHD), 675208 (OTS LHD), 669139 (FHC RHD), 681420 (FHC LHD), 667212 (DHC RHD) and 678271 (DHC LHD).

May 1954: Introduction of OSL-type gearbox as alternative on some cars, from 661171 (OTS RHD), 675543 (OTS LHD), 669170 (FHC RHD), 667280 (DHC RHD) and 678347 (DHC LHD), but not found on any FHC LHD cars.

Jun 1954: Flat horn push instead of domed type, from 661172 (OTS RHD), 675926 (OTS LHD), 669194 (FHC RHD), 681481 (FHC LHD), 667280 (DHC RHD) and 678418 (DHC LHD).

1. *The Autocar* 14 Apr 1950

2. Knight in *XK Gazette* no.10 Jul 1998; Porter & Skilleter *Sir Williams Lyons* pp99, 109, 112

3. Schmid *Jaguar XK 120* pp54-55, detailed explanations with excellent photographs

4. *The Autocar* 14 Apr 1950, *The Motor* 16 Nov 1949

5. The figure quoted when the car was launched, *The Motor* 27 Oct 1948, and still used in 1954, eg. *Automobil Revue Katalognummer* Mar 1954

6. The figure quoted in *Automobile Engineer* Jul 1950

7. Jaguar Cars *Jaguar XK 120 Service Manual* pA.17; "dry" weight

8. Porter in *Jaguar World* Nov/Dec 1995, citing report by Bob Knight "Weight Reduction on XK 120" 12 Oct 1949, and other material

9. Schmid p265

10. *The Motor* 16 Nov 1949

11. Skilleter *The Jaguar XKs A Collector's Guide* p40

12. *The Autocar* 2 Mar 1951; *The Motor* 7 Mar 1951; *Australian Jaguar Magazine* nos. 108, 2003, and 119, 2005; see also discussion of this car, chassis 679002, in chapter 9

13. Jaguar Cars *Service Bulletin* no.95 "Tuning Modification on XK 120 Cars for Competition Purposes", Jun 1951, 2nd issue

with amendments in Jun 1952

14. *The Autocar* 22 Jun and 17 Aug 1951; *The Motor* 4 Jul 1951

15. Jaguar Cars *Service Bulletin* no.109, Sep 1952

16. Jaguar Cars *Service Bulletin* no.121, Mar 1953

17. Jaguar Cars *Service Bulletin* no.133, Sep 1953

18. Based on Jaguar price lists, see also chapter 6

19. *Auto Sport Review* Jun 1953

20. See also tables for Sales by Agent

21. It is a typed sheet headed "English Retail Prices" 15 Jan 1954, JDHT archive; prices quoted here do not include Purchase Tax

22. Porter *Original Jaguar XK* 2nd ed. p134; he quotes the C-type head as being available from April 1953 at a cost of £150

23. *The Motor* 1 Apr 1953; *The Autocar* 3 Apr 1953

24. Porter pp128, 134

25. *Road and Track* May 1951, cited by *The Motor* 23 May 1951

26. Porter pp94-95, 130

27. Jaguar Cars *Service Bulletin* no. 95 Jun 1951; *The Autocar* 22 Jun and 17 Aug 1951; *The Motor* 4 Jul 1951

28 Finishes as listed in a Jaguar price list dated 15 Jan 1954

29 Jaguar Cars *Service Bulletin* no.95B

Chapter Six

Production and Sales

Best of both worlds? The attractive drophead coupé combines the civilised and comfortable interior of the fixed-head, including wind-down windows and a more protective hood than the open two-seater, with the option of open-air motoring.

The foremost requirement needed for Jaguar to survive as a viable manufacturer in the post-war period was to establish a world-wide distribution and sales network. Before the war, exports had accounted for an average of only 7.4 per cent of SS and Jaguar sales.[1] Post-war, the British Government set an official target for exports of 50 per cent of production.[2] Pre-war SS and Jaguar exports had mostly been to a mixture of European countries (in particular Switzerland, Spain until 1935, Holland and Portugal) and the British Empire (Australia, India, South Africa and Malaya). Only Argentina and the USA were among the 10 best markets falling in neither category.[3] Most American sales, however, had been in a brief period from 1935 to 1937, and up until 1947 the company's representation in the USA was woefully inadequate. In any case, Jaguar only began to make left hand drive cars in October 1947,

and the only model of pre-war type with a serious sales prospect in the USA was the 3½-litre drophead coupé, re-introduced at the beginning of 1948.

The first post-war Jaguar importer in the USA was Fergus Motors in New York, which also handled Standard, Triumph and Daimler. On the recommendation of Bertie Henly of the London distributorship, in 1947 a certain Max Hoffman in New York had been appointed as the East Coast distributor, replacing Fergus. In March

1948 Lyons, together with Henly, paid his first visit to the USA.[4] After a short interim when Roger Barlow's International Motors in Los Angeles was the West Coast distributor, Lyons now appointed Charles ("Chuck") Hornburg, also in Los Angeles.

Hoffman was an Austrian-Jewish *emigré* who acquired a mixed reputation as part showman, part wheeler-dealer, and he was eventually to lose his Jaguar business – after a great deal of acrimony and at great

However, as the folded hood is rather bulky and windows are quite prominent, the drophead does not quite have the same purity of line as the open two-seater, or for that matter the fixed-head. It still looks good, or even better, with the hood up.

A later photo of a convoy of XK 120s for export, snapped by the roadside on a winter's day on the way to the port. This time, hoods are folded, and hubcaps as well as spats have been stowed. (JDHT)

In December 1949, an early batch of 14 alloy cars for export mostly to the USA was lined up outside the Foleshill factory, and the delivery drivers were photographed with the cars. Note the front number plates mounted above the left-hand bumper, and that many of the cars do not have headlamps. (JDHT)

This was the original showroom of "Maxie" Hoffman on Park Avenue in New York. It was later re-designed by Frank Lloyd Wright and acquired a more impressive glass frontage. (JDHT)

cost to Jaguar – at the end of 1955, after Jaguar had set up an American sales company as a wholly-owned subsidiary, managed by Johannes Eerdmans.[5] Hoffman had also introduced the Volkswagen to the USA, and later dealt in Mercedes-Benz, BMW and Fiat. He had Frank Lloyd Wright design his Park Avenue show-room, as well as his private house. Hornburg lasted little more than six months longer than Hoffman as a main importer, but was allowed to retain a Jaguar distributorship which continued to flourish.

Other new distributors already appointed, or about to be, included Jack Bryson in Australia, Madame Joska Bourgeois in Belgium, James L Cooke in

In April 1950 Lyons paid his second visit to America. Here he is, flanked by actor Ray Milland (an enthusiastic Jaguar owner) and "Chuck" Hornburg in the latter's showroom on Sunset Boulevard in Los Angeles. (Jaguar Cars North America Archives)

Toronto together with others in Canada, and RM Overseas in Germany. They joined some of the established pre-war importers – Ehlert in Argentina, Delecroix in France, Lagerwij's in Holland, and Emil Frey and Garage Claparede both in Switzerland, among others – and Jaguar's map of the world soon looked much better. By June 1949, Jaguar was represented in just over 50 export markets, and the list grew further over the years.[6] When the XK 120 was introduced and initial demand quickly outstripped supply, the burning question became how to meet the orders as they flooded in. Hornburg, who had come to London for the 1948 Motor Show, wanted to order

An XK 120 fixed-head coupé and a Mark VII photographed outside the California mansion that was Hornburg's home. (Jaguar Cars North America Archives)

In early 1953, Lyons travelled to the USA with his newly appointed manager of the American subsidiary company, Johannes Eerdmans. Here they are on Hoffman's stand at the New York Motor Show, with the new XK 120 drophead coupé, a photo of Lyons accepting the Dewar trophy for 1951 behind them, and on the right behind the Jaguar … a VW Beetle! I fear that the Le Mans trophy on the left may have been part of the adjacent Mercedes-Benz display, however – compare with the photo on page 199. (JDHT)

It is now late 1950, and production of the steel bodies is forging ahead at Foleshill. Here the front end is being assembled, and the operator behind the car has begun to weld in the headlamp pod. Note the jig and fixtures to keep the panels precisely aligned. (Paul Skilleter/Jaguar)

A general shot of the XK 120 body shop at Foleshill in 1951. In the foreground, individually sub-assemblies are being fabricated and stored, while the body assembly takes place in the background. It seems to be a spray booth on the right, while on the left is a glimpse of the rectification area, with a single Mark VII, but we also see some Mark V drophead coupés. (JDHT)

the entire first year's production.[7] Hoffman master-minded the Jaguar display at the 1949 New York Motor Show, where the XK 120 made its American debut. Even before then he was taking orders, as reported by Fl Lt John Bentley in his "New York Notebook" in *The Autocar*:

"The new XK Jaguars, unheralded as yet by anything more substantial than catalogues, photos and descriptions, are selling as briskly as hot cross buns on Good Friday. Max Hoffman, whose sumptuous Park Avenue corner showroom has become a New York landmark for European cars, tells me he already has firm orders for over ninety of these two-seater 'Jags' alone… Max sees the Jaguar growing into 'the biggest European car business ever transacted in the US… The Jaguar sells itself because it's exactly what the American enthusiast has wanted for a long time. It has the power to outspeed, outperform and outmanoeuvre anything built over here, and the price is right'."[8]

No car for sale would reach the USA until August

1949. Of that year's production of 96 cars, 44 were earmarked for the USA, 26 for Hoffman and 18 for Hornburg, and barely 20 of these had actually reached American shores by the end of 1949. Among the privileged early owners was Briggs Cunningham, and Clark Gable's car arrived in time for Christmas, while other Hollywood stars including Gary Cooper, Robert Montgomery, Robert Stack and Dick Powell were kept waiting.[9] At the time of the 1949 London Motor Show, it was stated that Hoffman had ordered the entire production of the XK 120 for the next six months.[10]

Once the steel-bodied car had gone into production in April 1950, production figures quickly increased and built up towards the figure of 200 per month. As the USA was turning out to be the most important market for the car, Jaguar was no doubt materially assisted by the fact that, in September 1949, the British Government had devalued the pound against the US dollar from $4.03 to $2.80 to the pound. This, in theory, would reduce the ex-factory price in US

dollars of a British car by 30 per cent. This provided a fillip for exports, and the number of British cars exported to the USA increased from 6716 in 1949 to 19,980 in 1950.[11]

An early advertisement for the XK 120 issued by International Motors in Los Angeles and using a picture of the 1948 show car quoted a price of $4745 which, assuming this was pre-devaluation, would equate to £1177.[12] While the devaluation resulted in a price reduction in the USA, by 1950 the XK 120 was quoted at $3945 (New York port of entry price, including Federal Tax but less any state sales tax), or £1409. This was the equivalent of the cost of three basic Chevrolets or Fords, while the cheapest Cadillac then cost $2761, and the XK 120 was, by a clear margin, the most expensive British car imported in quantity; an MG TD cost $1850.[13]

At the time of the 1950 Annual General Meeting of Jaguar Cars Ltd, William Lyons stated that "the demand from the USA and Canada for the new XK

In the interest of improved rear visibility, this drophead hood has a much larger rear window than original, approximately the shape and size of the zip-out panel of the original hood, or of the rear window on XK 140/150 dropheads.

The drophead door trim, in contrast to that of the fixed-head, had a finger grip door pull on top of the wood capping, and a door pocket. The chrome finisher was attached to the drop glass.

As seen elsewhere on the fixed-head, this drophead has the final 1954 layout of instruments and minor controls.

Both coupé models had external door handles. This is the drophead; the fixed head had for some reason slightly different handles.

The drophead boot. Note that the fuel filler flap (with the lock on the flap) is further back than on the other models, and the rear tonneau panel shorter. This is also a good view of the rear bumpers (or overriders) and their brackets. This car has the twin exhaust system which on the drophead, even to SE specification, was always an option.

120 is taxing our resources to the utmost. This car… is acclaimed in America… and it will undoubtedly prove to be a big dollar earner… We have not been able to release any of these models to the home market."[14]

A different note was struck two months later, when Lyons reported to the Jaguar board on his latest visit to the USA, concerning the sales situation in the USA: "Mr Lyons said that he felt the position was precarious, and we should have to rely mainly upon the XK model together with a coupé model, for future business in America."[15] The reference here to a "coupé" model may be to the Mark V drophead coupé, and the statement may reflect disappointing sales of the Mark V saloon in the USA. US dealers wanted only sports cars and convertibles, and Hoffman resorted to "sharp practice" in his efforts to make dealers take saloons as well.[16]

American sales soon ran into problems, and while exports from Britain to the USA were increased, sales of British cars in the USA did not keep pace. Actual American sales of British cars had been 10,713 in 1949 and rose to only 14,341 in 1950.[17] Among the possible causes for this must be listed the fact that immediate post-war demand for cars in the domestic US market had now been met, and a degree of satura-

This unusual overhead view shows the integral body colour windscreen frame of the drophead, the bucket seats fitted to this car, and the cover for the folded hood, but also the non-original shelf behind the seats with what appears to be individual trapdoors for each battery.

Stiffening panels were fitted under the bonnet to either side of the grille, also acting as air ducts. The internal release bonnet lock was supplemented by a safety catch.

months later, it was almost 250 cars.[18] The decision was therefore taken to suspend production of this model and other left-hand-drive cars for the time being, instead concentrating on right-hand-drive cars, as can be gauged from the following statistic.

tion had been achieved, leading to a cyclical decline in new car sales. This was probably exacerbated by the outbreak of the Korean war in June 1950.

The result for British car manufacturers who had geared up to supply the American market was that stocks of new unsold cars in the USA quickly rose. Some makers (Austin, Morris) resorted to having cars shipped back to the UK, some of which were rebuilt from left-hand drive to right-hand drive and sold in the home market. Jaguar was also affected. In the case of the XK 120 two-seater with left-hand drive, the factory stock during the summer holiday in August 1950 had already reached over 90 cars. Three

	XK 120 OTS		Mark V* Saloon		DHC		Mark VII Saloon		Total
	RHD	LHD	RHD	LHD	RHD	LHD	RHD	LHD	
Nov 1950	150	34	307	66	15	44	2	1	619
Dec 1950	135	0	171	140	34	0	3	2	485
Jan 1951	136	0	354	8	41	0	4	8	551
Feb 1951	73	1	228	0	60	0	32	14	408
Mar 1951	10	0	7	0	3	0	1	6	27
Apr 1951	43	0	85	0	36	0	3	25	192
May 1951	25	108	54	0	29	43	37	126	422
Total	572	143	1206	214	218	87	82	182	2704

*Mostly 3½-litres; the figures include only 43 2½-litre models

Here the finished front and rear assemblies are being mated up with the body sills, while in the foreground is a bare chassis frame, although this is perhaps only intended for trial fitting to ensure that the body is correctly aligned. (Paul Skilleter/Jaguar)

The assembly lines at Foleshill, probably during 1950, with Mark Vs and XKs on parallel tracks. (JDHT)

The problem was then compounded by the fact that Jaguar was hit by a seven-week industrial dispute that ran from 1 March to 16 April 1951.[19] The combined effect of the temporary collapse of the US market and the strike was that calendar year production fell from 7206 cars in 1950 to 6496 in 1951, this from a factory that was already then capable of turning out 10,000 cars per year.

During this period, an American *ex*-XK 120 owner wrote a critical commentary on the XK 120's performance in US sports car races and also stated that, as a fast sports tourer, "the car has little purpose in the American market, this probably being the reason that you will find [second-hand] Jaguar XK 120s advertised for sale every Sunday in the *New York Times* and there is now no trouble in getting immediate delivery of these automobiles".[20]

Despite all this, American demand did not entirely dry up, and during the early months of 1951 20-odd right-hand-drive cars were shipped over, mostly to

Hoffman in New York. Furthermore, from mid-1951 onwards the American market revived and, once resumed, production of the XK 120 open two-seater with left-hand drive averaged 100 cars a month for the rest of the year. The advantage of this episode was that it enabled Jaguar to catch up with home market demand for the XK 120. No less than 250 open two-seaters were built for the home market during 1950 and 199 during 1951 (see Statistics for Sales by Agents), or just over 400 cars in the 1950-51 sales year, a figure that represented two-thirds of all XK 120 open two-seaters sold in the UK.

From 1951 to 1954, American sales and thus production increased steadily, but there was another problem to come. In 1952, Australia introduced sharply increased tariffs and restrictions on cars imported complete, as opposed to imports of chassis

In the car despatch bay at Foleshill with its characteristic wooden floor – a legacy of its World War One origin as a shell filling factory: wooden floors meant no sparks from hob-nailed boots, so less risk of an explosion! – XK 120s, mostly to US specification with number plate above the left-hand bumper and no headlamp units, are waiting to be dealt with. In the background is a selection of Mark Vs. (Paul Skilleter/Jaguar)

or cars in CKD form (Completely Knocked Down for local assembly). This was a continuation of Australia's historical policy originally introduced to support her local body-building industry, but now reinforced to protect her infant national car, the Holden. From 1951 to 1952, sales of British cars in Australia dropped by one-third.[21] In the following year, Lyons stated that "we look forward to a resumption of volume sales in Australia and New Zealand".[22]

The larger British car makers now increasingly set up assembly or manufacturing operations in Australia. Jaguar and its main importer, Bryson Motor Industries in Melbourne and Sydney, were too small to contemplate this step. The consequence was that XK 120 production for Australia fell from 134 in 1950 and 58 in 1951, to precisely 1 in 1952, 21 in 1953 and 9 in 1954 (of all body styles). In general, Jaguar

A 1950s aerial shot of Jaguar's then new Browns Lane factory. More than fifty years later, the surroundings are still quite rural. (JDHT)

exports to Australia dropped to a fraction of previous figures, this in a market that had taken almost 3000 Mark Vs, and which, barring the tariff, would have been a better outlet for the Mark VII.[23]

The introduction of the additional fixed-head coupé model[24] which went into regular production in left-hand-drive form in the summer of 1951 gave a boost to XK production, which, as will be seen, more than doubled from 1951 to 1952. Unsurprisingly, again the majority of fixed-head coupés went to the USA, and the home market had to wait. The new model only began to reach UK customers in early January 1953, with exceptions for favoured VIPs such as Peter Whitehead and Stirling Moss, who both had left-hand-drive examples.

There was, though, another break in production at the end of 1951, as from late November 1951 to mid-January 1952 no XK 120s of any kind were built. Factory stock levels at this time do not appear to have been unduly excessive, so the obvious explanation is that Jaguar simply chose to concentrate on building

Mark VII saloons at a time of year when sports car demand was at its lowest.

The big upheaval of 1952 was the transfer of production from the old Foleshill factory to the newly acquired factory in Browns Lane, Allesley. As the move was carried out gradually over a period of months, department by department, it is frustratingly difficult to pin-point when XK 120 production did move, but in so far as the *Car Record Books* offer any clue, it would appear to have been in July 1952. It is evident that the move took longer than planned. At one time Jaguar had anticipated completing it by the end of 1951, but a later estimate was of April 1952, and even then there were further delays.[25] XK 120 assembly was probably at Browns Lane after the summer break finished in August 1952 and, in fact, cars may already have been built in the new factory from mid-July onwards.

It would also appear, however, that body production continued for a while at Foleshill, even into October 1952. I believe that the switch of body production from Foleshill to Browns Lane – where a new paint plant was being constructed – co-incided with the change from cellulose to synthetic paint. This was effected gradually, depending on the colour of cars produced, from 21 October onwards, and was completed a month later. (Curiously, for three months hardly any red cars were built!) When all was in order, Jaguar held a convention for dealers, suppliers and the press on 28 November 1952 to show off the new factory.[26] Only at the end of 1952 did Lyons report to

California circa 1953 – young lady with XK 120 drophead coupé seeks tennis partner. (Jaguar Cars North America Archives)

The XK chassis assembly line at Browns Lane, a very modest affair! (JDHT)

The new paint shop at Browns Lane, with XK bodies mounted upside down on conveyors, going through the spray booths. (JDHT)

the board that the company was now well established in the new factory and that "the paint shop was operating as satisfactorily as we could hope",[27] a comment that probably indicates there had been some teething troubles in that area.

A third body style for the XK 120 appeared in the shape of the drophead coupé, which went into production at the end of January 1953 and for the first six months was built exclusively with left-hand drive for export.[28] There was the by-now-customary delay before the release of the model on the home market, but this was finally announced on 28 August, and the first UK deliveries were made in September.[29]

It is evident from the statistics that in later years, in the home market and many other export markets, the coupé models were preferred, and a larger proportion of the open two-seaters were sold in the one market of the USA, where demand for this version actually increased. No doubt this was assisted by the remarkable price reductions in the USA, which were announced at the end of September 1953, and included a greater reduction in percentage on the open two-seater. The old and new prices were as follows:[30]

Model	Old price in US $	Equivalent in £	New price in US $	Equivalent in £	Reduction
OTS	$4035	£1441	$3345	£1195	17.1%
FHC	$4065	£1452	$3875	£1384	4.7%
DHC	$4250	£1518	$3975	£1420	6.5%

(The Mark VII was actually increased in price in the USA at the same time)

This is the final assembly area at Browns Lane, probably in 1952, with Mark VIIs as well as open and fixed-head XK 120s. The cars on the right bear stickers on the rear number plates with warnings such as "Avoid Damage" and "Damage Means Dismissal". A typical Lyons touch! The assembly lines are rudimentary – an endless chain with hooks, between two guide rails. (Paul Skilleter/Jaguar)

One wonders what prompted this, but we cannot overlook the possibility that Jaguar was aware of the potential competition from the new, cheaper Austin-Healey 100 sports car and the Triumph TR2, as well as the Chevrolet Corvette, that had come on the market at $3513. As it was, the Corvette would not yet constitute a threat to Jaguar's sports car sales in the USA with a mere 315 sales in the 1953 model year, and only 4629 altogether for the first-generation Corvette through the 1955 model year.[31]

By 1954, the overall picture had settled down. Production of the XK 120 stopped in July (fixed-head) and August (open two-seater and drophead) in readiness for the introduction of the XK 140, but it

The "wedding", a gleaming fixed-head coupé body is lowered on to the chassis. (JDHT)

turned out to be the best ever year for the open two-seater, with 1871 cars produced. Of these, more than 1800 went to the USA. The fixed-head had peaked in 1952 and the drophead in 1953 (see detailed figures in the tables below).

Of all the 12,059 cars produced, the USA took the lion's share, with 9096 cars (not even including tax-free, home-delivery personal-export cars supplied in the UK to American service personnel and visitors, or cars sold to American citizens in countries such as Germany or Japan). This included 5772 open two-seaters, 2083 fixed-heads and 1241 dropheads. Sales were split fairly evenly between east and west; 4832 cars were consigned to Hoffman in New York, 4264 to Hornburg in Los Angeles. The USA therefore took 75.4 per cent of total production.

Altogether, the home market received 612 two-seaters, 152 fixed-heads and 262 dropheads, a total of 1026 cars, or around 8.5 per cent of production. A total of 470 cars were consigned to Henlys as the distributor for London and all of the south and east of England, and the firm also handled 38 of the Personal Export sales. In the sales year of 1951-52, Jaguar's overall sales performance had contained an astonishing 89 per cent of export sales, but this quickly dropped to figures more typically around 50-55 per cent.[32] Jaguar's pride in its export achievements was evident in the typically bullish statement issued in May 1952:

"…the delivery position in the home market is unchanged. [The] present overseas market is showing no signs of diminution and [the] proportion of exports has long stood at 85 per cent of total output. The home market waiting list for Jaguar cars includes unsatisfied orders dating back to 1946, and… deliv-

Some times you wonder how Americans imagine "merrie olde England". These chaps in hunting pink and the ladies in ball gowns make unlikely partners for a lilac(!) XK 120 on the cover of the American Car Life magazine. (Jaguar Cars North America Archives)

eries will continue to be made in strict rotation."[33]

Quite so. One can just imagine the provincial solicitor or doctor, who had ordered a 1½-litre saloon in 1946, and had waited patiently for six years, being contacted by the distributor to ask whether he would accept delivery of a C-type instead…

Apart from the USA, the UK and Australia (236 cars), important markets for the XK 120 included France (227 cars), Canada (222 cars) and Germany (196 cars), the latter unsurprising as most British cars exported to Germany at the time were sold to British

A well-filled despatch department at Browns Lane, with Mark VII saloons as well as XK 120s, in both open and fixed-head forms. (JDHT)

As Jaguar became a world-famous brand, the XK 120 found its way to some then unlikely markets. Here are XK 120s photographed at Motor Shows in Turkey and Finland. The open two-seater in Turkey must be 671346, the only one of its type to be exported there in late 1951. The fixed-head coupé in Finland is probably 679453, the first of two fixed-heads for this country. (JDHT)

and American service personnel, although some also found German buyers. Similarly, the 33 cars that went to Japan most likely found American buyers. Other good markets included Belgium (161 cars) and Switzerland (93 cars) – Switzerland took more RHD than LHD cars, as many Swiss customers continued to prefer RHD cars for mountain driving. Then there was Brazil (55 cars), Morocco (46 cars), Malaya (43 cars), New Zealand (37 cars), Venezuela (29 cars), Holland and Mexico (28 cars each), Sweden (27 cars) and Bahrein (21 cars). 145 cars were supplied tax-free under the Home Delivery Export Scheme in the UK.

Although Jaguar could probably have charged more for the XK 120, it was a well known part of William Lyons's philosophy to sell his cars at the lowest possible price in order to keep production up and spread the overheads over the largest possible number of cars. In consequence, he often astounded industry

and trade colleagues, the press, and the public with the very reasonable prices he charged. Another consequence, however, was that the company was sometimes run on a shoestring. No money was spent unless absolutely necessary, while the modest dividends were often a cause of complaints from shareholders.

The following table quotes the UK prices for the XK 120 model, ex-factory as well as including Purchase Tax, throughout the production period. Although there were two price increases, as will be seen, the greater variations resulted from changes to the level of Purchase Tax. In 1948, this was one-third of the wholesale price of a car with a factory price of less than £1000, but in 1951 was increased to two-thirds of the wholesale price of all cars, irrespective of factory price. Obviously, Jaguar strove to keep the factory "basic" price down to below the £1000 level until 1951…

Date	Model	Factory price	Purchase Tax	Total	Note
1948	XK 100/XK 120 "Super Sports"	£988	£275.3.11	£1263.3.11	From launch
10 Apr 1951	XK 120 OTS	£988	£550.7.9	£1538.7.9	Tax increased
19 Jul 1951	XK 120 OTS	£1078	£600.7.9	£1678.7.9	Prices increased
	XK 120 FHC	£1088	£605.18.11	£1693.18.11	
24 May 1952	XK 120 OTS	£1130	£629.5.7	£1759.5.7	Prices increased
	XK 120 FHC	£1140	£634.16.8	£1774.16.8	
15 Apr 1953	XK 120 OTS	£1130	£471.19.2	£1601.19.2	Tax reduced
	XK 120 OTS SE	£1245	£519.17	£1764.17	
	XK 120 FHC	£1140	£476.2.6	£1616.2.6	
	XK 120 FHC SE	£1245	£519.17	£1764.17	
28 Aug 1953	XK 120 DHC	£1160	£484.9.2	£1644.9.2	DHC model added
Late 1953	XK 120 OTS SE	£1210	£505.5.10	£1715.5.10	SE prices reduced
	XK 120 FHC SE	£1210	£505.5.10	£1715.5.10	
	XK 120 DHC SE	£1230	£513.12.6	£1743.12.6	
By 15 Jan 1954	XK 120 OTS SE	£1195	£499.0.10	£1694.0.10	SE prices reduced
	XK 120 FHC SE	£1195	£499.0.10	£1694.0.10	
	XK 120 DHC SE	£1215	£507.7.6	£1722.7.6	

(based on circulars and price lists issued by Jaguar Cars Ltd)

This is Henlys' London showroom in Piccadilly. As the posters proclaim that Jaguar has won the Tourist Trophy again, the photo must have been taken after Moss drove the C-type to victory in 1951. (JDHT)

Production figures for the XK 120 models have been quoted at various levels, and some published figures have been uncritically based on the statistics of cars sold as opposed to produced. In the following simplified table are the overall figures, split by body style, RHD/LHD, and calendar year. These figures have been compiled by an examination of the actual production records in the *Car Record Books*, and the total figures are broadly similar to the known range of chassis numbers issued.

	OTS RHD	OTS LHD	OTS combined	FHC RHD	FHC LHD	FHC combined	DHC RHD	DHC LHD	DHC combined	All models
1948	1		1							1
1949	26	70	96							96
1950	493	1026	1519							1519
1951	414	700	1114	2	214	216				1330
1952	111	1592	1703	2	1357	1359	1		1	3063
1953	107	1203	1310	107	735	842	167	1101	1268	3420
1954	24	1847	1871	84	177	261	127	371	498	2630
Total	1176	6438	7614	195	2483	2678	295	1472	1767	12059

(the above figures are based on "date chassis completed" from the *Car Record Books*, and include chassis only, CKD cars, and experimental cars or chassis)

In the tables which follow, I have split the production figures by model and calendar year, further by agents (distributors and importers), and also shown separate figures for, respectively, standard and Special Equipment models, cars supplied in chassis form, and Completely Knocked Down (CKD) cars. The dates on which these statistics have been based, are the dates of build ("date chassis completed" according to the *Car Record Books*). While similar statistics were maintained by Jaguar at the time, and are, indeed, now kept in the JDHT archive, these original statistics are arguably less helpful, for the following reasons:
• They were not split between RHD and LHD cars
• They were based on dates of despatch, rather than dates of build

• They were compiled by sales year from 1 August to 31 July, rather than calendar year
• They lump too many sales into a "miscellaneous" category
• They fail to account for cars which were retained by the company rather than sold.

The tables I have compiled are, in fact, based on electronic database versions of the complete XK 120 production records, and I accept that the transcription into a computerised format may have led to the occasional error. Nevertheless, I believe the results are reasonably accurate, and in so far as comparisons are possible with the original statistics, the final total figures are very similar.

OTS RHD – Home market:		1948	1949	1950	1951	1952 Std	1952 SE	1953 Std	1953 SE	1954 Std	1954 SE	Total
Birmingham	P J Evans			12	11	1		7	1		1	33
Belfast	Victor			4	2	1			1			8
Bolton	Parker's			13	7	1		3	1			25
Cardiff	Exclusive Cars			1	2			2			1	6
Carlisle	Scottish Motor Traction			2	3							5
Coventry	SH Newsome			3	2							5
Derby	Sanderson & Holmes			2	2	1						5
Douglas, Isle of Man	WH Shimmin				2							2
Edinburgh	Rossleigh			9	12	1		4	1	1		28
Glasgow	Ritchies			8	8			2	1			19
Grimsby	Roland C Bellamy			3	3	2						8
Harrogate	Glovers of Ripon			7	7	1						15
Hull	WL Thompson			2	3							5
Jersey, Channel Islands	St Helier Garage			2	2	1		1	3			9
Leeds	Appleyards			12	10			6				28
Leicester	Walter E Sturgess			4	3	1		1				9
London	Henlys			119	79	44		26	6	2	2	278
Malvern	Rothwell & Milbourne			2	2	1		1				6
Manchester	Henlys			18	13	2	1	3	2			39
Nottingham	CH Truman			4	2	1		1				8
Preston	Ashton Preston Garages			4	3	1		3				11
Sheffield	Ernest W Hatfield			4	4	1		1	2			12
Shrewsbury	Wales & Edwards			1	3							4
Stoke-on-Trent	Tom Byatt of Fenton			3	3	3		2		1		12
Wolverhampton	Charles Attwood			4	6			1			1	12
Miscellaneous	Jaguar Cars etc*	1	1	7	5	2		3	1			20
TOTAL		1	1	250	199	65	1	67	19	4	5	612
TOTAL by calendar year		1	1	250	199	66		86		9		612

*including chassis 660010

FHC and DHC RHD – Home market:		FHC 1951	1952 Std	1952 SE	1953 Std	1953 SE	1954 Std	1954 SE	Total	DHC 1952 Std	1953 Std	1953 SE	1954 Std	1954 SE	Total
Birmingham	PJ Evans					4	6	2	12	5	1	7	1		14
Belfast	Victor					1			1	1					1
Bolton	Parker's					2			2		6	4			10
Cardiff	Exclusive Cars				1		2		3				3		3
Carlisle	Scottish Motor Traction				1				1		1		1		2
Coventry	SH Newsome				1		1		2		2	1			3
Derby	Sanderson & Holmes				2				2		2		1	1	4
Edinburgh	Rossleigh				2	1	2		5		4		2		6
Glasgow	Ritchies				2		2		4		5		3		8
Grimsby	Roland C Bellamy					2		5	7		1			1	2
Harrogate	Glovers of Ripon				1	2			3		4		1		5
Hull	WL Thompson				1				1			2	1	1	4
Jersey, Channel Islands	St Helier Garage						2		2		1			1	2
Leeds	Appleyards				5	2	4		11		6	1	7	5	19
Leicester	Walter E Sturgess					1	1		2				1		1
London	Henlys				26	6	17	10	59		79	5	44	5	133
Malvern	Rothwell & Milbourne								0			4	1		5
Manchester	Henlys				7		4	3	14		11	2	4		17
Nottingham	CH Truman				1				1			1			1
Preston	Ashton Preston Garages				2		2	1	5		1	1	1		3
Sheffield	Ernest W Hatfield				1		2		3		3		4		7
Shrewsbury	Wales & Edwards								0				1		1
Stoke-on-Trent	Tom Byatt of Fenton				1		1		2		1	1	3		5
Wolverhampton	Charles Attwood				4		2		6		2		1		3
Miscellaneous	Jaguar Cars etc	2			1	1			4	1	2				3
TOTAL		2	0	0	59	22	45	24	152	1	137	14	94	16	262
TOTAL by calendar year		2		0	81		69		152	1	151		110		262

OTS RHD – Export markets:		1948	1949	1950	1951	1951 Chs	1951 CKD	1952 Std	1952 SE	1952 Chs	1953 Std	1953 SE	1954 Std	1954 SE	Total
Aden	Besse							1							1
Australia, Adelaide	Dominion		2	9	5						1				17
Australia, Brisbane	Anderson's Agencies		2	5	5						2				14
Australia, Melbourne/Sydney	Brylaw, later Bryson		7	119	46					1	2				175
Australia, Perth	MS Brooking		2	1	2						1				6
Austria, Vienna	Georg Hans Koch			2											2
Bahamas, Nassau	Commission Merchants			2											2
Belgium, Bruxelles	Jaguar Car Distributors/Belgian Motor Company			4	8	2		1							15
China	Biddle Sawyer							1							1
Cyprus, Nicosia	Tseriotis												1		1
Egypt, Cairo	Universal Motor Co							1							1
Eire, Dublin	Frank Cavey			3	1		12								16
France, Paris	Charles Delecroix			6	5			1							12
Germany, Düsseldorf	RM Overseas			1	1			1							3
Germany, Hamburg	Fendler & Luedemann							1							1
Gibraltar	Alfred Bassadone			1				1							2
Gold Coast, Accra	Berberi			2	1			1							4
Holland, The Hague	JW Lagerwijs		1	1											2
Hong Kong	Gilman & Co		2	2	1			1	1				1		8
India, Bombay	BD Garware			6	3										9
India, Calcutta	French Motor Car Co							1							1
India, Madras	Reliance Motor Co			1											1
India, New Delhi	Pearey Lal		1	1				1							3
Italy, Milano	Compagnia Generale			1							1		1		3
Italy, Torino	CEAT			1											1
Japan, Tokyo	Neil Buchanan				2										2
Japan, Tokyo	Jidosha								1						1
Kenya, Nairobi	Lowis & Hodgkiss			1	4			3	1			2			11
Malaya, Singapore	Brinkmann's		1	3											4
Malaya, Singapore	Cycle & Carriage				20			6			6		3		35
Malta, Gzira	Muscat's Garage				1			1							2
Morocco, Casablanca	Moto Maroc			3	2										5
Mozambique, Lourenço Marques	Gundle							2							2
New Zealand, Auckland	Shorter's Garage		1	2	3	1									7
New Zealand, Christchurch	Archibald			1	4									1	6
New Zealand, Wellington	Independent Motor Sales		1	3	13										17
Nigeria, Lagos	British West African Corp				1										1
Pakistan, Karachi	Polad & Co			1				1							2
Portugal, Oporto	Auto Omnia			5											5
Rhodesia, Bulawayo	Sager's Motors			3	3									1	7
South Africa, Cape Town	Robb Motors				1			2							3
South Africa, Johannesburg	John B Clarke				1										1
Spain, Madrid	ATA				1										1
Spain, Madrid	C de Salamanca													1	1
Sweden, Stockholm	Fredlunds Automobil			4						1					5
Switzerland, Geneva	Garage Place Claparede		1	14	4	2					1				22
Switzerland, Zürich	Emil Frey		2	11	15			3		1	1		1	3	37
Thailand, Bangkok	Assia			2	2			2							6
Trinidad, Port of Spain	FJ Miller & Co			1											1
USA, New York	Max Hoffman		2	6	27			4	1		1	1			42
USA, Los Angeles	Charles Hornburg			4	2			1			1			2	10
PED, Harrogate	Glovers of Ripon			1											1
PED, London	Henlys			3	6										9
PED, direct sales	Jaguar Cars Ltd			6	7							1			14
Unknown location	Heath Booth			1											1
Unknown location	Lewis & Peat											1			1
Unknown location	Paramount Traders				1										1
TOTAL of export sales		**0**	**25**	**243**	**198**	**5**	**12**	**38**	**5**	**1**	**17**	**5**	**7**	**8**	**564**
Plus home market sales		**1**	**1**	**250**	**199**			**65**	**1**		**67**	**19**	**4**	**5**	**612**
TOTAL of all sales		**1**	**26**	**493**	**397**	**5**	**12**	**103**	**6**	**1**	**84**	**24**	**11**	**13**	**1176**
TOTAL by calendar year		**1**	**26**	**493**			**414**			**110**		**108**		**24**	**1176**

OTS LHD – Export markets:		1949	1950	1951	1952 Std	1952 SE	1952 Chs	1953 Std	1953 SE	1954 Std	1954 SE	Total
Argentina, Buenos Aires	Ehlert (Nash) Motors	2	4					1			1	8
Bahamas, Nassau	Commission Merchants					1						1
Bahrein	M & A Koohiji				8			4	2			14
Belgium, Bruxelles	Jaguar Car Distributors/ Belgian Motor Company	1	21	14	22				6	1		65
Belgian Congo, Leopoldville	IMOCO			1	1							2
Brazil, Rio de Janeiro	Goodwin Cocozza	3	24	9	9							45
British Guyana	Campbell Booker Carter				1							1
Egypt, Cairo	Universal Motors	2		1								3
Finland, Tampere	SM Kauppa	1	1	1	3							6
France, Paris	Charles Delecroix	3	20	26	17			12	4		1	83
Canada, Halifax	Murch Motors							2				2
Canada, Montreal	Budd & Dyer	1	6	1	1			7		1		17
Canada, Montreal	National Motors							4	1			5
Canada, Newfoundland	MJ Duff				1							1
Canada, Ottawa	Waverley Motors		2						1		1	4
Canada, Toronto	James L Cooke	4	20	3	10	1		9	5	5	3	60
Canada, Vancouver	Thomas Plimley	2	14	4	1			4	1			26
Chile, Santiago	Importadora Fisk		2									2
Columbia, Barranquilla	Hutchinson			2								2
Columbia, Bogota	Anglo-Columbiana			1	3							4
Cuba, Havana	Frank Seiglie	3	3									6
Dutch West Indies, Curaçao	Kusters		1									1
Germany, Düsseldorf	RM Overseas		34	40	32	3		16	3	1		129
Germany, Hamburg	Fendler & Luedemann		2	1								3
Gibraltar	Alfred Bassadone		1					1				2
Gold Coast, Accra	Berberi		1									1
Greece, Athens	CD Coulentianos		1	3	2				1			7
Hawaii, Honolulu	British Motor Imports		1									1
Holland, The Hague	JW Lagerwijs		6	1	2							9
Hong Kong	Gilman & Co	1	1									2
India, Calcutta	French Motor Car Co								1			1
India, Madras	Wallace Cartwright				1							1
India, New Delhi	Pearey Lal			1								1
Indonesia, Djakarta	WB Govaars				1							1
Italy, Milano	Compagnia Generale				2	1		1				4
Japan, Tokyo	Neil Buchanan				2							2
Japan, Tokyo	Jidosha				10	3		3	2			18
Lebanon, Beirut	IJ Saad				4			1		2	1	8
Libya, Tripoli	Gordon Woodroffe			1	1					1		3
Mexico, Mexico City	Jorge Barranco		1	4	3	3						11
Mexico, Mexico City	Auto Europeos					1		1	2			4
Morocco, Casablanca	Moto Maroc		5	3	6	2		2		2		20
Norway, Oslo	Standard Autos							1				1
Panama, Panama City	Guardia & Cia				2	1						3
Peru, Lima	Fenix	1	6					1				8
Philippines, Manila	Luzon Industrial Corp		1									1
Portugal, Oporto	Auto Omnia		2		2							4
Portugal, Lisbon	Martins & Almeida								2			2
Puerto Rico, San Juan	Esteve		1									1
Puerto Rico, San Juan	Grosch								1			1
South Africa, Johannesburg	John B Clarke				1							1
Sweden, Stockholm	Fredlunds Automobil		9						1			10
Switzerland, Geneva	Garage Place Claparede		7		1							8
Switzerland, Zürich	Emil Frey	1	3				1					5
Thailand, Bangkok	Assia			1								1
Trinidad, Port of Spain	FJ Miller & Co							2				2
Turkey, Istanbul	Otokar Ticaret			1								1
USA, New York	Max Hoffman*	24	436	358	621	107		303	286	405	604	3144
USA, Los Angeles	Charles Hornburg	18	361	214	496	177		127	365	225	593	2576
Uruguay, Montevideo	Pablo Aicardi		1	1								2
Venezuela, Caracas	Mercantil Anglo (CAMAV)	1	7		2			2				12
PED, Glasgow	Ritchies				1							1
PED, London	Henlys		3	5	3			3				14
PED, Nottingham	CH Truman		1									1
PED, direct sales	Jaguar Cars Ltd		9	2	3			4	1			19
PED	UK Exchange Service		4	3	14	2		5	2			30
Works cars	Jaguar Cars Ltd**	1	2									3
Unknown location	Heath Booth											
TOTAL		**70**	**1026**	**700**	**1289**	**302**	**1**	**515**	**688**	**643**	**1204**	**6438**
TOTAL by calendar year		**70**	**1026**	**700**			**1592**	**1203**		**1847**		**6438**

*incl. chassis no. 670001
**incl. an insurance write-off in 1950

FHC and DHC RHD – Export markets:		FHC 1951	1952 Std	1952 SE	1953 Std	1953 SE	1954 Std	1954 SE	Total	DHC 1952 Std	1953 Std	1953 SE	1954 Std	1954 SE	Total
Australia, Adelaide	Dominion				4				4		2				2
Australia, Brisbane	Anderson's Agencies					1			1		1				1
Australia, Melbourne/Sydney	Brylaw, later Bryson				2	1	5	1	9		3		3		6
Australia, Perth	MS Brooking								0		1				1
Belgium, Bruxelles	Belgian Motor Company					1			1						0
France, Paris	Charles Delecroix							1	1						0
Gold Coast, Accra	Berberi				1	1			2						0
Hong Kong	Gilman & Co				1	1			2				2	1	3
India, Madras	Wallace Cartwright							1	1				1		1
Jamaica, Kingston	Daytona Sales								0				1		1
Kenya, Nairobi	Lowis & Hodgkiss				1				1				1		1
Malaya, Singapore	Cycle & Carriage				2				2		2				2
New Zealand, Auckland	Shorter's Garage				1				1		1				1
New Zealand, Christchurch	Archibald								0					1	1
New Zealand, Wellington	Independent Motor Sales				3				3		1				1
Rhodesia, Bulawayo	Sager's Motors		1		4				5		1	2			3
South Africa, Cape Town	Robb Motors								0		1				1
Spain, Madrid	C de Salamanca							1	1						0
Sweden, Stockholm	Fredlunds Automobil					1	1		2				1		1
Switzerland, Geneva	Garage Place Claparede								0				1		1
Switzerland, Zürich	Emil Frey						1		1						0
Thailand, Bangkok	Assia						1		1				1		1
Trinidad, Port of Spain	Engineering Ltd						1		1						0
USA, New York	Max Hoffman								0				1	1	2
PED, London	Henlys				1		1		2			1	2		3
Unknown location	Lewis & Peat			1			1		2						0
TOTAL of export sales		0	1	1	20	6	11	4	43	0	13	3	14	3	33
Plus home market sales		2	0	0	59	22	45	24	152	1	137	14	94	16	262
TOTAL of all sales		2	1	1	79	28	56	28	195	1	150	17	108	19	295
TOTAL by calendar year		2	2		107		84		195	1	167		127		295

FHC and DHC LHD – export markets		FHC 1951	1952 Std	1952 SE	1953 Std	1953 SE	1954 Std	1954 SE	Total	DHC 1953 Std	1953 SE	1954 Std	1954 SE	Total
Algeria, Algiers	Bouloch & Reynaud				1				1		1			1
Angola, Luanda	Pereira								0		1			1
Argentina, Buenos Aires	Ehlert (Nash) Motors					1	1	1	3	3		1	4	8
Austria, Vienna	Georg Hans Koch		1			1			2	2		1		3
Bahrein	M & A Koohiji		1			2			3			3	1	4
Belgian Congo, Leopoldville	IMOCO					1			1					0
Belgium, Bruxelles	Jaguar Car Distributors/ Belgian Motor Company	6	37	12	2	6		3	66	7	6		1	14
Brazil, Rio de Janeiro	Goodwin Cocozza	1	8		1				10					0
Burma, Rangoon	Peacock Motors		1						1					0
Canada, Montreal	Budd & Dyer	1	4	1	3		1	1	11	1	1	2		4
Canada, Montreal	National Motors				3	1			4	2				2
Canada, Newfoundland	MJ Duff								0			1		1
Canada, Ottawa	Waverley Motors					1			1	3	3	1		7
Canada, Toronto	James L Cooke	1	10	5	5	8	3	2	34	9	6		5	20
Canada, Vancouver	Thomas Plimley		11		1	1			13	5	1	1		7
Canada, Vancouver	Oxford Motor Co						1		1			2		2
Ceylon, Colombo	Brown & Co		1						1					0
Columbia, Barranquilla	Hutchinson								0			2		2
Columbia, Bogota	Anglo-Columbiana			1	1	1			3				1	1
Columbia, Medellin	Autobritanica								0				1	1
Cuba, Havana	Frank Seiglie	1			1				2				1	1
Denmark, Copenhagen	E Sommer								0	2		2		4
Dutch W.I., Curaçao	Kusters				1				1					0
Ecuador, Guayaquil	Aviles Alfaro & Co								0			1		1
Egypt, Cairo	Universal Motor Co	1	1						2					0
Finland, Tampere	SM Kauppa		1		1				2					0
France, Paris	Charles Delecroix	11	34	2	6	11	7	1	72	20	11	21	7	59
Germany, Düsseldorf	RM Overseas	23	4			7	1	1	36	11	4	7		22
Germany, Hamburg	Fendler & Luedemann								0		1	1		2
Greece, Athens	CD Coulentianos		1						1					0
Holland, The Hague	JW Lagerwijs	2	6				1		9	2		5	1	8
Iceland, Reykjavik	Orka								0		1			1
Iran, Tehran	Abolhasssan Diba & Co								0			1		1
Italy, Milan	Compagnia Generale								0	1		1		2
Italy, Rome	Fattori & Montani								0				2	2
Japan, Tokyo	Jidosha		5		2	2			9	1				1
Kenya, Nairobi	Lowis & Hodgkiss		2						2					0
Lebanon, Beirut	IJ Saad				1				1	1		2		3
Libya, Tripoli	Gordon Woodroffe		1		1				2					0
Madagascar, Tananarive	R Weinberger								0				1	1
Mexico, Mexico City	Jorge Barranco	3	3	1					7					0
Mexico, Mexico City	Auto Europeos				1	2			3	1	1		1	3
Morocco, Casablanca	Moto Maroc	2	6		3	3	5	1	20	1				1
Norway, Oslo	Standard Autos								0			1		1
Nicaragua	Nicaragua Machinery Co								0	1				1
Panama, Panama City	Guardia & Cia		1		1				2					0
Peru, Lima	Fenix		1						1					0
Philippines, Manila	Products Inc								0			1		1
Portugal, Oporto	Auto Omnia	1	1						2					0
Portugal, Lisbon	Martins & Almeida				1				1		1	1	1	3
Puerto Rico, San Juan	Grosch					1			1			1		1
Rhodesia, Bulawayo	Sager's Motors		1						1					0
South Africa, Johannesburg	John B Clarke		2						2					0
Spain, Madrid	C de Salamanca				1				1				2	2
Sweden, Stockholm	Fredlund		1		1	1	1		4	1	1	2	1	5
Switzerland, Geneva	Garage Place Claparede	2	4		1				7	2			1	3
Switzerland, Zürich	Emil Frey	1	2	1	2	1			7	2				2
Trinidad, Port of Spain	FJ Miller & Co								0		1			1
Turkey, Istanbul	Otokar Ticaret	1							1					0
USA, New York	Max Hoffman	85	514	102	101	209	20	8	1039	295	203	19	88	605
USA, Los Angeles	Charles Hornburg	69	430	118	151	165	46	65	1044	252	232	33	117	634
Venezuela, Caracas	Mercantil Anglo (CAMAV)	1	3		5	2	3	1	15			2		2
PED, Coventry	SH Newsome	1							1	1				1
PED, Glasgow	Ritchies								0	3	1	3		7
PED, London	Henlys		4	1	2	2	1		10					0
PED, direct sales	Jaguar Cars Ltd	1	3	1	1	2			8	3	1	2		6
PED	UK Exchange Service		4	2	2		3		11	4	1		2	7
Works cars	Jaguar Cars Ltd		1						1					0
TOTAL		**214**	**1110**	**247**	**314**	**421**	**94**	**83**	**2483**	**636**	**466**	**130**	**240**	**1472**
TOTAL by calendar year		**214**	**1357**		**735**		**177**		**2483**	**1102**		**370**		**1472**

1. Porter & Skilleter *Sir William Lyons* p280, based on statistics in JDHT archive

2. Announced by Sir Stafford Cripps, President of the Board of Trade, at a dinner of the SMM&T in November 1945; Plowden *The Motor Car and Politics in Britain* (Pelican ed.) p321, citing *The Times* 16 Nov 1945

3. Porter & Skilleter p280, based on statistics in JDHT archive

4. *Ibid.* pp103-06; Dugdale *Jaguar in America* p13

5. Porter & Skilleter pp136-37

6. Dealer list in 1949 XK 120 handbook

7. Porter & Skilleter p109

8. *The Autocar* 14 Jan 1949; Bentley soon ordered his own XK 120 which he had by the summer of 1950, *The Autocar* 4 Aug 1950, 29 Dec 1950

9. *The Autocar* 30 Dec 1949, 17 Jan 1950

10. *The Motor* 19 Oct 1949

11. *The Motor Industry of Great Britain* (SMM&T annual handbook), various years

12. Stein *British Sports Cars in America* 1946-1981, p63

13. Whisler *At the End of the Road*, table VII.2, p197, citing PRO SUPP 14/332 "The Market for British Cars in the USA"

14. Jaguar Cars Ltd, Lyons's "Statement to Shareholders" 4 May 1950

15. Jaguar Cars Ltd, minutes of board meeting 27 June 1950, JDHT archive

16. Porter & Skilleter pp116-17

17 .*The Economist* 24 Oct 1953, p298; slightly different and conflicting but broadly similar figures quoted by Dugdale pp18, 29-30

18. Figures compiled by comparing build and despatch dates as found in the *Car Record Books*

19. Porter & Skilleter pp122-23

20. AE Goldschmidt in *Motor Sport* Jan 1951

21. From 93,430 to 64,230; *The Times Survey of the British Motor Industry* Oct 1955 p42

22. *The Times Survey of the British Motor Industry* Oct 1953 p55

23. See on this subject also Elmgreen & McGrath *The Jaguar XK in Australia* and annual statistics by sales year in Porter & Skilleter p281

24. *The Autocar* 2 Mar 1951; *The Motor* 7 Mar 1951

25. Jaguar Cars Ltd, minutes of Board Meetings 27 Jun 1951, 2 Jan 1952, JDHT archive

26. *The Motor* 3 Dec 1952; Whyte *Jaguar The History of a Great British Car* p139

27. Jaguar Cars Ltd, minutes of board meeting 31 Dec 1952, JDHT archive

28. *The Motor* 1 Apr 1953; *The Autocar* 3 Apr 1953

29. Jaguar Cars Ltd circular letter 28 Aug 1953, JDHT archive

30. Jaguar Cars Ltd press release 25 Sep 1953; *The Motor* 7 Oct 1953. Figures in £ quoted here have been slightly adjusted to reflect the exchange rate of $2.80 to the £.

31. *50 Years of American Automobiles* pp99, 476

32. Porter & Skilleter p281

33. *The Motor* 28 May 1952

Chapter Seven

The Hectic Years – Competition 1949-1953

In this chapter, the competition history of the XK 120 is given more or less chronologically, including both the works cars and many of the private entries. Many of the successes are chronicled in the detailed Appendix in Lord Montagu of Beaulieu's *Jaguar – A Biography* (1961 and later editions). For additional race information, I have principally made use of Paul Skilleter's *Jaguar Sports Cars* (1975) and the late Andrew Whyte's *Jaguar Sports Racing and Works Competition Cars to 1953* (1982). Bernard

Viart's *Jaguar XK – Le Grand Livre* (1993) is especially good on many Continental events which are little covered in British publications.

The XK 120 was not designed as a racing car, but as a fast road-going sports car for touring use. There was, however, undoubtedly some pressure on the company to prove that it also had a potential race winner on its hands, especially after the demonstration of the new model's performance at Jabbeke in May 1949 (see chapter 8). After this event, Bill Boddy commented in

In the paddock before the 1949 Silverstone race. The white HKV 500 is nearest to the camera, still with the rear number plate mounted on the boot lid. Behind it is HKV 455, now painted blue with a yellow steering wheel, but the absence of the external fuel filler gives it away. This was Bira's car in the race. Works mechanic Frank Rainbow and a colleague are busy with something! (Paul Skilleter)

Here is Leslie Johnson in full flight, making up lost time after his encounter with the errant Jowett Javelin. (Paul Skilleter)

Motor Sport that "we believe that [Jaguar's] policy is against racing… because they regard the XK as a normal touring car and because they consider that better publicity results if successes are achieved by private owners."[1]

A revival of motor racing in Britain after the end of World War II was initially handicapped as two of the premier venues, Brooklands and Donington Park, had both been lost. There was, however, a surplus of war-time RAF bases, and many of the new post-war circuits were converted from former air fields. These included Silverstone and Goodwood, which both opened in 1948. The first race at Silverstone was the 1948 British Grand Prix run over a somewhat improvised course. In 1949, the British Racing Drivers' Club took over management, laid out a three-mile circuit on the perimeter roads, and staged the first International Trophy Race with sponsorship from the *Daily Express*.[2] As part of this meeting, scheduled for 20 August, the BRDC would hold a Production Car Race, in itself a milestone as it marked the start of organised racing for touring cars in Britain. It attracted a wide entry, originally reported as no fewer than 100 cars, but was whittled down to 30 starters, including pre- as well as post-war saloons and sports cars.

This race represented an opportunity for Jaguar, but since the reputation of both the company and the new model would be at stake, it was deemed necessary first of all to establish whether the XK 120 had the speed and the stamina to be a winner. Accordingly, an XK 120 was taken to Silverstone and "flogged round for three hours" by "Lofty" England, "Wally" Hassan and

The three XK 120s line up in front of the pits before the start of the 1949 Silverstone race. (JDHT)

Bira and Lyons confer with none other than Earl Howe in the pit before the start of the 1949 Silverstone race.

A Frazer Nash, possibly Culpan's, sandwiched between the XK 120s of Walker and Johnson. (JDHT)

The unlucky third man: Bira in HKV 455 before his retirement at Silverstone. (JDHT)

"Bill" Rankin. Even Lyons himself turned up and put in a few laps. He jumped into the car where Rankin was sitting in the passenger seat and set off smartly with the words "Hey Rankin, I've left my specs behind, tell me where the corners and braking points are…" He then proceeded to lap nearly as fast as the rest, finally pulling in, much to the relief of the long-suffering Rankin.[3]

The results of the test run were sufficiently good for Jaguar to confirm the entry of three XK 120s in the race, with drivers "B Bira" (Prince Birabongse of Thailand), Leslie Johnson, and Peter Walker. Their cars were just about the only three XK 120s which the

company had available to race, and were painted blue (Bira's car), red (Walker) and white (Johnson). Johnson's car, in fact, was the Jabbeke record car (see chapter 8). The strongest opposition in the race came from the Frazer Nash Le Mans replica, the Healey Silverstone and the Allard J-type, but it deserves mention that there was a *fourth* Jaguar in the race – Cyril Mann's pre-war SS Jaguar 100.

The result of the race was neither a foregone conclusion nor was it achieved entirely without incident. Although one of the Allards was first away from the Le Mans-type start, it was soon overtaken by the XKs. Bira initially took the lead, with Johnson and Walker close behind, and Culpan in a Frazer Nash snapping at their heels. As the XK drivers lapped the field, over-taking the slower cars, Johnson was in collision with a Jowett Javelin but continued, although temporarily in fifth place. Then Bira suffered a blown-out rear tyre, which sent his car spinning into the straw bales lining the track. This forced his retirement when his jack dug into soft ground, thereby preventing him from changing the wheel. At the end of the hour-long race, Johnson was first across the line, followed 5.6 seconds later by Walker, and Culpan's Frazer Nash in an equally close third place. Johnson had covered 28 laps and averaged 82.8mph (133.25km/h). In fourth place, a lap behind, was Rolt's Healey, and the best-placed Allard was eighth.

Leslie Johnson gave the XK 120 its debut in American racing when he took 670001, Walker's red car from Silverstone, out to the USA for the SCCA (Sports Car Club of America) event at Palm Beach in

The XK 120 enjoyed mixed fortunes in American sports car racing, but both importers were quick to seek publicity for the car. This XK 120 was lent by Hoffman as a course car for the Watkins Glen sports car grand prix. (JDHT)

January 1950. He finished fourth overall and second in class, behind an ex-Indianapolis Ford Duesenberg special, a Cadillac-engined Healey Silverstone, and a Ferrari. The American drivers Bill Spear and Sam Collier also drove XK 120s in this race but were eliminated with brake trouble, and Johnson himself was said to have no brake linings left at the end of the race.[4] The first overseas win for an XK 120 came when Alfonso Gomez Mena won a production car race in Havana, Cuba in February, against a very mixed bag of entrants.[5]

By the spring of 1950 the six specially works-prepared XK 120s were ready (see chapter 8), and the first race for any of these cars was the Targa Florio in Sicily on 2 April, where Clemente Biondetti entered 660043. He led for a time and was still in second place when number three con rod fractured across the big end, and found a way out through the hole which it made in the side of the engine. This was immediately reported back to Bill Heynes by Jaguar mechanic John Lea, who added Biondetti's mostly favourable comments on the car, but also mentioned the tendency for the brakes to fade.[6]

A replacement engine was sent out and fitted so that Biondetti's car was ready for the Mille Miglia three weeks later, where three other of the works cars were also entered – by Nick Haines, Leslie Johnson and Tommy Wisdom. As a four-times past winner of this race, Biondetti may have been the favourite, but he was delayed for three-quarters of an hour while an improvised repair was made to a broken rear spring. Although he then pressed on magnificently, gaining

much of the lost time, he was unable to finish better than eighth, about an hour behind the winning Ferrari. Johnson, with John Lea as riding mechanic, had a relatively trouble-free race and finished fifth, while the two other cars retired. The Haines car crashed and lost too much time, and on Wisdom's car the front universal joint broke.

Wisdom went on to Oporto in Portugal where, on 18 June, he came third in a sports car race which was also contested by a locally owned XK 120. Wisdom, too, now experienced braking problems, and after the race Ken Bowen, the Jaguar service representative, "found the front shoes completely worn to a knife

By contrast, this XK 120 took part in the Elkhart Lake Rally organised by the Sports Car Club of America in 1952. (JDHT)

The three XK 120s lined up in numerical order before the start of the 1950 Le Mans. From left to right the Haines/Clark car, the Whitehead/Marshall car, and the Johnson/Hadley car. (JDHT)

California in November 1950, with Hill's brother-in-law Don Parkinson in second place in a similar car.[9]

Despite these successes, the XK 120 was far from having its own way in American sports car racing. The aforementioned A E Goldschmidt had become so disillusioned that he swapped his XK for a Cadillac-engined Allard, with which he won the International Grand Prix at Watkins Glen, lapping all the XKs. He related his experiences in a letter to *Motor Sport*.[10] This was supported by Bill Boddy's analysis of American sports car races in 1950: in nine races, there was only one win for Jaguar, two second places and three third places. The Cadillac-engined Allard J2 was then very much the car to beat on the American racetracks – 3cwt lighter than the XK, and with an engine of 5.4 litres producing up to 180bhp in tuned form.[11] The battle against not only the Allards but also the Ferraris and the new Cunninghams continued into 1951. The XK 120s rarely got the best of it, although Don Parkinson won the Palm Springs Cup Race of 150 miles in November 1951 in his special-bodied XK 120, possibly chassis 670191 (see chapter 10).[12]

The most important event for the Jaguar works cars in 1950 was the 24-hour race at Le Mans on 24-25 June. Although the cars were officially private entries

edge".[7] Also in June 1950, Phil Hill finished second in the Santa Ana race in California in his newly-acquired XK 120, with J McAfee in a similar car in third place. Similarly, a third place behind a Cadillac-engined Allard and a Ferrari had been the best for Goldschmidt's XK 120 at Suffolk County Airport, Westhampton, Long Island, in May 1950.[8] Later in the season, Hill won the Pebble Beach Cup Race in

Perhaps the most famous photo ever taken of an XK 120: Ian Appleyard on the Furka Pass during the 1950 Alpine Rally. (JDHT)

Peter Clark at the wheel of car number 15 during the 1950 Le Mans. He and co-driver Haines finished as the best of two surviving XK 120s, in 12th place. (JDHT)

This is a still from the film Endurance – A Fantasy of Le Mans, *shot by the Dunlop Company at Le Mans in 1950, featuring the Jaguar team.*

by their owners, extensive works preparation was undertaken on the three cars, with a Jaguar works mechanic allocated to each. England and Heynes were also on hand, just to see how things went! England acted as unofficial team manager, while John Eason-Gibson organised the pit. Nick Haines's car was number 15, co-driven by Peter Clark. It was the race debut for Peter Walker's car, which was driven by Peter Whitehead and John Marshall under number 16, while Leslie Johnson and co-driver Bert Hadley were allocated number 17.

The field of 60 starters included many bigger-engined cars, such as the Talbots with 4.5-litre engines, Rosier's car was described as a road-equipped grand prix car, an Allard with an even bigger Cadillac engine, as well as the two Cadillacs of the

At the start of the race, with a Talbot coupé in the lead, followed by a Delahaye and the three Jaguars. (JDHT)

The original owner of JKV 116 (660082) was S Y Barsley (or Barslay) so presumably this is him and his wife, in the 1950 Alpine Rally, with a very odd ship's ventilator fitted on their bonnet. (Paul Skilleter)

This is the Swiss driver Habisreutinger on the 1950 Alpine Rally, in his early alloy-bodied car 660023, with the starting handle hole in the radiator just visible. (Paul Skilleter)

Cunningham team and 4.5-litre Delahayes. There were also five Ferraris, with 2- or 2.3-litre engines, which were the favourites (a Ferrari had won the 1949 race) together with the Talbots. Other entries included Aston Martin DB2 and Frazer Nash. In the race, the Jaguars far from discredited themselves. The Johnson/Hadley car was running in second place after 15 hours and, notwithstanding brake fade, was actually speeding up when the clutch centre ripped out and ended the pair's race. Whitehead and Marshall also had brake trouble but managed to finish 15th. Haines and Clark were at one time in eighth place but were slowed when oil leaked into the clutch, and they finished 12th, averaging 80.6mph (129.7km/h).

The winner was Rosier's Talbot at 89.71mph (144.37km/h), followed by a second Talbot, after all the Ferrraris had retired. In third place, the Allard was the highest-placed British car, followed by a Nash-Healey and a brace of Aston Martins, while the ninth place for the 2-litre Frazer Nash of Stoop and Mathieson was an outstanding effort. Not a stunning result for Jaguar, perhaps, but it was deemed to be sufficiently encouraging to entertain the idea of building a more specialised lightweight racing model which, in the words of chief engineer Heynes, might stand a chance of winning Le Mans "given reasonable luck".[13] The result was the C-type, which was ready for the 1951 Le Mans – and won it. It may be added that the Jaguar entry at Le Mans in 1950 was used as the setting for a film shot by the Dunlop Company, called

Endurance – A Fantasy of Le Mans, starring Jean Lodge and Guy Middleton.[14]

I have not so far mentioned the sixth of the works-prepared cars, NUB 120, which was allocated to Ian Appleyard for rallying. Its first appearance was in the Tulip Rally in April 1950, and Appleyard completed the road section without loss of marks but made an error in the final driving test which cost him first place. He next entered the Morecambe Rally, but the International Alpine Rally in July would provide a more serious test. Appleyard had run in three successive Alpines, with his SS 100 in 1947 and 1948, and in a Healey Silverstone in 1949. He had two class wins and an Alpine Cup to his credit already. On the 1950 rally, NUB 120 was joined by the sister car of Nick Haines as well as other XK 120s entered by the Swiss driver Habisreutinger, and by Barslay.

The newly married Appleyard took his wife Patricia, the elder daughter of William Lyons, along as navigator. They were bothered by the by-now probably expected brake wear so, in his efforts to spare the brakes, Appleyard used first gear as much as possible – until it locked up. It soon freed itself but then kept on jamming intermittently for the rest of the rally. The worst episode was when he hit a wall on a very tight hairpin bend, pushing the right-hand front wing valance on to the tyre so that, eventually, the valance had to be cut away. Despite their woes, the Appleyards came through without losing any marks. They put up the best performance on all sections bar one, and set fastest time over a flying kilo-

A busy Silverstone paddock before the 1950 sports car race. In the foreground, "Lofty" England is sitting in Tommy Wisdom's car, chatting to Phil Weaver with his back to the camera. Behind are the cars of Nick Haines and Leslie Johnson. HKV 500 is missing, and so is Peter Walker's car. (JDHT)

Tazio Nuvolari is sitting in HKV 500 after his practice run at Silverstone in 1950, with William Lyons standing next to him. The ailing maestro was persuaded to give up his seat to Peter Whitehead. (JDHT)

metre on an Italian *autostrada* at no less than 109.6mph (176.4km/h). They also won the acceleration and braking test at Cannes at the end of the rally. The result was a class win and another Alpine Cup, and they were effectively the winners of the rally.[15] Of the other XK 120 drivers in the 1950 Alpine, Haines had brake trouble and collided with a lorry, while Habisreutinger

This photo deceives to flatter. Leslie Johnson was first away from the start of the 1950 TT, but had already passed the camera which here has caught Stirling Moss in JWK 988, chassis 660057. He went on to a famous victory. Between the works Aston Martins can be seen Peter Walker in HKV 500, he finished second, while Johnson in JWK 651 was third. (JDHT)

went off the road trying to avoid a collision. Barslay finished 21st. Appleyard ran NUB 120 in a number of British events during the remainder of 1950, winning the East Anglian Motor Club's Clacton rally and coming second in the Lakeland Rally and the MCC 1000-mile rally.

The second Production Car Race at Silverstone was held on 26 August 1950 and five XK 120s took part. This race was so popular that there were two heats; one for cars of less than two litres and the other for those over. The eventual winner would be the car that set fastest time, irrespective of engine size. Leslie Johnson, Peter Walker and Tommy Wisdom drove their own cars, while Nick Haines's car was driven by Tony Rolt, and finally there was the old war horse HKV 500. At one time this was going to be driven by Tazio Nuvolari, but when he felt unwell after practising it was taken over by Peter Whitehead. Whitehead was freakishly unlucky as his sump plug came loose and the engine lost all its oil, causing him to retire. It also caused some uncomfortable moments for Johnson, who had had a bad start and then ran straight into the oil spilled from Whitehead's car.

In the end, it was Walker and Rolt who took first and second places in the large-car heat and, with Wisdom and Johnson finishing further down the list, the Jaguars took the team prize. In the aggregate result, however, the 2-litre Ferraris of Ascari and Serafini were first and second; Ascari's average was 83.72mph (134.73km/h), against Walker's 81.88mph

After the race, the winning car was proudly displayed by Henlys in their London showroom. (JDHT)

(131.77km/h). Walker, Rolt and Johnson took the manufacturers' team prize.[16] Walker followed his success at Silverstone by setting fastest time in the class for Production Cars over 3000cc at Shelsley Walsh in September, with a climb in 44.61 seconds, although he was actually beaten by three Frazer Nashes. On this occasion, the hill was opened by Ian and Pat Appleyard in NUB 120.[17]

The next important event in the calendar was the first post-war Tourist Trophy race, held in appallingly wet conditions at the Dundrod track near Belfast. Four XK 120s were entered but Haines crashed his car in practice, and this car was not seen in racing again. Whitehead again had charge of HKV 500, now fitted with a new engine, Johnson drove his own car, and the newcomer to the team was a young up-and-coming driver called Stirling Moss, who had persuaded Tommy Wisdom to lend him his car. In practice, while the roads were still dry, Moss posted a fastest lap of 81.39mph (130.98km/h). In the race itself, Moss was content to let Johnson lead from the start, but after one lap overtook him, as did Whitehead. Moss, Whitehead and Johnson finished in that order on speed and Moss's race average was 75.15mph (120.94km/h). He and Whitehead were also first and second on handicap, with Johnson seventh. This was the race result that well and truly not only put the XK 120 on the map, but gave Moss a significant leg-up in his career – and a contract as a Jaguar works driver.

After the TT, Leslie Johnson turned his attention to

record breaking. He booked the Monthléry track for a 24-hour run on 24-25 October 1950, and enlisted Stirling Moss to share the driving in three-hour stints. The car was Johnson's usual mount, JWK 651, which was specially prepared by Jaguar, and works mechanics John Lea and Frank Rainbow joined the party. There were no problems, and the 24-hour run was completed

None other than John Coombs ran PPA 777 in the Rallye des Sestrières in February 1951; here he hunkers down, pensively, by the front wheel, while the co-driver enjoys what we hope is a nice cup of tea. (Paul Skilleter)

Jackie and Mrs Cooper, owners and drivers of KDU 164, chassis 670400, enjoy a cup of tea at the Shell Garage on the Promenade des Anglais (how fitting) in Nice during the Rallye des Sestrières in 1951. (Paul Skilleter).

The Rallye Soleil-Cannes also at one time threatened to become a preserve for les Anglais. Of four XK 120s here lined up during the 1952 event, two hail from Birmingham. (Paul Skilleter)

... and here is a Coventry registered Personal Export Delivery car in the same rally, KHP 251 was chassis 660215. (Paul Skilleter).

at an average of 107.46mph (172.94km/h), with individual laps at higher speeds of up to 126mph (202.7km/h).[18] The experience gave Johnson a taste for record runs, and on 12 March 1951 he took JWK 651 back to Monthléry after the engine had been further tuned by Jaguar to give 184bhp and the car fitted with aerodynamic aids. The intention was to drive as fast as possible for one hour, and Johnson covered 131.20 miles (211.15 km), with a fastest lap of 134.43mph (216.34km/h).[19] Johnson would cap both of these efforts with the 1952 seven days run in the XK 120 fixed-head coupé discussed in chapter 8.

In 1951, there was a dramatic scene shift. The Jaguar XK 120 C – or C-type – made its debut appearance at Le Mans in June and instantly relegated

the XK 120, as far as the works team was concerned, to an also-ran. On the other hand, as explained in chapter 6, comparatively large numbers of XK 120s now reached private enthusiasts in the home market, and were entered in all sorts of competitive events. However, before the C-type appeared, there were still some important races to be contested by the works or works-prepared cars.

XK 120s were now regularly seen in rallies, both in the UK and on the continent. In the Rallye des Sestrières in February 1951 the model was not competitive against Italian entrants, and best result was a 16th in class for Bellorini in the over 1.5-litre class, followed by Herzet, and John Coombs in PPA 777.[20] In the Lyon-Charbonnières in March, best-placed XK was the car of Herzet and Baudoin, who came second in the over 3-litre class[21] – their mount was not yet the Oblin coupé. In April, a mixed bag of private French and British entrants took their XK 120s on the Rallye Soleil-Cannes. The Jaguar dealer of Lyon, Henri Peignaux, took first place, while Taylor was second and Bray third, also in XK 120s, followed by sister cars in fourth as well as sixth place.[22] In the Scottish Rally in May, there was a 1-2 for the XK 120, Leslie Wood finishing ahead of Alex McGlashan.[23]

The first major road race of the season was the Mille Miglia at the end of April. Two XK 120s were sent out; Johnson's normal car JWK 651 with John Lea as co-driver was one, while Stirling Moss drove HKV 500 with Frank Rainbow in the passenger seat. In addition, Biondetti fielded his Jaguar-Ferrari special fitted with the original engine, now rebuilt, from his XK 120 JWK 650. None of them got very far in the race, which was blighted by pouring rain. Both Johnson and Moss crashed their cars some 20 miles after the start, in a spot where Ascari had already crashed his Ferrari. Johnson's fuel tank was damaged and he retired, while Frank Rainbow managed to get the Moss car going again, although the steering gear was damaged. The car later jammed in reverse gear, and the resulting delay put them out of the race. Biondetti took a bump at high speed, and the radiator fan cut through the bottom hose. A fourth, privately entered XK 120 (670431, Gianotti) was also an early retirement.

The third *Daily Express* meeting at Silverstone was held in May rather than August, and this saw an overwhelming entry of XK 120s, works supported as well as private cars. Moss was driving the first steel-bodied XK 120, JWK 675, and Johnson was in KHP 30, 660228, a later steel car which had been the company press car. Wisdom and Walker were still in their original alloy-bodied cars. As well as these there were half a dozen private XK 120s, their drivers including

Duncan Hamilton, George Wicken, and Charlie Dodson, the pre-war Austin Seven racer, who made a one-off appearance in Jack Broadhead's car.

Again this year, the race was held in two heats according to engine size, and the winner of the 2-litre class was Tony Crook in a Frazer Nash at 83.63mph (134.59km/h). Nevertheless, the aggregate result was a victory for Moss at 84.50mph (135.99km/h), followed by Dodson in second place at 83.65mph (134.62km/h). In the over 2-litre race, Hamilton was third, Wicken fourth and Johnson fifth. Of the other Jaguar drivers, Holt was eighth, Wisdom ninth, Gee 12th, Moore 14th and Walker 15th.

Johnny Claes's career was tragically cut short when he died from tuberculosis in 1956. The young Belgian had established himself as a popular jazz musician with his band, Johnny Claes and the Clae-Pigeons (*sic*), and as a promising racing driver who had started in the British Grand Prix in 1950. With the help of Madame Bourgeois of the Belgian Jaguar importers, he obtained the loan of one of the works XK 120s in 1951. This would appear to be none other than HKV 500, the original Jabbeke car, although some photos suggest that, despite bearing the number plate HKV 500, it might have been HKV 455 (cp. chapter 8).

Whatever the identity of the car, Claes drove it to victory in the production sports car race at Spa-Francorchamps on 20 May. Together with motoring writer Jacques Ickx, father of the Le Mans winner of the same name, in August 1951 he entered the famous Marathon de la Route, Europe's toughest rally, at that time running from Liège to Rome and back. This was virtually a 90-hour road race, run to a very tight timetable over some of the most challenging roads in Europe, and was considered to be impossible to finish without loss of marks. Claes and Ickx, however, achieved the seemingly impossible, as for the first time in the history of the rally, they lost no marks and thus won the rally outright. In second place were Herzet and Baudoin, now in the Oblin-bodied XK 120 coupé (see chapter 10), and a French-entered XK 120 finished sixth.

Although it was the C-type which stole the show at Le Mans, there was still one XK 120 entered – by the two privateers Robert Lawrie and I Waller from Lancashire. This was chassis 660449, registered AEN 546. It was Waller's only Le Mans entry, but Lawrie had finished 11th in an Aston Martin 2-litre in 1949 – apparently his first motor race! – and 17th in a Riley 2½-litre in 1950.[24] Interestingly enough, their 1951 entry marked a very early appearance for an XK 120 with wire wheels. They finished in 11th place, having completed 236 laps at an average of just over 82.5mph

(132.8km/h) – better than the winning average in 1949. Furthermore, this was actually the best place achieved by an XK 120 at Le Mans![25]

It was also a good year in rallying for Ian Appleyard and NUB 120. Apart from wins in minor British rallies, including the Morecambe Rally in May and the London Rally in September, Appleyard had three victories in major international rallies. First was his win in the Dutch Tulip Rally in April, a success that was followed by winning the RAC Rally in June, and the Alpine Rally (and another Cup) in July. In the Tulip Rally, it was third time lucky for Appleyard who had been narrowly beaten in the two previous years, and it was a double triumph for Jaguar as the Swiss privateer Habisreutinger came second in another XK 120.

The 1951 RAC Rally was the first post-war version of this event, still more like the pre-war events in being

Two of the works cars contested the 1951 Mille Miglia: Johnson and John Lea in JWK 651, start number 429, together with Moss and Frank Rainbow in HKV 500, start number 432. Both were early retirements. (JDHT)

JWK 675, the first steel-bodied car now converted to right-hand drive, was Stirling Moss's car in the 1951 Silverstone production car race, which he won. (JDHT)

Leslie Johnson ran the works car KHP 30 in the 1951 Silverstone race, finishing fifth in the over 2-litre race. (JDHT)

In the Alpine Rally in July 1951, Maurice Gatsonides and W A Mackenzie ran the works car, KHP 30, and not a speed camera in sight. (Paul Skilleter)

a gentle road run rather than the much tougher event it would later become, but at least with a speed test at Silverstone and a few other timed special stages. It was memorable for attracting no fewer than 37 XK 120s, including the young John Lyons, William Lyons's son, with co-driver Ted Lund, and numerous privateers. Appleyard arrived at the Bournemouth finish with the smallest number of penalty points and was effectively the winner, although there was no general classification. He was followed in the list by two Morgans, but Jaguars then occupied all the places from fourth to eighth, with John Lyons finishing seventh.

Apart from the Appleyards, there were again several XK 120s in the Alpine Rally, including Habisreutinger, and Gatsonides (of speed-camera fame) with co-driver McKenzie in the works car KHP 30 which Johnson had run at Silverstone, as well as private entrants. Gatsonides dropped out when his water

pump failed, but Appleyard and Habisreutinger both came through without loss of marks, and both won Alpine Cups. In the tie-breaking speed test at the end of the rally there were three equal-best times; Appleyard, Eric Winterbottom in George Duff's Frazer Nash, and Walter Norton in another XK 120. As Norton had lost marks on the road section, effectively the Appleyards and Duff/Winterbottom were joint winners. The team prize went to the Jaguars of Appleyard, Habisreutinger and Soler.

The last major rally of the season was the first Tour de France Automobile of more than 5000km, held over 13 days in August and September. It attracted seven XK 120s, mostly of French drivers. Sadly, Henri Peignaux was in a bad accident in which a spectator was killed, he himself was badly injured, and his car was destroyed. Four of the others were well-placed at the finish, led by Hache and Crespin in fifth place and winning their class, with John Simone and Schlee eighth overall and second in class, and Descollas/Gignon third in class.[26] Simone went on to win the *Coupe de Salon* sports car race at Montlhéry in October 1952 before he switched to the C-type XKC-027.[27]

Ecurie Ecosse, Scotland's own racing team, was the inspiration of Edinburgh amateur racing driver David Murray.[28] Together with race mechanic "Wilkie" Wilkinson, he assembled a team of three other young Scottish XK 120 owners; Bill Dobson, Ian Stewart and Sir James Scott-Douglas, who all painted their cars in the distinctive "Flag Blue Metallic" colour which became the team's trademark. They first raced at Turnberry in April 1952, where Stewart scored a debut win in the over-2500cc sports car race, and he and Scott-Douglas were second and third in a *formule libre* race. The team contested 14 race meetings that season, mostly in the mainland of Britain but with excursions to the Isle of Man, Jersey, Ulster and to the sports car race held at the French Grand Prix meeting at Reims.

Murray himself drove only once, in the British Empire Trophy race in the Isle of Man in May, only to go off course when the brakes failed, but Scott-Douglas won the over 3-litre class. Scott-Douglas was also third in the Reims sports car race, which was won by Moss in the C-type.[29] While Ian Stewart won the Jersey Road Race, he did so in his new C-type; his team mates in XK 120s were fifth and sixth. For the 1953 season, however, Ecurie Ecosse replaced the XK 120s with C-types, setting the team on course for their later successes, including two wins at Le Mans with the D-types in 1956 and 1957. The final outing for an Ecurie Ecosse XK 120 was the 1000km Nürburgring

race in 1953, where Scott-Douglas crashed his C-type in practice and reverted to his road car, in which he and Ninian Sanderson finished 10th, and helped Ecurie Ecosse and Jaguar to win the team prize.[30]

Other than the Ecurie Ecosse campaign, the XK 120 had almost disappeared from the important sports car races in 1952, with C-types being used for the works entries, and also reaching selected private owners. The C-type would soon arrive in the USA, but meanwhile Schott's and Carroll's XK 120 tied for second place on distance in the first 12-hour race at Alex Ulmann's airfield race track at Sebring in Florida in March 1952 (a Frazer Nash won, and a Siata-Fiat was equal second).[31] The model was also successful in other US races in 1952 – at the Bridgehampton meeting in May, there was a first for Carroll, and second and third for other drivers, including Hansgen and Fitch, in other races at the same meeting. They continued to race with increasing success in 1952, whereas Phil Hill, Sherwood Johnston and other drivers had mixed fortunes in Hornburg's lightweight XK 120s in 1951-52 (see chapter 8). Johnston, however, became SCCA's champion sports car driver in 1952, having run his XK 120 with a special narrow open-wheel body in 11 of the 13 qualifying races.[32]

For the *Daily Express* International Trophy meeting at Silverstone in May 1952, Stirling Moss took a double victory for Jaguar, with the C-type in the sports car race, and with the Mark VII saloon in the touring car race. But there was a *third* race which rated as a side show – the five-lap "International Race of Champions" contested by "Bira" from Thailand, Claes from Belgium, Tony Gaze from Australia, "Tulo" de Graffenried from Switzerland, Moss from Britain and Paul Pietsch from Germany, all in standard XK 120 open two-seaters with left-hand drive – cars which were subsequently exported to the USA. Just for a change, Moss won.[33]

The 1952 rallying season for the XK 120 began with the RAC Rally in April, where Broadhead and Appleyard finished second and third in their XK 120s, while Leslie Johnson would have been third in JWK 651 but was penalised for running without rear wheel spats on his disc-wheeled car. Denham-Cooke was outright winner of the Highland Rally, and in the Rallye Soleil there was a first-in-class for the XK 120 of the Taylors, followed by the Swiss pair of Habisreutinger and Horning. The latter were first in the over 3-litre sports car class in the Tulip Rally, with Mr and Mrs Grounds in another XK 120 second in class. The Appleyards chose the relative comfort of a Mark VII saloon to finish second overall. In the Morecambe Rally, Pat Appleyard did the driving of NUB 120 and

was rewarded with the ladies' prize. Denham-Cooke took a class win in the RSAC Scottish Rally in June.

The Alpine Rally of 1952 was the third time that the Appleyards had entered this event with NUB 120. The car had now been modified to the new Special Equipment specification, with tuned engine and wire wheels. Winning was not the main priority, but Appleyard wanted another Alpine Cup – which he achieved – and was awarded the first Alpine Gold Cup for having won three cups in a row. Maurice Gatsonides had borrowed a new XK 120 (660986, MDU 524) for this event, and he came second overall, won his class and an Alpine Cup. This car would later gain fame as the 1953 Jabbeke record car (see chapter 8).

In the 1952 Liège-Rome-Liège rally, French drivers Laroche and Radix won their class and finished second overall in the special-bodied XK 120 coupé (670028;

The XK 120 was probably the car to have for private rally entrants in the early 1950s. Here are eight of them, all taking part in the Isle of Wight rally. (JDHT)

LOB 300 is one of the cars seen in the previous photo, (above) and here it is again, this time in the Clacton rally. (JDHT)

MDU 544, seen here on the right in Jaguar's service department, was chassis 660989, a Personal Export Delivery in June 1952. It has an extraordinary boot lid mounting for a second spare wheel. (JDHT)

Jaguar was denied success in the strenuous Mexican Carrera Panamericana road race. In the 1952 race, Douglas Ehrlinger finished 10th in class with this XK 120. (JDHT)

see chapter 10), being 20 minutes behind schedule and five minutes behind the winners Polensky and Schluter in a Porsche. The 1951 winners, Claes and Ickx, again tried their luck, this time in MDU 524, but retired after collision with a road marker.[34] The Swiss XK 120 drivers Bohni and Hahne came 10th. There were again several XK 120s in the Tour de France, incuding the Oblin coupé driven by Herzet and Bianchi, and Guy and Raymonde Berthomier were first in the over 3-litre class in their standard fixed-head.[35] Berthomier, who was famous for always

having race number 13, also raced this car in Morocco, and would later own and race the C-type XKC-036.[36] In the MCC *Daily Express* Rally, of the XK 120 drivers the Taylors finished fifth and won their class, and Broadhead was 11th. In 13th place and also winning his class was Stirling Moss, driving the two-tone coloured left-hand-drive fixed-head coupé (679282), which was his Jaguar "company car" and which he also entered in other rallies, including the 1952 Lyon-Charbonnières.

Reporting on the sports car race at the British Grand Prix Meeting on 18 July 1953, Bill Boddy wrote "It is interesting that the XK 120 is now completely outmoded for sports-car racing and none ran"[37] whereas seven privately-owned C-types did. Of course, the works C-types took the honours in the two important sports car endurance races, at Le Mans and Reims, while private drivers both in C-types and in XK 120s, including Head, Howorth and Protheroe, had mixed fortunes. However, XK 120 successes continued in rallies. Henri Peignaux, now recovered after his crash in the 1951 Tour de France, won the Lyon-Charbonnières Rally in an outwardly standard XK 120 SE model, but there was speculation that the engine was tuned to C-type specification. The other French XK 120 driver, Descollanges, retired with a blown engine.[38] Peignaux and Descollanges, together with their "gang" of Crespin, Hache, Heurtaux and Montabert, had previously used Peignaux's rally car for a record attempt at Montlhéry in October 1952, but this had had to be aborted because of poor weather conditions.[39]

Here is MDU 544 again, on the Stelvio pass during the 1952 Alpine Rally. Presumably the extra spare wheel was fitted for rallying.

Ian Appleyard had intended to enter a C-type in the major 1953 rallies, but changed his mind and once again fielded NUB 120, by now three years old, in Special Equipment form as seen in the 1952 Alpine Rally. As open cars were not eligible for the Monte Carlo, he drove a Mark VII and was rewarded with a second place in the first event counting towards the new European Rally Championship. In the RAC Rally, the biggest threat in the sports car class came from Imhof's Cadillac-engined Allard, but Appleyard in NUB 120 beat him in the special tests to take overall victory. Of the other XK 120 drivers, Broadhead this year came fourth, Air Vice-Marshal "Pathfinder" Bennett and Mrs Bennett fifth, and Frank Grounds (and Mrs Grounds!) eighth. The XK 120s also took the team prize. Appleyard entered a Mark VII in the Tulip Rally (and came fifth overall), but he was to use NUB 120 on one final occasion, the Morecambe Rally, which he won for a second time in May 1953, after which the car went into honourable retirement.

For the Alpine Rally, Appleyard had ordered a new XK 120, 661071, registered RUB 120, a Special Equipment open two-seater. This was specially prepared with a few modifications, including a C-type cylinder head, so that the engine gave 182.5bhp.[40] This made Appleyard the winner of four out of six special tests. The other two tests were won by Swiss driver Horning, also in an XK 120, but he went off the road later in the rally. The final result favoured the smaller-engined Porsches with German driver Polensky as the winner, but Appleyard was still fifth

overall and won his class. The XK 120s of Fraikin and Gendebien, and of Reg and Joan Mansbridge (their car was the fixed-head coupé GFE 111) were second and third in class, and all three Jaguars were awarded an Alpine Cup.

The Bennetts contested a few minor European rallies, including the Rallye de Soleil and the Evian-Mont Blanc Rally where they won their class. In Greece, Nicholas Papamichail won the Acropolis Rally in his XK 120, and came second to a Porsche in the Yugoslav Rally. Porsches were now coming to the fore in European rallying, and so was the Lancia Aurelia GT. Johnny Claes switched to an Aurelia for the

This is Henri Peignaux, the Jaguar dealer in Lyon, and his "gang" with the XK 120 that they ran at Montlhéry in October 1952, hoping to set long-distance records up to 5000 km and 5000 miles. The car is 660981 with which Peignaux won the Lyon-Charbonnières rally, and which later ended up with the Barou barchetta body. (Paul Skilleter)

Liège-Rome-Liège, which he won after a remarkable performance, driving almost single-handed, but Gendebien and Fraikin were second overall in their XK 120 fixed-head coupé.

In the Norwegian Viking Rally, only four-seaters were eligible, and Appleyard had RUB 120 re-built with a new drophead coupé body equipped with two symbolic rear seats. In the end he gave in to the organisers who suggested he should run his Mark VII instead, which he did, only to run off the road. He did, however, use the drophead-bodied XK 120 in the Lisbon Rally, where he was placed second overall. Of the 10 rallies which counted towards the Championship, Appleyard had entered six, and had achieved one first, two second and two fifth places. This gave him a total of 80 points towards the championship. His main rival, Helmut Polensky, had similarly entered six rallies and had achieved two firsts, a second and a third, for a total of 74 points. However, in the final tally only the four best results of each driver counted, which meant that Appleyard's score was reduced to 68 points whereas all of Polensky's points still counted, making him the first European Rally Champion.[41]

Although there were few appearances for the XK 120 in first-line sports car races by 1953, it deserves

Borgeaud and Conte were among many French drivers who adopted the XK 120 as a rally car, here caught in a beautiful setting on the 1953 Alpine Rally. Despite the factory's recommendation, they rallied not only a disc wheeled car but left the spats in place! (Paul Skilleter)

Unusual mount for Ian and Pat Appleyard, this is RUB 120, their second XK 120 which replaced NUB 120, here in the 1953 Alpine Rally. (Paul Skilleter)

mention that Giron's XK 120 finished eighth in class in the famous Carrera Panamericana road race in Mexico (while a C-type did not) – Jaguar's best result in this event.[42] However, as discussed in chapter 8, the works XK 120 registered MDU 524 (660986) on two occasions achieved remarkable speeds on the Jabbeke motorway in Belgium, on the second outing in October being timed one-way at over 173mph (over 278km/h). M de Ridder, a local Jaguar dealer, ran his own streamlined and tuned XK 120 on the second occasion, and reached an almost equally remarkable 154mph (almost 248km/h).

There were steadily fewer XK 120 appearances or successes in 1954. Ian Appleyard had effectively retired, and had sold RUB 120 to Denis Scott. There was no sign of the XK 120 repeating former glories in the RAC Rally, where a Mark VII in 10th place was best Jaguar overall. There were, however, still six XK 120s in the Lyon-Charbonnières Rally, including Peignaux in the Barou barchetta and one of the Barou coupés, although both retired. Auriach and Briat in a standard fixed-head coupé, however, were seventh overall and third in class.[43] There were also XK 120s in the Tulip Rally but the best Jaguar was again a Mark VII in fourth place.[44] In the Alpine Rally, there was at least some semblance of the good old days, as the XK 120 of Haddon and Vivian was first in class, but through loss of marks did not gain an Alpine Cup. They followed this by winning the open sports car class in the MCC Rally in November, where Stross in a drophead coupé won the closed sports car class. Perhaps the most outstanding race result for an XK 120 in Australia also came late in the model's career, when a fixed-head coupé (669015, see chapter 9) won

A quite irresistible photo of a young Stirling Moss with William Lyons, possibly taken at Silverstone in May 1951 where Moss won the sports car race in JWK 675. "Does my bum look big in this?" (JDHT)

a 24-hour race in New South Wales.[45]

Ironically, after production had stopped, in 1955 the XK 120 was finally admitted to the Monte Carlo Rally – but only in fixed-head coupé form, and two such cars were entered. French drivers Auriach and Grail finished 73rd while the Anglo-American team of Delling and Lavell were placed 271st out of 272 finishers. As Viart says, "it would be difficult to achieve a worse result". In 1956 Delling, now with co-driver Shorter, improved on this result by finishing 213th out of 233 finishers…

A few other die-hards kept the XK 120 going in some Continental events, thus Michel Parsy ran his fixed-head coupé in the 1954 Mille Miglia, and won the Rallyes des Routes du Nord in February 1955. The Barou coupé appeared, with different drivers, in

One of the later rallies for the XK 120 was the 1954 Alpine which still attracted a fair number of Jaguar drivers, here RJH 400, driven by Haddon and Vivian. (Paul Skilleter)

RUB 120 was later rebuilt with drophead coupé bodywork, to enable Appleyard to rally it as a "closed car", but he eventually disposed of it, and the car appeared in the 1954 Alpine Rally in the hands of Scott and Cunningham. (Paul Skilleter)

Almost at the end of the XK 120's active life, the model became eligible for the Monte Carlo Rally, in fixed-head coupé form. The American driver Delling tried his best but finished second from last in 1955. Here he and co-driver Shorter have been caught during one of the driving tests in the 1956 rally. This time he came 213th out of 233 finishers. (Paul Skilleter)

the 1955 Lyons-Charbonnières, and again in the Liège-Rome-Liège, but did not finish.[46] In May 1955, Meunier in an XK 120 fixed-head coupé was third in the Grand Prix des Frontières at Chimay, and as late as 1956, he finished 20th in the Liège. Delling ran his fixed-head coupé in the 1958 Sestrières Rally,[47] and Schwindenhammer his open two-seater in the Rallye de Lorraine-Alsace in the same year.[48]

The XK 120 also continued on the racetracks, even after production had stopped. In American SCCA racing, Charles Wallace won the C-production Championships in both 1954 and 1955. In the UK, Bob Berry was extremely successful in 1954 in his D-type-engined, lightweight-bodied ex-works car (see chapter 8). Dick Protheroe and Peter Sargent continued to race their XK 120s into the early 1960s. They were joined by Eric Brown in the modified drophead coupé registered 1 ALL, Rhoddy Harvey-Bailey in the old Biondetti car JWK 650, and, notably, John Pearson's plastic-bodied XK 120, which was consistently successful in modified sports car racing into the early 1970s. This was described as "the fastest Jaguar ever to have raced on a British circuit" and inevitably earned its creator the sobriquet John "Plastic" Pearson.[49] When this car ended its career, the day was not far off when the XK 120s would begin to re-appear in historic motor sport…

The drophead registered 1 ALL with the characteristic headlamps set low in the front wings was raced for many years by Eric Brown. Here it is seen at Goodwood.

1. *Motor Sport* Jul 1949
2. Georgano (ed) *The Encyclopaedia of Motor Sport* pp141-42
3. Skilleter *Jaguar Sports Cars* p81; Porter & Skilleter *Sir William Lyons* p111
4. *Motor Sport* Feb 1950
5. Whyte *Jaguar Sports Racing and Works Competition cars to 1953* p284
6. Letter from Lea to Heynes 3 April 1950, cited in full in Whyte pp90-91
7. Bowen's report cited in Whyte p93
8. Skilleter p85; *Motor Sport* Jul 1950 cited a Ford Special as coming second
9. Whyte p286
10. *Motor Sport* Jan 1951; Feb and Mar 1951 for the predictable rebuff, from both British and American correspondents, including a letter from Alan Clark
11. *Motor Sport* Mar 1951
12. Whyte pp289, 292
13. Skilleter p88; Whyte p98
14. *Motor Sport* Oct 1950
15. For Appleyard's own story, see Whyte pp108-19
16. *Motor Sport* Sep 1950
17. *Motor Sport* Oct 1950
18. *The Motor* 8 Nov 1950; *Motor Sport* Dec 1950
19. *The Motor* 21 Mar 1951; *Motor Sport* Apr 1951; Whyte pp105, 121-22
20. Viart *Jaguar XK Le Grand Livre* p259
21. *Ibid.* p260
22. Whyte pp146-47; Viart p260
23. Viart p261
24. Moity and Tubbs *The Le Mans 24-Hour Race 1949-*

1973, index *et passim*; Skilleter p97
25. Skilleter p97; Whyte p139; Viart p262
26. Viart p264
27. Whyte pp279, 382
28. David Murray *Ecurie Ecosse* pp30-35 *et passim*; W E Wilkinson with Chris Jones *"Wilkie"* pp129-37; Skilleter pp100-01
29. *Motor Sport* Aug 1952
30. Murray pp43-44; Wilkinson p139; Whyte p235
31. *Motor Sport* Apr 1952
32. Skilleter pp93, 98; Whyte p287
33. *Motor Sport* Jun 1952; Skilleter p100; Whyte p162
34. Whyte p197
35. Viart pp271-72
36. *Ibid.* p264; Larson *C-type Register* pp54-55
37. *Motor Sport* Aug 1953
38. Whyte p247, citing Gregor Grant in *Autosport*; Viart p273
39. Whyte p280; Viart p272
40. Whyte p252
41. *Ibid.* p255
42. Whyte pp235-38, 284
43. Viart pp282-83
44. *Ibid.* p283
45. Whyte p283; Elmgreen & McGrath *The Jaguar XK in Australia* pp83-85
46. Viart pp286-91, also for discussion of other events in 1955-56
47. Skilleter p110
48. Viart p292
49. Skilleter pp110-12 for further details

Chapter Eight

The Prototypes and Works Competition Cars

In this chapter are detailed car histories by chassis numbers of the XK 120 prototypes, and other cars that were used by the company (or private drivers supported by Jaguar) in competition, especially the early alloy-bodied cars. The three original prototypes, which were all raced, were as follows:

660001 HKV 455. No date of build is recorded for this first right-hand-drive car, which was registered on 23 May 1949. The first engine recorded for this car is a prototype, 248/03, which was replaced by the first production engine W 1001, and it had the first body, F 1001. It was originally painted Bronze, with Biscuit trim, but was subsequently repainted in Birch Grey. It is normally asserted that this was the 1948 Motor Show car, which was certainly a right-hand-drive car finished in Bronze, although photos show it with two-tone trim. The show car had a number of identifying features such as low-mounted front bumpers of a different type from the later standard bumper – probably partly painted body colour – and the front number plate mounted on a plinth, or at least on triangular brackets at either end. It seemed, originally, to lack air intakes in the front valances. The rear bumper was a simple strip mounted on the lower edge of the boot lid while the rear lamps were in smaller housings and mounted lower than normal. The rear number plate was mounted directly on the boot lid without a plinth. There was no boot lid handle, but instead a catch mounted on the underside of the rear

Unmistakeably "Lofty" England, with HKV 455 taken in front of the Service Department at Foleshill. (JDHT)

As befits a 1950 rally car, NUB 120 sports a bonnet strap, stone guards for the headlamps and for the extra-large single drivng lamp, while there is still an original Alpine Rally plate also on the car.

The boot of HKV 455, with the fuel filler in the top left-hand corner. (JDHT)

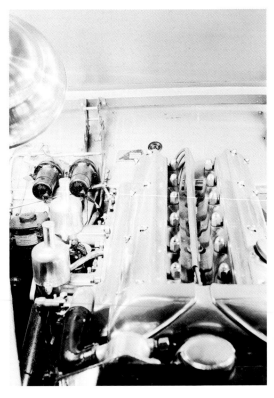

We know that this photo is the engine bay of 660001, a.k.a. HKV 455, since the chassis number plate is visible and it may just be possible to see the actual number. The twin fuel pumps and the shape of the scuttle were unique to this car. (JDHT)

sill. The fuel filler was in the boot and the wheel spats had no budget locks. The windscreen pillars were straight, fixed to the side of the scuttle with three screws, and had no visible rubber pad.[1]

It is believed that at the time of the show in October 1948, this car was fitted with a 3.2-litre XJ prototype engine, which could account for the strange engine number quoted above. Contemporary magazine articles were, however, careful to refer to it as the new "3½" litre sports car and to quote the capacity of 3442cc. Next to the car at the show were both four- and six-cylinder XK engines on stands. The under-bonnet photo published in *The Autocar* soon after showed a six-cylinder engine with twin SU electric fuel pumps mounted under the bonnet: a feature believed unique to 660001. Perhaps less likely, it has been speculated that the show car might originally have had a four-cylinder XJ or XK engine.[2]

It is probable that it was this car which chief test driver Ron "Soapy" Sutton tried out on the Keresley Road on the outskirts of Coventry in early December 1948, still with the 3.2-litre engine, and could initially only get up to around 102mph (164km/h). This was, perhaps, just as well as the brakes were "totally inadequate". The car also exhibited a number of other disconcerting characteristics, and was clearly in need of further development.[3]

The Earls Court car next appeared at the Belgian Motor Show in Brussels in January 1949, on which occasion it shared stand space with what seems to have been "Mark IV" 2½- and 3½-litre cars, as they were described as "assembled in Belgium". William Lyons and Madame Joska Bourgeois were photographed with the car. Also on the stand were the four- and six-cylinder XK display engines, and a display chassis with independent front suspension. The show date is too early for this to have been 660010, the "experimental chassis", which was only completed in September 1949, and the show chassis is most likely to have been from a Mark V. And in March, what must still have been the same XK 120 appeared on the Jaguar stand at the Geneva Show in Switzerland, together with the six-cylinder XK display engine and the Mark V.[4]

By August 1949, the car had been repainted blue with yellow wheels, and now had a yellow steering wheel.[5] By now, it had the standard-type front bumpers mounted higher up, air intakes in the front valance, as well as production-type rear overriders and rear lamps. The fuel filler was still in the boot. It was one of three XKs entered in the Production Car Race at Silverstone on 20 August, driven by "B Bira" (Prince Birabongse of Thailand) with race number 6. He retired after a rear tyre blew out, sending the car

spinning into the hay bales, with damage to the rear bodywork. This was soon repaired and the car, with the two others, appeared at Shelsley Walsh in September.

The car was then lent to *The Motor* for road test. On 26 October, Joe Lowrey and Harold Hastings, accompanied by "Wally" Hassan of Jaguar, took it to France and Belgium, measuring an average top speed on the Jabbeke motorway of 124.6mph (200.5km/h) with the hood up. On the list of company vehicles compiled for William Lyons on 28 October 1949, HKV 455 was included, chassis number 660001, still listed as blue. Also in the autumn of 1949, the car was used for a photo shoot for *Vogue* magazine by Don Honeyman.[6] In March 1950, the car went out to Switzerland for a second time to serve as a demonstrator at the time of the Geneva Motor Show. It was then registered locally under GE 12140 and was tried out by the Italian driver Clemente Biondetti. Photos of the car taken on this occasion confirm its identity by showing its uniquely shaped air intakes in the front valance,

It is now rather strange to think that the XK 120 and the Handley-Page Victor bomber are almost contemporaries – the Victor first flew in 1952! This preserved example is at Bruntingthorpe Aerodrome in Leicestershire.

This is Clemente Biondetti with HKV 455 when it had been taken out to Switzerland to be used as a demonstrator at the time of the 1950 Geneva Motor Show; note the local Geneva registration. (JDHT)

with semi-circular ends, as opposed to the normal D-shape with angled bottom corners. These air intakes can also be spotted in some photos of HKV 455 taken at Silverstone the previous August.[7] They are clearly different from the air intakes seen in photographs of HKV 500. The caveat must be added that it is difficult to judge such detail from the existing photos, and the front valances of the early cars may have been modified, changed, or repaired.

The trail then goes cold, but the *Car Record Book* states that the car (or its chassis) was used for the "Mark IV" fixed-head coupé prototype. The "Mark IV" designation is thought to relate to the XK 140.

John May has given me a copy of a letter which purports to confirm that a car described as a Jaguar XK 120 with the registration mark HKV 455 was sold through Henlys at Bournemouth to Jim Stephenson in June 1956, apparently with non-standard suspension and brakes, but the authenticity of this document has been called into question by him and other experts.[8] Harold Hastings believed that HKV 455 was later used for disc brake tests, and that he drove the car in this form.[9] The XK 140 fixed-head coupé prototype chassis number 804001 registered OWK 872 which may have been the car built on the chassis frame of 660001, was from 1954 to 1957 owned by the Dunlop Company which used it for testing disc brakes. This car had an XK 120 fixed-head coupé body and still exists.[10] Clearly, if a car based on the original HKV 455 was owned by Dunlop from 1954 to 1957, HKV 455 in its original form cannot have been sold in Bournemouth in 1956. There is currently one claimant to being HKV 455. This car was under restoration by Tom Zwakman in Holland at the time of writing but no details of its provenance were as yet known.[11] And there are others… although one has been written off as a fake. See also the story of 679002 in chapter 9.

670001. This was the first left-hand-drive car, and was never apparently road registered in the UK. The date of build is not known. It was originally Bronze in colour, but this was changed to White, later Red; trim was Biscuit and Red. The engine was originally 249/01, another prototype engine, but now probably of the definitive 3442cc capacity. It was later replaced by W 1016-8. The car had body number F 1002, so it

Right and opposite: The very first left-hand drive car, 670001, these are recent photos taken of the car as it appears to-day, having been re-painted in Bronze; the only car which still exists with the original type of straight windscreen pillars. (Jaguar Cars North America Archive)

was likely to have been the second car built.[12]

This was probably the car that was sent to the USA for the first New York International Motor Show in February 1949, the US debut of the new model. Photos show the XK 120 on the Jaguar stand.[13] It had left-hand drive, was dark in colour – presumably Bronze – with a light-coloured steering wheel. It had

the straight windscreen pillars and the front bumpers were like those of the Earls Court car, but were now fitted higher. There seems also to be a first attempt at carving air intakes in the front valance. The front number plate was on a plinth (or brackets), as it was on the Earls Court car. The car was rebuilt with right-hand drive and was painted Red for the 1949

A lovely contemporary colour shot of 670001, painted red and now with right-hand drive, before the 1949 Silverstone race where Peter Walker drove it into second place. (JDHT)

The Appleyard rally car NUB 120 is another car with its speedometer on the left (a kph instrument to suit the car's frequent Continental appearances), while the stop watches and map reading lamp in front of the passenger have a period feel. The grab handle has been removed, presumably the navigator had her hands full with rallying paraphernalia!

These louvres were added to the bonnet of NUB 120 during its active rallying life, presumably in an effort to overcome the XK 120's occasional tendency to overheat.

The luggage rack of NUB 120 is also seen in contemporary photos and presumably came in useful when the Appleyards travelled halfway across Europe to take part in rallies, bearing in mind that the boot was otherwise occupied. The car has the quick-release filler cap also seen on other works cars.

NUB 120 had the duo-blue interior trim and the colour split is well illustrated here. It is believed that the car has been at least partially re-trimmed, with the centre armrest over the prop shaft tunnel as well as the well-worn cockpit rails still being original.

The front wing vents on NUB 120 were a later addition, and are not of the standard type. The stickers refer to a recent rally appearance, while Norman Dewis was the Jaguar test driver in the 1950s, he did not drive NUB 120 at this time, but occasionally exercises the car more than fifty years later.

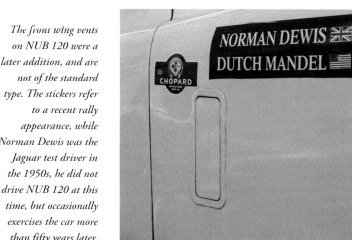

Silverstone race, where it was driven by Peter Walker, under number 8, to second place. Oddly enough, during the race it was fitted with a rear number plate with a spurious Birmingham registration FOJ 147, issued in 1939.[14] At this time, the steering wheel on 670001 was red to match the paint colour for the race.[15] In September, it appeared at Shelsley Walsh with the other Silverstone cars.

An unresolved mystery concerns the car that was used at the Goodwood press day at the time of the 1949 Motor Show,[16] where a photo was taken of Lyons as a passenger in the car. The driver is probably F I Connolly (of the famous curriers), who was then president of the SMM&T. This photo shows an unregistered right-hand drive car with *straight* windscreen pillars.[17] It has been suggested that it was 670001, and it has been claimed that the Goodwood car is on racing tyres similar to those worn by 670001 at Silverstone on 20 August, but the tyres on 670001 at Silverstone look very different from those seen on the car at Goodwood.[18] And it is difficult to decide

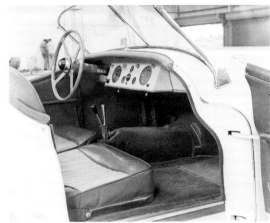

In May 1949, a series of photos were taken for use in the XK 120 handbook, including this shot of the interior of a left-hand drive car with straight windscreen pillars, which must be either 670001 (if it were white at this time), or 670002.

After having raced 670001 at Palm Beach in January 1950, Leslie Johnson posed with his trophies back at Foleshill – but it is believed that the car is not 670001, and therefore is most likely HKV 455. Perhaps deliberately, the photographer missed out the number plate! (JDHT)

whether the Goodwood car could have been red – it looks very dark in the black-and-white photo.[19] I have come to the tentative conclusion that the Goodwood car may have been the *second* car with chassis number 660003 which was black, and which could have been in existence at this time (see chapter 9).

On the list of company cars from October 1949, 670001 must be the car that figures as "XK.120. 3½-litre 2-str. Red. 1949 body. Chassis XK.120. Mk.2 No.2".[20] By New Year 1950, the car had been shipped to the USA again, where Leslie Johnson drove it to fourth place at Palm Beach on 3 January, and had no brake linings left at the end of the race. It is thought that the car was still red at this time. While post-race

photos were taken of Johnson with his Palm Beach trophy and an early XK 120 at the Foleshill factory, this car is thought to have been another of the straight-pillar cars (probably 660001), while 670001 remained in the USA where it was sold to Commander John ("Jack") Rutherford in Florida, who raced it until he got a C-type in 1952. It exists to this day; from the 1980s until 2004 it was in the collection of Walter Hill in Florida but was then sold. It was coming up for auction in 2005, but was apparently sold privately for a reputed £250,000, and stayed in the USA. It is still right-hand drive, although it now has a fawn steering wheel. After many years in white, it is now Bronze again, with single-colour trim. It has

Ron Sutton driving the car that we believe became HKV 500 (670002) on its exploratory trip to Belgium in the spring of 1949. The front bumpers still seem to be of the original type, and there are no rear over riders. The peculiar side lamps and extra rear lamps are visible; did Jaguar install improvised flashing indicators for this first European jaunt? (Paul Skilleter/Jaguar)

also received a 1954 XK 120 engine, with the rare 9:1 compression ratio.[21]

670002 HKV 500. The second left hand drive car had the most varied and interesting life of the early cars. It was registered on 1 May (or 23 May?) 1949. The original engine number is not in the *Car Record Book*, but according to the registration records this car also had engine number 249/01. It had the third body, F 1003. It was originally Red but was repainted in White, and was the car taken to Jabbeke for the record run in May 1949.[22]

In April 1949, a left-hand-drive XK 120 – which may have been Red, although some authors describe it as Bronze[23] – was sent out to Belgium to explore for the Jabbeke run. The car was driven out on trade plates and carried no number plate in most of the photos taken on this occasion, but we may conclude that it was most likely 670002. Unlike 660001 and

670001, this test car had the very odd feature of separate side lamps mounted on top of the front wings, as well as extra rear lamps mounted low down on the rear wings, but it lacked the rear overriders. It had an undershield at least at the front, and was already then sometimes fitted with the aero cowl in front of the driver instead of the normal windscreen, as later seen on the Jabbeke car. When the same car had a normal windscreen, it was of the straight pillar type. The rear

The press party about to board the chartered SABENA DC3 to fly out to witness the Jabbeke run. Lyons is on the far right; Bill Boddy of Motor Sport *is between the two hat-wearers, in front of the "M". (JDHT)*

One of the Belgian newspaper articles that upset Madame Bourgeois! Headlined "A Wonderful Racing Car", it shows HKV 500 on trade plates in the town hall square of Brugge, and it is claimed that Sutton had already broken the 200km/h barrier. (Paul Skilleter/Bernard Viart)

A mystery car… but it is tempting to assume that this left-hand drive car is HKV 500, painted white in readiness for the Jabbeke run. Its liberally fly-spattered state contrasts with the use of a show-type number plate. Points to note are the part-painted double-decker bumpers, the unusual bumper brackets, the air vents in the valance (just visible) and the hole for a starting handle in the radiator. The bulkhead and bonnet are very different from those seen earlier on HKV 455. (Paul Skilleter/Jaguar)

Ron Sutton in HKV 500 ready to be flagged of at the start of the record run. (JDHT)

… and here is Sutton trickling past the journalists at 10mph in top gear after the record run. Lyons is on the left, in a dark suit and hat. (JDHT)

The Jabbeke run was naturally made the most of in Jaguar literature and publicity, as witness this page from the 1950 XK 120 brochure. (Jaguar)

wheel spats had no external locks.

The test run was supposed to be a secret but was rumbled by a local Brugge newspaper which incurred Madame Bourgeois's displeasure as she had not been let in on it.[24] The driver on the exploratory mission was Ron Sutton, accompanied by John Lea as riding mechanic. They established that the car was capable of 130mph (209km/h) on the Jabbeke motorway, a speed that Sutton had already reached on roads near

Coventry.[25] "Bill" Rankin of Jaguar's publicity department therefore decided to go ahead with the proper Jabbeke run, and invited members of the press to attend on 30 May 1949; the party was flown out in a DC3, chartered from SABENA.

The pictures taken on the day show the car now registered HKV 500, painted white, with rear over-riders and normal side lamps, although apparently of a smaller-than-standard size, possibly as originally

After the Jabbeke run, "Wally" Hassan and Tommy Wisdom took HKV 500 on a test run through the Alps, during which the exhaust pipe detached itself and was tied to the front bumper. (JDHT)

Ron Sutton in the car at Jabbeke after the run, still with a tight grip on the steering wheel, at least he could manage a sort of smile for the photographer! (JDHT)

found on the 1948 show car. HKV 500 then seemed to retain them into 1950.[26] Sutton was again at the wheel, and the mission was accomplished. With the undershield, the aero screen and a cowl over the passenger seat, the two-way average speed over the measured mile was 132.596mph (213.393km/h), and with normal windscreen, and hood and sidescreens in place, the speed was still over 126mph (202.8km/h). The rear axle ratio was a higher than standard 3.27:1.

Sutton then drove past the assembled journalists at 10 mph – in top gear. The resulting publicity did much to establish the reputation of the new Jaguar sports car.

After the Jabbeke run, the undershield was removed, and "Wally" Hassan and Tommy Wisdom took the car on an extended test run through the Alps. HKV 500 was photographed at a Bugatti Owners' Club meeting at Silverstone in June 1949, and it was

A pre-race shot of HKV 500 at Silverstone in August 1949, still pristine, now sporting full chrome one-piece bumpers and external locks for the spats. (Paul Skilleter)

When HKV 500 appeared at Shelsley Walsh in September 1949, the body damage had been rectified, although the car still had the twin aero screens. (JDHT)

In the winter of 1949-50, HKV 500 was tested at the new MIRA track near Nuneaton. (JDHT)

probably this car which was tested at the same track shortly after.[27] It was still white in August 1949, but had then been rebuilt with right-hand drive, and in this form was entered for the Silverstone race, where it was driven by Leslie Johnson to victory (race number 7). It suffered damage to the left front wing after making contact with a Jowett Javelin during the race.

After the race, the still-damaged car was lent to writer Dennis May and photographer Guy Griffiths, preparing a feature for an American magazine,[28] and next appeared at Shelsley Walsh in September. In the company car list of October 1949, HKV 500 was included, colour white, chassis number 670002.[29] During the winter of 1949-50, the car was tested at the newly-opened MIRA track near Nuneaton, and by now had acquired external budget locks for the spats which were mentioned as an improvement on the 1950 model.[30] The actual Jabbeke car was part of a special feature display at the New York Motor Show in April 1950, shown here with the aero screen and half tonneau cover, and billed as "the fastest stock car in the world".[31] Then HKV 500 was entered in the second Production Car Race at Silverstone on 26 August 1950, at very short notice. In an internal memo dated 22 August, Phil Weaver of Jaguar's Experimental Department said: "It has now been decided to prepare XK.120 2-seater HKV 500 for the Production Car 1 hour race on August 26th." As part of the preparation, a black steering wheel was fitted, and the car was re-sprayed Red.[32]

This colour was supposedly in honour of the Italian racing driver Tazio Nuvolari, who was the intended driver and who practised in the car, but he felt unwell afterwards and decided not to take part in the race. Other sources suggest that Nuvolari had arrived at Silverstone expecting to drive a Healey, and the invitation for him to drive was a last-minute inspiration.[33] In the event, HKV 500 was raced by Peter Whitehead but promptly lost all its oil when the sump plug came loose. This probably did the engine no good at all, and after this episode HKV 500 was fitted with a new

powerplant, number W 2048-8, drawn from production. Also, in preparation for entering the car in the Tourist Trophy race, the car changed colour again, this time to Green "to comply with colour regulations".[34]

It was again Whitehead who drove HKV 500 in the TT at Dundrod in September 1950, finishing second to Stirling Moss in 660057 (JWK 988). In 1951, HKV 500 went to Italy for the Mille Miglia, held on 28 April, where it was driven by Stirling Moss with works mechanic Frank Rainbow as co-driver.[35] The car suffered braking problems and they crashed within 20

This is Johnny Claes in the sports car race at Spa in 1951. The car had a Belgian number plate on this occasion. The straight windscreen pillars are evident. (JDHT)

Jacques Ickx and Johnny Claes with the winning car in the 1951 Liège-Rome-Liège, HKV 500 according to the number plate, but was it really HKV 455? (JDHT)

The boot of NUB 120 is full of second spare wheel, mounted above the larger than standard petrol tank. The use of wire wheels, as well as the twin exhaust pipes, betray that this car was modified to Special Equipment specification later in life. The number 414 painted on the hub of the wheel is the starting number in the final Alpine Rally of this car. This was intended to prevent wheel swaps which were not allowed under rally regulations.

The quick release filler cap and luggage rack are original, as is the rally plate from the car's final Alpine Rally, but the other stickers and signs are recent and reflect the still-active retirement led by NUB 120.

miles of the start, causing damage to the steering gear, and were then delayed when the gearbox seized in reverse. Retirement was inevitable.

Repairs were, however, done quickly, as HKV 500 was next sent to Belgium where Johnny Claes won the production sports car race at Spa Francorchamps on 20 May 1951. Claes, with co-driver Jacques Ickx (father of the Le Mans winner of the same name), then entered HKV 500 in the Liège-Rome-Liège Rally (the Marathon de la Route) in August, winning this tough event outright; the first time the winner had not lost a single point. One other suggestion is that the car which ran at Spa and in the Liège was HKV 455. Photos show the car driven by Claes at Spa with a Belgian number plate, and clearly it is a very early XK 120, with the straight windscreen pillars. A photo taken after the Liège shows a car with the number plate HKV 500, but with air intakes which look suspiciously like those on HKV 455 discussed above.[36] This

seems to have been the end of the career of HKV 500, which, according to the *Car Record Book* was "reduced to produce".

According to the registration records, it was last taxed to the end of December 1951 when it was still owned by Jaguar, but the registration book was not surrendered. Other documents held by the Coventry registration office were destroyed at the end of 1956, five years after the car was last taxed. I have now discovered that its later engine W 2048-8 was subsequently fitted in a RHD production car chassis number 660939 built on 22 February 1952, and this may provide another clue to the date that HKV 500 was scrapped.[37] Some parts were used on 669002, the "seven days and seven nights" record car (see below).

The three cars discussed so far all had the straight-sided windscreen pillars, and originally all had light-coloured steering wheels. Both of these features had been seen on the 1948 Motor Show car. I believe

The under bonnet view of NUB 120 strongly suggests that a later engine was fitted, or at least that the engine was brought up to later specification. The routing of the ignition leads (although here in a non-standard bracket) and the position of the front coil are typical of engines after November 1952. The extra coil at the rear is special to this car. The cam covers have the post-April 1952 extra studs, while the carburettors are of the short neck type. The expansion tank seen behind the engine is likely also to be a later fitting.

they also all had the odd under-sill catch for the boot lid, which can still be seen on 670001, and the rear number plate mounted directly on the boot lid. These three cars were literally the only cars in existence through to the early summer of 1949.

The cars built from July 1949 onwards were regular production cars, with the exception of 660010, 26 October 1949, for which the entry in the *Car Record Book* is blank, except for the statement that this number was allocated to the Experimental Department. Other authors have reached the conclusion that it was not built up as a complete car and that there is certainly no missing body number that could have been allocated to this car.[38] The discussion of 679002 in Chapter 9 may have some bearing here. Incidentally, 660010 was not included on the list of development department cars compiled around this time.[39]

In the winter of 1950 it was decided to lay down a small batch of right hand drive cars to allocate to well known drivers for competition use, with the company's support, even if the cars were sold by Jaguar to the nominated drivers. There were, at first, five of these, with consecutive numbers, soon joined by a sixth car, as follows:

660040 engine number W 1144-8. Chassis completion date 1 March 1950. Colour Cream, with Pigskin trim. Despatched 17 March. Registered JWK 651 for Leslie Johnson.

660041 engine number W 1145-8. Chassis completion date 1 March 1950. Colour Pastel Blue, with Pigskin trim. Despatched 28 March. Consigned to Jaguar Car Distributors of Brussels in Belgium. It was allocated to LH "Nick" Haines, an Australian who helped set up the Belgian import operation,[40] and the car was registered in Belgium under 750837, but was later brought back to the UK and registered under MGJ 79.

660042 engine number W 1146-8. Chassis completion date 1 March 1950. Colour Olive Green, with Suede Green trim. Despatched 26 April. Registered JWK 977 for Peter Walker.

660043 engine number W 1147-8. Chassis completion date 1 March 1950. Colour Red, with Biscuit and Red trim. Despatched 23 March. This car alone remained the property of Jaguar and was registered JWK 650 for the Italian driver Clemente Biondetti, a past winner of the Mille Miglia.[41]

660044 engine number W 1148-8. Chassis completion date 1 March 1950. Colour Cream, with

JWK 651 was Leslie Johnson's car, chassis 660040, seen here at Montlhéry on the occasion of its 24-hour record run in October 1950. (JDHT)

Here JWK 651 is back in the service department at the Foleshill factory, while behind it is the Studebaker Champion that Bill Heynes had acquired for evaluation. (Paul Skilleter/Jaguar)

Duo-Blue trim. Despatched 12 April to Appleyard, Jaguar distributors in Leeds, for the use of Ian Appleyard, and registered in Leeds NUB 120.

660057 engine number W 1311-8. The penultimate RHD alloy-bodied car. Chassis completion date 2 March 1950. Colour Apple Green with Biscuit trim. Despatched 14 April to Henlys, London, for Tommy Wisdom, and registered JWK 988.

In two memos, Phil Weaver of the Experimental Department gave the detailed specification of these cars. The earlier memo is not dated but, from the context, was written around 1 February 1950 and lists only the first five cars, while the second memo was compiled on 26 April 1950, after the cars had been built, and includes the sixth car.[42] Work was in hand by the time the first memo was written, and chassis

and engines had "been drawn from production as frames, parts being drawn as required". It is of interest that at least NUB 120 was built on a chassis frame originally intended for a *left* hand drive car, as were perhaps some of the others.[43]

The modifications carried out were not too radical. The crankshaft was fitted with indium lead bronze bearings, and the "ports in cylinder head [were] modified to Silverstone standard – [valve] inserts radiused and inlet manifold matched to head". Pistons with 8:1 compression ratio were fitted. A 2-inch Monza-type quick-release oil filler cap was fitted. All drain plugs and taps were wire locked and, similarly, "all suspension and steering attachment bolts [were] specially reamed and fitted with castle nuts and split pins. All other bolts and nuts wired or split pinned".[44]

A special 25-gallon petrol tank was fitted, with an extra 10-gallon tank on chassis 660040 (the Johnson car) taking up the lower spare wheel space; otherwise the cars were equipped to carry two spares. An external 4-inch petrol filler of bayonet type from Derringtons was fitted, and provision was made for a racing-type filler cap. The brake pedal ratio was altered and the master cylinder repositioned. Special brake drums with cooling vanes were being made, together with brake shoes with 0.25in thick M14 linings, as an alternative to standard shoes with 0.1875in M15 linings. Consideration was given to fitting centre lock wire wheels and 6.50x16 tyres but in the end standard disc wheels and tyres were fitted.[45]

Otherwise there were only relatively minor changes from standard, as well as detail differences between the individual cars, but it is clear that they were all built with special care and modifications to ensure reliability even during 24-hour races – already, then, somebody had an eye on Le Mans! During the following 12 to 18 months, however, further changes were made to some of the cars as they were prepared for later races.

The subsequent competition careers of the six works cars were as follows:

660040 JWK 651. The race debut for this car came in the 1950 Mille Miglia, where Johnson and co-driver John Lea finished fifth, which was to be the best-ever result for Jaguar in the classic Italian road race. It was then entered for Le Mans, where Johnson shared the driving with Bert Hadley, an experienced Austin Seven racer who also drove for Jowett. The race number was 17. Regularly in fifth place or better, they were lying second when, after 21 hours, the clutch gave out. Johnson's best lap time was 97mph (156km/h).

Its next race was the Production Sports Car race at Silverstone on 26 August, where Johnson, after a bad start, finished eighth in the heat for over 2-litre cars. In the Tourist Trophy race at Dundrod in September, Johnson's car was one of three XK 120s that started, and he finished third on speed but was placed seventh on handicap.

Johnson then came up with the idea of using the car for a long-distance record run and enlisted the help of Stirling Moss, who had just won the TT in 660057. They took JWK 651 to the Montlhéry race track near Paris and over 24-25 October 1950 drove for 24 hours at an average speed of 107.46mph (172.94km/h), with a fastest lap of 126mph (202.8km/h).[46] On 12 March 1951, after the engine had been tuned to give 184bhp, Johnson completed a one-hour run at Montlhéry at 131.20mph (211.15km/h) with a fastest lap of 134.43mph (216.34km/h).[47] Johnson and John Lea took the car out to Italy for the Mille Miglia (where Moss drove HKV 500) but they crashed early on, wrecking the fuel tank. For a change, in 1952 Johnson contested the RAC Rally with the car and came close to finishing third, but was penalised for running without rear wheel spats.

Johnson sold the car in 1952. It passed through several owners and, in the 1960s, was fitted with wire wheels, a 3.8-litre engine and disc brakes. After a few more changes of owner, and the reinstatement of the original engine, it was sold at Coys auction at Rockingham in 2001 for £230,000. It was offered for re-sale by Gregor Fisken in 2004. In 2005 it was being restored for its new owner.[48]

Walker leads Duncan Hamilton during the 1951 Silverstone sports car race. On this occasion, Walker had to be content with a 15th place. (JDHT)

660041 original Belgian registration **750837**. Nick Haines started this car in the 1950 Mille Miglia with co-driver Rudi Haller, but they crashed 140 miles from the finish and lost too much time to be classified. It was the second of the three XK 120s at Le Mans, Haines sharing driving with Peter Clark, under race number 15. They finished in 12th place at an average speed of 80.6mph (129.7km/h), some 9mph slower than the winning Talbot with a 4.5-litre engine. The next month, Haines started the car in the Alpine Rally but brake trouble caused him to have a collision with a lorry.

The damaged car was brought back to the UK and prepared for the Silverstone race in August, where it was driven by Tony Rolt, who came second in the over 2-litre race. Next, it was entered for the TT but Haines crashed in practice. Despite a damaged radi-

Biondetti (and his mate Bianco) collecting JWK 650 from Foleshill, but probably not when the car was new as it has lost its rear spats. Although the date is uncertain, it is still believed to be in 1950. (JDHT)

The first race for JWK 650 was the 1950 Targa Florio, here Biondetti awaits the start at Palermo. (JDHT)

ator, it was subsequently driven back to Coventry. Soon afterwards, Haines gave up racing altogether. The car was registered in the UK in 1951 under MGJ 79. Haines sold it on, and the car disappeared from sight for many years, until acquired by John and Ursula Pearson in 1986.[49]

660042 JWK 977. This car made its racing debut at Le Mans in June 1950, although here it was driven by Peter Whitehead and John Marshall rather than by its owner, Peter Walker. Its race number was 16, and it finished in 15th place, having been delayed by numerous pit stops.

Walker was behind the wheel at Silverstone in August, where he won the race for over 2-litre cars but, in the overall result, had to be content with a second place to a 2-litre Ferrari. He subsequently used the car for hill climbs, at Prescott and Shelsley Walsh, and was placed 15th in the 1951 Production Car Race at Silverstone.

The car was sold to Hugh Howorth, who fitted it with a C-type rear axle and suspension. It passed through several owners, receiving a D-type dry-sump engine in 1956, and still exists.

660043 JWK 650. This one was taken out to Italy by works mechanic John Lea for Biondetti to enter in the Targa Florio on 2 April 1950, but met with an accident on the way to Dover. It was taken back to the

A conundrum. This is a left-hand drive steel bodied car, but also seems to have the number plate JWK 650! The lady is Mrs Nick Haines and it is her concours-winning car. (JDHT)

factory, where it was rebuilt on a new chassis frame (there is no record of a change in the chassis number).[50] The rebuilt car was driven to Palermo, but in the race a con rod broke while Biondetti was in second place. A replacement engine was sent out from the factory and fitted before the Mille Miglia later in the same month; the date, however, is too early for this engine to have been W 2026-7 (see below). The original engine was subsequently rebuilt, Biondetti intending to use this in a "special". In the Mille Miglia, Biondetti had trouble with plugs and over-heating, and a rear spring leaf broke, but he still managed to finish a creditable eighth overall.

The car was then left with Biondetti in Italy, and he entered it in local races but was involved in a crash in the Giro dell'Umbria which badly bent the chassis. This accelerated Biondetti's plan to build a special round the original engine from the car. This turned out to have the Jaguar engine in Biondetti's own chassis,[51] with Ferrari-like front suspension and cloaked in a body from a Ferrari 166, with cycle-type wings. Biondetti ran this car in the Grand Prix at Monza but retired.

Apart from other minor events, Biondetti entered his Ferrari-Jaguar special in the 1951 Mille Miglia although his race lasted only 140 kilometres, at which point the fan cut through the bottom radiator hose. Nor did Biondetti have much luck for the rest of the 1951 season, and engine trouble prevented him from

The car that Clemente built, the first single-seater Biondetti special using an XK 120 engine. (JDHT)

The XK 120 engine installed in the Biondetti car. (JDHT)

The second Biondetti special with its barchetta body, built around an XK engine and other Jaguar components. It was first seen in the 1952 Mille Miglia. This photo of the restored car was taken in the 1980s. (Paul Skilleter/Bernard Viart)

entering the special in the Targa Florio. This car survives, albeit in much modified form, and was last reported in Denmark where I saw it at the Copenhagen Classic Cup in the summer of 2000.

Biondetti then built another special around an XK engine (number unknown) and other components supplied to him by Jaguar, with a Maserati-like chassis with, unusually, quarter-elliptic rear springs. This car was bodied somewhat in the manner of the C-type Jaguar and appeared in the 1952 Mille Miglia driven by Pezzoli and Cazzulani. They were almost 30 minutes behind the race leader at Ravenna, and then dropped out. Biondetti himself drove a Ferrari in this race, but was back in the second special at Bern in May 1952, when the engine ran its bearings. The car had a final fling when Barone drove it to victory in the Circuito de Reggio Calabria. It then disappeared, but re-surfaced in the 1980s. It was fully restored and Paolo Dabbeni ran it in the Mille Miglia. A further appearance was in the 2003 Mille Miglia re-enactment.[52]

The original 660043 must have returned to Jaguar because a note in the *Car Record Book* reveals that it

was sold second-hand to a Mr Hagen on 29 October 1952, when it was fitted with engine W 2026-7 dating to approximately September 1950. It was bought by A H Harvey-Bailey in 1957 and raced by his son Rhoddy Harvey-Bailey with great success in the 1960s.

660044 NUB 120. Almost immediately after taking delivery, Ian Appleyard, with his wife Pat – the elder daughter of William Lyons – as navigator, started the car in the International Tulip Rally in April 1950. They seemed set for an overall win but lost out by being penalised in a driving test because his front wheels were two inches short of a white line. He next entered the Morecambe Rally and took the award for best performance for a production car. In July 1950, he set out on the Alpine Rally where he had won a Coupe des Alpes with his venerable SS 100 in 1948. After an eventful rally, during which he hit a wall causing damage to the front end, Appleyard's car was the only one to finish without losing any points, and he was effectively the winner, being rewarded with another Alpine Cup. During the remainder of 1950,

This is the farewell appearance of NUB 120, now with wire wheels and other "Special Equipment" modifications, fog-bound in the 1953 RAC Rally, where Appleyard was again victorious. (JDHT)

JWK 988 was the "works" car of Tommy Wisdom, here seen in the over 2-litre race at Silverstone in 1950 with a works Aston Martin DB2 and an Allard in hot pursuit. Wisdom finished seventh. (Paul Skilleter)

Appleyard gave NUB 120 further exercise in a number of British rallies. It was also lent to Montague Tombs of *The Autocar*.[53]

The 1951 season began well, with the Appleyards getting their revenge by winning the Tulip Rally outright, and repeating the feat in the Morecambe Rally. The big event was the first post-war RAC Rally where John Michael Lyons, the son of William Lyons, was one of 37 starters in an XK 120. He did well, finishing in seventh place, but his big sister and brother-in-law topped the score sheet with the lowest number of penalty points.

In the Alpine Rally the Appleyards won another Alpine Cup and were joint winners. For a change, Gordon Wilkins was Ian Appleyard's navigator in the London Rally, which they won, and Ian and Pat continued to enter other British events, with Pat doing the driving in the 1952 Morecambe Rally, where she was rewarded with the ladies' prize.

NUB 120 was the only one of the original six works cars that was kept going in first rank events after 1951. The C-type had quickly replaced the XK 120 in racing, but rallying was a different matter, and the Appleyards continued their run of successes, although they had to be content with a third place in the 1952 RAC Rally. For the Alpine Rally in July, NUB 120 was fitted with wire wheels, improved brakes, and the engine was tweaked with 1⅝in exhaust valves – the specification being effectively that of the new Special

Equipment version of the XK 120. Appleyard was not trying for outright victory (which, incidentally, went to the pre-war BMW 328 driven by Baron Alex von Falkenhausen) but simply wanted another Alpine Cup to make it three in a row. This was duly accomplished as the Appleyards finished fourth, and as a result Ian Appleyard became the first driver to be awarded a gold cup for having won three Alpine Cups in a row, and in the same car.

In January 1953, the Appleyards drove a Mark VII into second place in the Monte Carlo Rally, as two-seaters were not eligible. His intention had been to adapt a C-type for rallying, but he changed his mind and instead entered NUB 120 for its third RAC Rally, winning this for a second time. He again used a Mark VII in the Tulip, coming fifth, but gave NUB 120 a final outing when he won the Morecambe Rally in May. He then sold NUB 120 back to Jaguar for the works "museum"[54] and the car remains there to this day, now in the JDHT collection.[55] It was replaced by a new XK 120, RUB 120 (S 661071, see below).

660057 JWK 988. Tommy Wisdom's car was the fourth XK 120 in the 1950 Mille Miglia. It suffered broken wheel studs and finally the front universal joint broke 40 miles from the finish causing his retirement,[56] although some reports say the gearbox jammed. It next appeared in a race at Oporto in Portugal on 18 June, where Wisdom finished third

A later colour shot of JWK 988, now with wire wheels. (JDHT)

The first steel-bodied car, with left-hand drive, was road tested by The Autocar *in 1950.*

having driven almost 1500 miles to get to the start. Also in this race was a locally owned alloy XK 120, probably 670157.

Wisdom drove the car at Silverstone in August, the fourth out of five XK 120s to contest this event, and came seventh in the race for over 2-litre cars. The four Jaguars that finished clinched the team prize for the marque.

The car was then lent to a young racing driver called Stirling Moss, and entered in the first post-war Tourist Trophy race held at Dundrod outside Belfast in September 1950 on the day before Moss's 21st birthday. In a race memorable for the miserable weather conditions, Moss finished first, on both speed

and handicap, followed by Peter Whitehead in second place in HKV 500. JWK 988 was then refitted with road equipment for Wisdom's use. In May 1951, Wisdom drove the car to a ninth place at Silverstone, and then went out to Portugal again for the grandly named "Portuguese Grand Prix" but retired, as did two private XK 120s. It is believed that this car is now in the Bamford collection.[57]

The following later steel-bodied cars were also prototypes, competition or works cars:

670172 JWK 675. This was the first left-hand-drive steel-bodied car, which was road tested by *The Autocar*, but was later converted to right-hand drive.[58] It was entered for Stirling Moss to drive in the third Production Car Race at Silverstone in 1951, brought forward from August to May. Moss duly won this race, which was a Jaguar benefit, and XK 120s took the first five places and numbered 10 altogether among the first 15 cars in the race for the over 2-litre cars. The car was eventually dismantled and reduced to produce.[59]

660228 KHP 30. Built 3 October 1950, this was a works press car – it was possibly the 1950 Earls Court Motor Show car – and was road tested by Bill Boddy for *Motor Sport*.[60] It was originally fitted with engine W 2589-7 but this was later replaced by W 1543-8.[61] It became Leslie Johnson's mount in the Silverstone Production Car race on 5 May 1951. He finished fifth, after Moss in first place in JWK 675 and three privately-entered XK 120s, one of which was driven

Bob Berry's car, chassis 660917, built in September 1951, originally registered LRW 174, was re-registered under MWK 120 on 18 November 1952. Here it is complete with badges for the Bugatti Owners' Club and the BARC, before Berry fitted the lightweight body; but note: As seen here, it has the body-colour side lamp housings only introduced in September 1952, and the colour is probably not the Silver which was original on 660917. (JDHT)

by Duncan Hamilton. The car next appeared in the 1951 Alpine Rally in the hands of Maurice Gatsonides and Bill McKenzie, but was eliminated when the water pump failed. Afterwards it was sold through Sanderson & Holmes, the Jaguar distributors at Derby, now with yet another engine, W 2683-7, despatched on 18 December 1951.[62] I believe it survives in Italy, fitted with a fourth engine!

Some of the cars discussed below were strictly speaking not works cars, but were nevertheless built or prepared in the factory for competitions. This was certainly the case for the lightweight XK 120s of 1951. The story behind these cars is that Lyons ordered three aluminium bodies for XK 120 chassis from Abbey Panels in 1951 as a fallback in case the new C-types weren't ready. They had a solid rear panel, no boot lid, and the rear wings were in one piece with the bodywork. There were sills below shortened doors, and a louvred lift-out panel instead of the normal bonnet. Two of these bodies were mounted over a tubular framework on XK 120 chassis and, according to the *Car Record Book*, were both completed (but perhaps in chassis form?) on 17 April 1951. Other competition features included a 40-gallon tank and wire wheels, a single aero screen and a cowled mirror. The cars (or perhaps only the bodies as yet unmounted – expert opinions differ[63]) were then spotted in the factory by Los Angeles importer "Chuck" Hornburg in June 1951. He bought them and had them sent out to California on 1 August 1951. Hornburg called these two cars "XK 120 Silver-

stones", and raced them in the 1951 and 1952 seasons.

660741 body LT 3, colour white. Phil Hill was placed third at Elkhart Lake in August 1951, and third again at Palm Springs in November. Hill raced this car into 1952 with mixed results until Hornburg got a C-type for him. LT 3 went to a Jaguar dealer in St Louis and stayed in that area until Tom Hendricks in Washington acquired the car in the 1970s. He still owned it in 2005.

660748 body LT 2, colour green. Pedro Malbrand finished in fourth place at Elkhart Lake in August

Bob Berry (on the left) and mechanic John Lea with Berry's XK 120 with its new lightweight body. Note the short doors and the small louvred lift-out bonnet.

Berry with the lightweight MWK 120 in action at Goodwood. (JDHT)

A well-known photo, of LWK 707 on the banking at Montlhéry during the seven days run in August 1952. (JDHT)

LWK 707 was the centrepiece of the Jaguar stand at the 1952 Earls Court Motor Show in this elaborate display. (JDHT)

1951. The car was then damaged in a crash during a race at Reno, Nevada (driver Bill Breeze) and was eventually rebuilt with a C-type-like front end. It was raced by Sherwood Johnston at Pebble Beach in April 1952 but retired with overheating. Charles Fifield used the car for races and hill climbs in 1955, winning at Buffalo Bill Mountain in Colorado. At one stage it was fitted with a V8 engine. It returned to the UK in 1971, where it was restored to original appearance by Lynx Engineering. For some time it was registered JSV 482,

but after passing into the ownership of Chris Jaques in 1974 it acquired its present number, CJ 120.[64]

660917 LRW 174, 27 September 1951. This was originally a company car but in February 1952, it was sold second-hand to Bob Berry of Jaguar's publicity department, who had it re-registered as a "re-build" in November 1952 under MWK 120. It may have been re-bodied around this time. He began racing the car in the 1953 season but then fitted it with the surplus lightweight body LT 1 (which he disarmingly described as "an early type alloy body" in an article in *Jaguar Apprentices Magazine*[65]). This saved some 4cwt in weight, and Berry won the Lyons Trophy race in June 1954. The car was eventually fitted with a 3.8-litre D-type engine with Weber carburettors, and was the fastest XK racer in the country, but Berry sold it when he got a drive in a D-type. A later owner was David Cottingham but he sold MWK 120 to Bill Mackin of Vancouver in Canada in 1968. It raced at Laguna Seca in 1976 and in the early 1980s. It was bought back by Cottingham in 1990 and he drove the car at the Goodwood Festival of Speed in 1993.[66]

It has occasionally been claimed that Jaguar made more than these three lightweight bodies, but experts are unanimous in refuting such claims. A number of replicas, though, have been made, both in the UK and the USA.

669001. This was the white prototype right hand drive fixed-head coupé, which displayed some unusual features such as trafficators built into the front wings and a vertical rear quarterlight pillar.[67] It had the separate, chromed, side lamp housings otherwise not seen on coupés, except possibly the first LHD cars built in early 1951. 669001 was built in early 1950, as it was photographed in April of that year. It is thought that it originally had engine W 1979-7 which, by the spring of 1951, was removed and was supposedly being installed in KHP 30 (660228) for the Silverstone one-hour race on 5 May 1951.[68] The white coupé later had an experimental 2-litre, four-cylinder XK unit and was eventually scrapped (see chapter 2).

669002 LWK 707, 23 November 1951. This was the second fixed-head coupé with right-hand drive. It was built more than a year before production of RHD cars started in earnest, and it is interesting that it actually used a left-hand-drive bodyshell[69] – LHD cars were made in quantity from July 1951 onwards. LWK 707 was registered in January 1952 and was finished in Bronze with Tan trim. It was allocated to the Experimental Department. Leslie Johnson persuaded Bill

Heynes to release the car for his "seven days and seven nights run" at Montlhéry in August 1952 and had it prepared in the factory, with a high rear-axle ratio, large fuel tank and a Pye two-way radio. The wire wheels, twin-exhaust system, and mildly tuned engine mirrored the Special Equipment specification that was by then available for the XK 120. The heavy-duty prop shaft and the 25-gallon fuel tank came from HKV 500, further evidence that this old warhorse had been scrapped in 1952 (cp. above).[70]

Johnson was one of four drivers, together with Jack Fairman, Bert Hadley and Stirling Moss. Early into the run a rear tyre burst and an errant piece of thread cut the main battery lead. That was fixed, and having re-started on 5 August, the team duly accomplished what they had set out to do, as the car covered 16,852 miles (27,121 km) at an average of just over 100mph (161.4km/h), and set a number of official world records. However, as a rear spring broke on the fifth day, and had to be replaced by a spare not carried in the car, no more records could be approved after that. The car was exhibited on the Jaguar stand at the Paris and Earls Court Motor Shows the following October, and ever since has been a museum piece, now cared for by the Jaguar Daimler Heritage Trust.[71]

660986 MDU 524, 27 May 1952. This car was first prepared for Maurice Gatsonides to run in the 1952 Alpine Rally, where he came second overall, first in class, and won an Alpine Cup. It was then lent to Johnny Claes and Jacques Ickx for another attempt at the Liège-Rome-Liège, but they retired after hitting a road marker stone in the Alps. This was probably the car that Gatsonides drove in the 1953 RAC Rally, and it was entered for Tommy Wisdom and his wife "Bill"

With the pit crew wildly cheering LWK 707, this is probably at the end of the seven days run. (JDHT)

to drive in the Alpine, but the entry was withdrawn after Wisdom had an accident in a Bristol at Le Mans and ended up in hospital.

Meanwhile, MDU 524 had been taken out to the

The four drivers with the car after the run: Hadley, Moss, Johnson and Fairman. (JDHT)

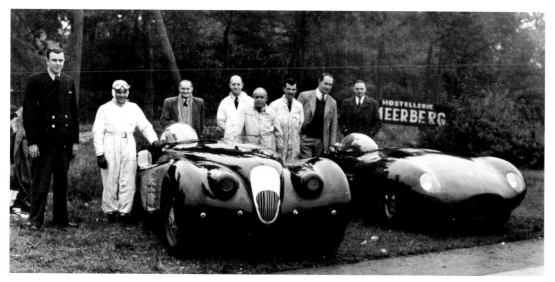

MDU 524 returned to Jabbeke in October 1953, now fitted with the bubble top and other aids to improve the aerodynamics. "Lofty" England and Norman Dewis (who is quite a small chap) are to the left of the car. On the right is the interim "C/D-type"

From the relaxed posture of Dewis we may speculate that this is after the 172mph record run. (JDHT)

Jabbeke highway in Belgium on 1 April 1953, in company with a Mark VII saloon and a C-type (XKC-012) which was run with both the 1952 Le Mans long-nose bodywork and in standard guise. The aim was for the XK 120 to reach 140mph, which it beat in the hands of test driver Norman Dewis, who reached 140.789mph (226.579km/h) over the flying mile and 141.846mph (228.280km/h) over the kilometre.[72]

When a Pegaso was timed at Jabbeke at over 150 mph, Jaguar felt it must demonstrate that it still had the quickest production car. Accordingly, MDU 524 was

Ian Appleyard replaced NUB 120 with RUB 120, with which he contested the 1953 Alpine Rally. The car then had its original two-seater body but was later fitted with a drophead body (photo in chapter 7).

streamlined. Among other changes it lost its distinctive front indicators set in the leading wing edges,[73] and was most prominently fitted with an aircraft-type Slingsby bubble canopy over the driver's seat and a metal tonneau cover over the passenger seat. The engine was tuned with a 9:1 compression ratio and 2-inch carburettors, and the rear axle was fitted with a 2.92:1 ratio final drive. On 20 October 1953, the car returned to Jabbeke, where Dewis set up an amazing average of 172.412mph (277.471km/h). Less the bubble canopy and fitted with an aero screen, the car was still timed at 168.539mph (271.238km/h).

The respected Jaguar specialists Guy and Jeremy Broad of Coventry built a replica of the Jabbeke car in the 1990s, the "XK 180" or "XK 200" project car, based on a chassis and body acquired from XK racer Jim Tester. They demonstrated the near-finished car at the Jabbeke 50 event in 1999, with the help of Norman Dewis. The 3.8-litre engine was persuaded to yield 325bhp, while the car had a modern gearbox and disc brakes. They then took the car to a Lincolnshire airfield in October 1999 where driver John Young achieved 184.92mph (297.6km/h), a new record speed for a Jaguar XK, albeit an "unofficial" record as it was not verified by any appropriate recognised organisation.[74]

S 661071 RUB 120, 12 May 1953. This car was Ian Appleyard's replacement for NUB 120 and was built to Special Equipment specification. He came fifth in it in the 1953 Alpine and won his fifth (and final) Alpine Cup. In the same car, now re-bodied as a drophead coupé, he came second in the first European Rally Championship. RUB 120 was then sold to Dennis Scott who entered a few more rallies with it but it was broken up in the 1960s. Appleyard subsequently appeared in a few rallies in an XK 140, registered VUB 140.

1. *Car Record Book*, JDHT archive; Viart *Jaguar XK Le Grand Livre* p81; Skilleter in *Jaguar World* Oct 1998
2. Recollections of "Lofty" England in *Jaguar Quarterly* spring 1989; Porter in *Jaguar World* Sep/Oct 1994, and *Jaguar Sports Racing Cars* p11; supported by photos, taken around the time of the 1948 show, in Viart pp81-82, and *XK Gazette* no.10 Jul 1998; *The Autocar* 17 Dec 1948; the four-cylinder engine has been mentioned by Richard Hassan, Walter Hassan's son
3. Sutton's report cited by Porter in *Jaguar Sports Racing Cars* pp11-12; *Jaguar World* Sep/Oct 1994
4. *The Autocar* 28 Jan 1949; *The Motor* 2 Feb 1949; Viart p117; *The Motor* 23 Mar 1949
5. Porter p11; Boyce *Jaguar XK Series – The Complete Story* p81

6. *The Motor* 16 Nov 1949; Hastings in *Collector's Car* Jan 1981; list of Development Department Cars, 28 Oct/1 Nov 1949, Lyons files, JDHT archive; *XK Gazette* no.50, Nov 2001
7. Skilleter *Jaguar Sports Cars* photos between pp66-67; Whyte *Jaguar Sports Racing and Works Competition Cars to 1953* pp79, 88; Boyce p33
8. Skilleter in *Jaguar World* Mar/Apr 1998, he links this letter to John Woods who then claimed to have found HKV 455 in the USA in 1994
9. Hastings in *Collector's Car* Jan 1981
10. Information and photocopies of log book and correspondence etc. courtesy of John May
11. Zwakman's website zwakmaneurope.com, 2004
12. *Car Record Book*, JDHT archive

13. *The Motor* 16 Feb 1949; Dugdale *Jaguar in America* pp19, 21

14. Photo by Louis Klemantaski in JDHT archive

15. Whyte, colour photo on the back of the dust jacket

16. Paul Frère's reminiscences, *XK Gazette* no.10, Jul 1998 and *Jaguar World* Nov 1998

17. Photo credited to Guy Broad, *XK Gazette* no.3 Dec 1997 p12

18. Compare the photo referred to in the note above to the photo of 670001 at Silverstone in *Jaguar World* Sep/Oct 1994 p55, and Sep 1999 p69

19. Skilleter in *Jaguar World* Mar/Apr 1998

20. List of Development Department Cars, 28 Oct/1 Nov 1949, Lyons files, JDHT archive

21. Whyte p86; Viart p116; *Jaguar Quarterly* summer 1990; *Jaguar World* Sep/Oct 1994; information courtesy of Paul Skilleter, and other sources

22. *Car Record Book*, JDHT archive; registration records, Coventry City archives

23. Whyte p69

24. *Ibid.*; Viart p24; "Lofty" England's recollections in *XK Gazette* no.20 May 1999

25. Telegram from Sutton 14 Apr 1949 confirming he had reached 130mph on the Autobahn, Lyons files, JDHT archive

26. For a discussion, see Boyce p32, although I do not agree with his suggestion that HKV 455 and HKV 500 changed identity at this time

27. *Ibid.* p34; Hassan's report dated 7 Jul 1949, cited in Whyte pp74-75

28. May's letter to *The Motor* 14 Jul 1950

29. List of Development Department cars, 28 Oct/1 Nov 1949, Lyons files, JDHT archive

30 *The Motor* 14 Sep 1949

31. *The Motor* 19 Apr 1950; *Jaguar World* Aug 1999

32. Weaver's memo in JDHT archive

33. *Autosport* 25 Aug 1950, cited by Whyte p100; Skilleter p90

34. Memo from Weaver dated 4 Sep 1950 in JDHT archive; also *Car Record Book*, ditto

35. Memo from Weaver dated 20 Mar 1951 in JDHT archive detailing preparation and modifications; here, and in some other memos, the chassis number is given erroneously as 620002 which was a Mark V 3½-litre saloon chassis number

36. Boyce p130; Skilleter *Jaguar The Sporting Heritage* pp64-65

37. Registration records, Coventry City archives; *Car Record Book*, JDHT archive

38. Porter *Original Jaguar XK* p139

39. List of Development Department Cars 28 Oct/1 Nov 1949, Lyons file, JDHT archive

40. Whyte p107

41. *Ibid.* p88

42. Both memos in JDHT archive

43. Information courtesy of John May

44. Appleyard's reminiscences to Don Law, *Jaguar World* Jan/Feb 1998; verified by restoration work on NUB 120 during 2004; information courtesy of John May

45. Memo from Claude Baily to Bill Heynes 14 Mar 1950, JDHT archive

46. *The Motor* 8 Nov 1950

47. *The Motor* 21 Mar 1951

48. *XK Gazette* no.78 Mar 2004; information courtesy of Paul Skilleter

49. *XK Gazette* no.1 Oct 1997

50. Whyte p88, citing letter from John Lea 18 Feb 1975, copy in England's Biondetti competition file JDHT Archive

51. Some times described as a Maserati chassis, *The Motor* 11 Apr 1951

52. Urban *Les Métamorphoses du Jaguar* pp108-12; *XK Gazette* no.71 Aug 2003, and no.74 Nov 2003, where Ole Sommer noted that the two Biondetti cars are often confused, for instance by Andrew Whyte

53. *The Autocar* 1 Sep 1950

54. *The Autocar* 10 Jul 1953

55. *Jaguar World* Jan/Feb 1998

56. Report from John Lea to Heynes 28 Apr 1950, JDHT archive

57. *XK Gazette* no.28 Jan 2000

58. *The Autocar* 14 Apr 1950

59. *Car Record Book*, JDHT archive

60. *Motor Sport* Apr 1951

61. Memo from Weaver, dated 4 Apr 1951, and *Car Record Book*, JDHT archive

62. *Car Record Book*, JDHT archive

63. *Jaguar Quarterly*, spring 1989

64. *XK Gazette* no.15 Dec 1998, no.32 May 2000

65. Cited by Whyte p320

66. *Jaguar Quarterly* summer 1990; *Jaguar World* Sep 1993; *XK Gazette* no.43 Apr 2001

67. Skilleter *The Jaguar XKs – A Collector's Guide* p40, Viart pp122-23

68. Memo from Phil Weaver to Mr Case dated 4 Apr 1951, JDHT archive

69. Information courtesy of John May

70. Memo from Weaver dated 8 Jul 1952, JDHT archive

71. Viart p127; *The Motor* 22 and 29 Oct 1952

72. *The Motor* 8 Apr 1953

73. These can be seen in Skilleter *Jaguar Sports Cars*, photos between pp66-67, and Whyte p201

74. *Coventry Evening Telegraph* 28 May 1999; *The Daily Telegraph* 16 Oct 1999; *Classic Cars* Jan 2000; *XK Gazette* no.42 Mar 2001

Chapter Nine

Some Famous XK 120 Cars

The Montlhéry record car has never been fully restored and thus appears very much in the form in which it completed the seven days and seven nights record run, including the extra driving lamps with yellow bulbs to French specification.

In this chapter are car histories of some of the more interesting XK 120s, including selected private race cars, as well as others that were of special interest, such as motor show cars or cars with famous first owners. For the early alloy-bodied cars, reference should also be made to the complete list which may be found in the appendix. The primary source for much of this information is the original *Car Record Books* kept in the JDHT archive at Browns Lane, but as well as the works quoted previously, John Elmgreen's and Terry McGrath's monumental *The Jaguar XK in Australia* (1985) has been particularly helpful with regard to those cars that went Down Under.

The three original prototypes discussed in chapter 8 were followed by one production RHD car in July 1949, then six production LHD cars during July-August, and one RHD and four LHD cars during September; a total of 12 cars, all bar one of which were exported. More regular production was underway by the second week in October 1949, and production during that month totalled 16 cars. Already, left hand drive cars greatly outnumbered right hand drive cars in production. By the end of 1949, total production including the prototype and experimental cars had reached 27 right hand and 70 left hand drive cars.

Right-hand drive alloy cars

660002, build date ca. June/July 1949, to Brylaws in Sydney on 21 July 1949. This is thought to be the first XK 120 released for sale. An early photo taken in Australia is believed to be of this car, although it shows two-tone interior trim when, according to the factory records, the trim was all red. It had curved rather than straight windscreen pillars, and a white steering wheel. After a chequered career, the car re-surfaced in the 1980s in poor condition, and came back to the UK where it was restored by Mill Lane Engineering. It has engine number W 1009-7 and the engine size is cast on the block as "3½ LTRE" rather than the common "3½ LITRE". It is now registered ESJ 563.[1]

The single car that did initially stay in the UK is of particular interest, as there appear to have been two cars with this chassis number.

660003, 13 September 1949. As originally built, this car *may* have had engine number W 1007-7 or W 1026-7, body number F 1016 and gearbox

number JH 670, all numbers that would tie in with a September "chassis completed date" (cp. below), although the original numbers for the first 670003 cannot be deciphered in the *Car Record Book*. I believe that this was the XK 120 which was on the Jaguar stand at the 1949 Earls Court Motor Show at the end of September. This was a right-hand-drive car in a light colour (probably Cream), it had light single-colour interior trim with, unusually, dark colour contrast piping. The steering wheel was black, the windscreen pillars were curved, and the car generally conformed to production specification.[2] By the time of the 1949 Motor Show, according to the "chassis completed date" in the *Car Record Book*, only three right-hand-drive cars had been built. Of other candidates for being the 1949 Motor Show car, we can exclude 660001, 670001 and 670002 (the latter two by now converted to right-hand drive) which all retained the straight windscreen pillars, while 660002 had gone to Australia in July, and 670003 onwards, of course, had left-hand drive.

For whatever reason, it was then decided to convert 660003 to left-hand drive, and in January 1950 it was issued with a new chassis number 670071, as clearly stated in the *Car Record Book* against this number. This was a Cream car with Cream trim, as the Motor Show car had been, and the numbers for 670071 in the *Car Record Book* were engine W 1026-7, body F 1016, and gearbox JH 670 – which would all appear to be much earlier than January 1950. In this form the car was eventually exported to France and sold in Monte Carlo, the first owner was the American ballerina Rosella Hightower (1920-2008), and it seems

likely that it is her car that was photographed at the Cannes concours; the unusual dark contrast colour piping on this car is also seen on the 1949 Earls Court car. This car does not appear to exist.

A new car was then built using chassis number 660003. For this one, the *Car Record Book* indicates changes of engine and body. The engine in this second car *may* have been W 1007-7 but this was replaced by W 1137-8. The body number was F 1093 but this was changed to F 1119. This second car was Black; as mentioned in chapter 8, this second car may have been the car used at the Motor Show press day at Goodwood in October 1949. It was later exported to

The first right-hand drive production XK 120 to leave the factory was 660002, here seen on display in the Bryson showroom in Sydney. Points to note are the curved windscreen pillars and the white steering wheel. (Terry McGrath)

Presumably this is the ballerina Miss Rosella Hightower of Monte Carlo, first owner recorded for chassis 660071, the left-hand drive conversion of the first 660003. The colour scheme and the contrast-colour piping for the trim is the direct link between the two cars. The photo was taken at a concours at Cannes in 1950. (JDHT)

Hoffman in New York. It has been suggested that it was the New York Motor Show car in April 1950, or one of them: There were two XK 120s on the Jaguar stand, but one was white, the other silver, and unfortunately they were both left-hand-drive cars.[3] In 1997, 660003 was re-discovered in the USA, still with right-hand drive, and was subsequently repatriated to the UK by Retro Classics. Now restored by Lynx, the car is believed to be in the Channel Islands.[4]

This is the car displayed at the 1949 Earls Court Motor Show, with its unusual colour scheme and contrast colour trim piping. Here it has been caught without its spats, probably during the stand build-up, when it was customary to tie the Jaguars down to appear as low as possible.

All the following alloy production cars, whether with right-hand drive or left-hand drive, were exported to a variety of destinations, none stayed in the UK, although some Personal Export Delivery cars were registered in Coventry before being taken abroad by their owners.

660007, 21 October 1949, to Brylaws, Melbourne. Another car exported to Australia where it was displayed at the 1950 Melbourne Motor Show.[5]

660022 Dutch registration PT-10-40, 29 November 1949, to Lagerwijs, The Hague in Holland. Sold to JL van Dieten, later owned by Rob Slotemaker, and raced by both. In 1960 it was bought by a Mr Mulder, and is still owned by his son.[6]

660023 Swiss registration SG 3818, 9 December 1949, to Emil Frey in Zürich. Sold to the Swiss rally driver Rolf Habisreutinger and driven by him in the 1950 Alpine Rally[7] – he later owned 660731 (see below).

660027 Swiss registration ZH 14061, 22 December 1949, to Emil Frey in Zürich. Sold to Kurt Klaus, and raced in Switzerland.[8]

660058, 3 March 1950, to Brinkmann in Singapore. The last RHD alloy car.

Left-hand-drive alloy cars:

670003, ca. August 1949, to Hornburg in Los Angeles. The first LHD production car. After many years owned by Wesley Clark in Texas, it came back to the UK and was restored by JD classics. It has been claimed to be Clark Gable's first XK 120, which furthermore Gable is supposed to have given to Rudolf Caracciola! The idea that "Rudi", who lived at Lugano in Switzerland after the war, should ever have owned a Jaguar – even if it were given to him – is, I think, an "urban myth"; surely he remained faithful to Mercedes-Benz until his death in 1959. Anyway, 670003 was Cream, and this does not match the photos of Gable in a darker car taken at the time. Gable's car had a light-coloured steering wheel and was registered 56A 2443, and John Dugdale says that his car was "the first Jaguar XK 120 in the West".

It has also been claimed that Gable's first car was Light Grey with Red trim, and that he sold this car in mid-1952. If so, the most probable candidate would be 670032 which was Gunmetal with Red trim. This car was despatched to Hornburg on 28 December 1949, and went through International Motors, but the first owner in the *Car Record Book* is A H Wittenberg Jr. Alternatively, 670029 was also Gunmetal, but had Pigskin trim; this too went to Hornburg on 28 December, and there is no first owner listed in the *Car Record Book*. A third theory is that the first Gable car was 670054 in Suede Green. This went to Hornburg on 5 January 1950

This is 660007 photographed at the Melbourne Show in 1950. (Terry McGrath)

and, again, the first owner is not recorded in the *Car Record Book*. However, supposedly Gable's car had arrived already in December, which would make it one of only four cars, 670003, 670006, 670010 (all Cream) or 670014 (Pastel Blue), none of which had Red trim… Another Hollywood owner of an alloy car was actor Ray Milland, but its chassis number has not been identified.[9]

Clark Gable on the right seems very pleased with his brand new alloy open two-seater. The starting handle hole confirms that this is one of the first seventy left-hand drive cars. The bonnet is different from the steel cars, as there is no front cross member. (Paul Skilleter)

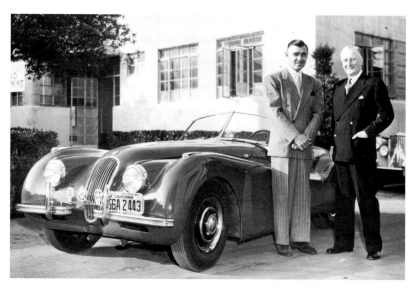

A famous image in Jaguar iconography: Clark Gable and William Lyons, together with Gable's car, during Lyons's visit to Los Angeles in April 1950. (JDHT)

Alfonso Gomez Mena took chassis 670052 to the first race win abroad for an XK 120, at Havana in February 1950. (JDHT)

670004, June/July 1949, to James L Cooke Motors in Toronto, Canada. The first XK 120 exported to Canada, this is regularly described as "the Montreal Motor Show Car", which must refer to the British Motor Show in Montreal in February 1950. However, there was also a Canadian National Exhibition opened in Toronto on 26 August 1949, where an XK 120 was exhibited.[10] The car was later customised, it is claimed by Barris in California, although the car was known to be in Montreal from ca. 1973 to 1998, when it was repatriated and restored by Guy Broad. It is now thought to be owned by Tom Zwakman in Holland. The car has one of the earliest-known XK engines, W 1006-8, which also has the engine size cast into the block as "3½ LTRE" and block number C2335 rather than C2335/1.[11]

670009, 13 September 1949, to Delecroix in Paris. This Cream car with Biscuit and Red trim was the first XK 120 to be exported to France, and was the 1949 Paris Motor Show car.

670022, 2 November 1949, to Ehlert in Buenos Aires, Argentina. Sold to Lucio Bollaert, who raced the car, and who later drove his second XK 120 across the Andes (see chapter 4). His alloy-bodied car still exists in Argentina.

670023, 3 November 1949, to Hoffman in New York. Sold to Briggs Cunningham, the yachtsman and racing driver who ran a Cadillac at Le Mans in 1950 and then went on to build Chrysler-engined sports racing cars under his own name until 1955. He later raced Jaguars at Le Mans, including the E2A prototype in 1960, and E-types in 1962 and 1963.

670052, 9 December 1949, to Seiglie in Havana, Cuba. Sold to Alfonso Gomez Mena who drove the car to victory in a race at Havana, on 24 February 1950, the first overseas race win by the XK 120.[12] It was the third of three alloy cars exported to Cuba.

670063 Swiss registration BS 18652, 21 December 1949, to Emil Frey in Zürich. Sold to Albert Scherrer who raced it.[13]

670068, 29 December 1949, to Universal Motors, in Cairo, Egypt. This was bought in Egypt by Dick Protheroe who brought it back to Britain in late 1952 and had it registered under GPN 635, and for many years raced it. It was fondly nick-named "The Ancient Egyptian".[14]

670100, 20 January 1950, to Hoffman in New York. This has been claimed to be Clark Gable's second XK 120 (compare above), but this seems unlikely as the car went to the East Coast. It was last reported in Germany. It would also have been odd for Gable to change his car as quickly as that, and some experts believe that Gable only had two XK 120s. These would be the first 1949-50 alloy car discussed above, later replaced by 672282 in 1952 (see below).[15]

670105, 24 January 1950, to Sommer in Copenhagen, Denmark. This was the Copenhagen Motor Show car, but as presumably nobody in Denmark could afford to buy an XK 120, it was re-exported to Fredlunds of Stockholm in Sweden.[16]

670138 JWK 496, 17 February 1950, to Hornburg. A Black car that was originally owned by Phil Hill, he brought it back with him to California after he had been trained as a Jaguar mechanic in the factory. When the car was registered in Coventry, however, (as a Personal Export car, under the Home Delivery Export Scheme), Hill was living at an address in Abingdon – MG country. He placed the car second in its first race at Santa Ana on 25 June 1950. Hill went on to win at Pebble Beach in November 1950, but disposed of the car in early 1951 to make way for a pre-war Alfa Romeo 8C2900, though not before he had bored out the engine by 0.125in (3.175mm) to 3.7 litres – conceivably the first to try this. The car was re-discovered in California in the 1990s after having been in the hands of the same owner for 36 years, and was being restored in 1996.[17]

670144 later LXK 48, 21 February 1950, to RM Overseas in Düsseldorf. The original owner is not known but the car later returned to the UK, possibly in 1951, and was for many years owned by the Jaguar historian Paul Skilleter. It still exists in the UK.

670159, 28 February 1950, to Hoffman. This car was finished in a special colour scheme; White with White trim, which matches one of the 1950 New York Motor Show cars.[18] The other show car was Silver with Red trim, and could have been any one of a dozen.

670178, 16 March 1950, to Hornburg. The remarkable "1000 mile" car owned by Bob Tucker, which has become a benchmark for the originality of alloy cars.[19]

670184, 22 March 1950, to Lagerwijs in Holland. The last LHD alloy car, it also had the highest alloy-body number, F 1240.

Steel-bodied open two-seaters, right-hand drive:

660059 JVC 66, 6 April 1950, to Brylaw in Melbourne, as a Personal Export Delivery car. The first steel-bodied car with right-hand drive, and still in existence.[20]

660075, 10 May 1950, through Henlys in London to W M Couper, St Albans. The first UK-delivered steel-bodied car – and the first normal customer delivery in the UK of any XK 120 – the original owner was Lt Col AT Goldie Gardner of MG fame who had driven his MG-based special with the Jaguar engine at Jabbeke in 1948.

660084 JVC 621 later BA 7641, 12 May 1950, to Brinkmann in Singapore. It was a Personal Export Delivery to Derek Bovet White who used this car to win Malaya's 1952 Johore Grand Prix with another XK 120 a close second – this was very much a formule libre event! – and then went on to win a

A rare colour photo of the Jaguar stand at the 1950 New York Motor Show. The white car is likely to be 670159. (JDHT)

Phil Hill and "Chuck" Hornburg – not in Hill's XK120, here they are slumming it in C-type XKC-007 that Hornburg bought for Phil to drive.

From across the cockpit we see the non-standard rev. counter and 180mph speedometer, probably borrowed from a C-type, while the stop watches, map reading lamp (hardly required at Montlhéry) and Halda speed pilot are probably later additions.

This is where the two six-volt batteries hide on all XK 120s. Curiously LWK 707 seems to lack the normal hinged parcel box behind the seats, perhaps this was omitted to make access to the batteries easier. The significance of the scrawled chalk marks is not known…

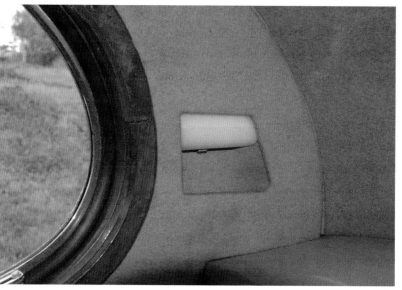

A small lamp was fitted in a recess in the trim panel in each rear quarter pillar of the fixed head coupé.

There are plenty of special features in the interior of the Montlhéry record car. The radio microphone is conveniently poised above the steering wheel, with its bracket attached to the dashboard on the right, where there is also an extra switch panel including switches for changing from the main to the auxiliary petrol tank, for the fog lamps, the windscreen washer and the additional electric fan (which must be a later addition).

The lucky fire chief of Adelaide had the use of this XK 120, 660094. (Terry McGrath)

The Maharajah of Jaipur with 660177. It may be pointed out that in a rare streak of egalitarianism for 1950, His Highness is wearing jeans. (JDHT)

Concours d'élégance.[23]

660094, 24 May 1950, to Dominion in Adelaide, Australia. This car caused local controversy when it was acquired by the Adelaide Fire Brigade as the fire chief's car! From the records relating to this incident, we know that an XK 120 at that time cost £1520 in Australia. The car was naturally Red, and still exists.[22]

660146, 21 July 1950, direct sale. Sold to Peter Whitehead, who was one of the drivers of the winning C-type at Le Mans in 1951. Later owned by "Jumbo" Goddard, who modified the car including a 4.2 E-type engine and all-synchro gearbox. The car migrated to Australia in the 1980s.[23]

660177, 10 August 1950, direct sale. Sold to the Maharajah of Jaipur.

660194, 10 August 1950, through Henlys to Martin Walter in Kent. Sold to Stanley Baker, possibly the film actor of that name.

660272 NMA 404, 10 November 1950, to Henlys in Manchester. Sold to Jack Broadhead, and driven by Charlie Dodson to second place in the 1951 Silverstone Race. Several race entries, for Jack Fairman in the 1951 TT among others. Broadhead came second in the 1952 RAC Rally, and fourth in 1953. This car still exists.

There were four Ecurie Ecosse team cars, which were as follows:

660276, 10 November 1950, to Rossleigh in Edinburgh. Sold to David Murray, the founder of the Ecurie Ecosse team, and raced at least once by him, in the British Empire Trophy Race in 1952, although Murray retired.

Chassis number not traced HWS 104. Registered Edinburgh November 1950, Bill Dobson's Ecurie Ecosse team car. He came fifth in the Jersey International Road race in July 1952, and won the sports car handicap at Goodwood in September 1952.[24]

660347 HWS 210, 24 November 1950, to Rossleigh. Registered Edinburgh December 1950, for Ian Stewart, Ecurie Ecosse team car, but quickly replaced by XKC-006.

660578 LXO 126, 9 January 1951, to Henlys in London. Sir James Scott-Douglas's Ecurie Ecosse team car. With this car, he came sixth in the 1952 British Empire Trophy race in the Isle of Man, third at Reims in June 1952, sixth in the Jersey International Road Race, third in the Wakefield Trophy Race, and second in the O'Boyle Trophy Race. This car also completed the 1000km race at the Nürburgring in 1953, after Scott-Douglas had crashed his C-type XKC-046 in practice. It is now owned by Dick Skipworth.[25]

660286 PFC 999, 14 November 1950, through Henlys in London to City Motors, Oxford. On 24 November 1950, sold to the then 22-year-old undergraduate Alan Clark, who kept the car until his death in 1999, and wrote about it on a number of occasions.[26] He even had this car prepared by Jaguar with a view to entering it in the 1953 Carrera Panamericana – although in the end, he decided against.[27] And surely it was the same Alan Clark who wrote a letter to *The Motor* in defence of the XK 120 in 1949, quoted in chapter 4?[28]

660328 NKL 444, 21 November 1950, to Henlys in London. Sold to GH Wicken, who finished fourth in the 1951 Silverstone Race.

660332 LXF 731, 21 November 1950, to Henlys in London. Sold to Philip Fotheringham-Parker who, together with Duncan Hamilton, drove to third place in the 1951 Silverstone Race. It is also described as Duncan Hamilton's first XK 120.[29]

660382, 30 November 1950, to Victor in Belfast. Sold to Dr Tinsley in Ulster. This car was driven by Louis Chiron in the 1951 Ulster Handicap Race.[30]

660449 AEN 546, 12 December 1950, to Parkers of Bolton. This was the car entered privately by Lawrie and Waller in the 1951 Le Mans, where they finished 11th. By 1970, the car was still in existence but had lost engine and gearbox, and was sold on as a bare chassis. It was bought and rebuilt by Bob Kerr in Scotland, and in 2002 it was acquired by Guy and Jeremy Broad, who took part in the Le Mans Classic with the car.[31]

660569, 8 January 1951, to Andersons in Brisbane, Australia. Sold to Les Taylor who gained notoriety when he drove from Darwin to Alice Springs, 965 miles (1553 km), in 10 hours and 32 minutes, averaging over 91mph (147km/h)! – and was promptly arrested for driving offences. The car still exists.[32]

660662, 2 February 1951, to Claparede in Geneva. This was the 1951 Geneva Motor Show car.

660682 JGB 414, 8 February 1951, to Ritchies in Glasgow. This XK 120 was at one time owned by Betty Haig, the famous woman rally driver, who drove it at Goodwood and Shelsley Walsh. The car still exists.[33]

660694 MKV 878, 13 February 1951. This was a Jaguar company car and was only registered in 1953 when it was sold second-hand to Henlys.

660696 KRW 923, 14 February 1951. The first XK 120 used by John Lyons, William Lyons's son. He took part in the Morecambe and RAC Rallies with this car, and was placed seventh in the 1951 RAC. It was later sold to a US Serviceman and, after spending many years in the USA, was repatriated by Chris Keith-Lucas of Lynx in 1999.[34]

660731 Swiss registration SG 3818, 1 March 1951, to Emil Frey in Zürich, Switzerland. Sold to Rolf Habis-

The valiant effort of Lawrie and Waller with 660449, AEN 546, at Le Mans in 1951 resulted in an 11th place. (JDHT)

Three of the Ecurie Ecosse cars, at Arthur's Seat in Edinburgh. From front to rear, Bill Dobson, Ian Stewart, and Sir James Scott-Douglas. (JDHT)

Both driver and car look a little worse for wear. Les Taylor with 660569, after his record run from Darwin to Alice Springs. (Terry McGrath)

The front end of LWK 707 shows several unusual features, notably the non-standard headlamps with the yellow bulbs adopted as a concession to French requirements, the additional Lucas fog lamps, and the two leather straps for the bonnet.

The quick-release filler cap is obviously a desirable fitting on a record car

Normally the rear lamp housings on XK 120s were chromed over a cast-alloy base, but on LWK 707 they are painted body colour.

reutinger who came second in the 1951 Tulip Rally, and won an Alpine Cup in the 1951 Alpine Rally (see also 660023, Habisreutinger's earlier car).

660742, ca. 16 March 1951, to Frank Cavey in Dublin, Ireland. This car was assembled from a Completely Knocked Down (CKD) kit in April 1951, and was sold to Cecil Vard, who famously entered his Mark V in the Monte Carlo Rally, finishing third in 1951 and fifth in 1953. There were two batches, each of six cars, which went to Dublin in CKD form.

660865 LHP 866, 26 July 1951. Originally a Jaguar demonstrator and press car, sold second-hand to Henlys in June 1953. At one time owned by the late Dr Harvey Postlethwaite, the famous Formula One car designer, it was for sale through Duncan Hamilton in 2001.[35]

660870 LRW 747, 10 August 1951, direct sale (Personal Export Delivery). Sold to Lt Col Ronnie Hoare who later became the Ferrari importer in Britain. The car still exists and is believed to have seen action at Prescott. Hoare subsequently owned a C-type, two D-types and a succession of E-types.[36]

660882 MBJ 298, 27 August 1951, through Henlys to Howes & Son of Ipswich. Originally owned by Giles the cartoonist, it is said to have been given to him by a grateful Lord Beaverbrook. It featured in quite a few of his drawings for the *Daily Express*, and was kept by him until his death in 1998. It is now owned by Mike Ridley.[37]

660926 LWK 799, 24 October 1951, Personal Export Delivery through Murketts in Cambridge. Sold to the British High Commissioner of Pakistan.

660971, 18 March 1952. Development car, so-called "Mark III", retained by Jaguar's experimental department, where it was apparently fitted with rack and pinion steering.[38] In other words, a stage in the development of the XK 140 model.

S 660983, 6 May 1952, to Brylaw in Sydney. The first OTS RHD car to Special Equipment specification.

S 661001 MXJ 954, 25 June 1952, to Henlys in Manchester, sold to Ferodo Ltd, and **661153** OLF 626, 30 December 1953, to Henlys in London, sold to M Levy in London. There are two cars here which have been confused in *XK in Australia*, where it is stated that it was 661153 which was registered MXJ 954 and sold to Ferodo. In fact chassis 661153, registered OLF 626, was bought by Dick Protheroe in1959, he raced it, and had it re-registered under CUT 6. It was kept by Rosemary Protheroe after Dick's death in 1966, but after her death the car emigrated to Australia in 1978. It was by then much modified with later XK parts, including disc brakes, rack and pinion steering, and an XK 140 engine.[39] Chassis S 661001, registered MXJ 954, was raced by Rob Beck in the 1960s, it was exported to the USA in 1971 where it was subsequently broken up.[40]

661023, 8 September 1952, to Hoffman in New York. This was one of many RHD cars supplied to the USA, and it has been claimed that Hoffman raced it – not personally, I would assume, although Hoffman did occasionally race Porsches.[41] A driver or later owner may have been Alex Ulmann of Sebring race track fame. RHD cars were often preferred for racing as most tracks are circumnavigated in a clockwise direction. This particular car, which still exists, apparently now has a fully race-prepared engine to SE or even C-type specification, although it was originally built as a standard model.[42]

661028, 10 October 1952, to Henlys in London. The *Car Record Book* describes this as an "ex showroom car" and I think it might have been the 1952 Earls Court Motor Show car. It was Cream (or White), with special Orange trim, and the date of despatch was quite late; 3 December 1952.

661051, 5 February 1953, to Claparede in Geneva. The 1953 Geneva Motor Show car.

661078 RDU 864, 26 May 1953. Originally a company show car and demonstrator, sold second-hand to Mansbridge in Lincoln two years later. The car was purchased by the late A F Rivers Fletcher, at that time working for BRM, who rebuilt it as a single-seater racing car in the mould of the contemporary BRM, and raced it for some years. The car eventually ended up in France in the collection of Roland Urban, who continued to race it,[43] but by 2003 I believe it had moved to Denmark.

661106 RDU 431, 29 September 1953, and **661112** RDU 932, 2 October 1953. John Lyons's name is in the records against both these cars – could he have used both of them? I suspect that one of them must have been the 1953 Earls Court Motor Show car, as both were Grey with Tan trim; the colour scheme of

The engine of LWK 707 has the additional front studs to the cam covers introduced in April 1952 – in fact this is puzzling as the car had an earlier engine, according to the records. Another anomaly is that the carburettors have the individual pancake air filters normally only found on open two-seaters: The coupés had a remote air filter mounted in front of the radiator fitted in this location (left) where we instead see the extra electric fan.

the show car.[44] Both were disposed of second-hand in the spring of 1955, *before* John's untimely death. Both still exist today.[45]

S 661176, 23 August 1954, to Archibalds in Christchurch, New Zealand. The last RHD open two-seater.

Steel-bodied open two-seaters, left-hand drive:

670185, 27 March 1950, to RM Overseas in Düsseldorf, Germany. The first steel-bodied car with left-hand drive, apart from 670172 (see chapter 8). The first steel-body number F 1241 was found on chassis 670270, 12 May 1950, which also went to Germany and was bought by an American serviceman.

670214, 14 April 1950, to RM Overseas. This car was for the Berlin Motor Show, held in May-June 1950.

670327, 15 June 1950, to Jaguar Car Distributors in Brussels. Sold to HH Raja Surendra Sinh of Alirajpur.

670400 KDU 164, 3 July 1950, to Hoffman in New York. Personal Export Delivery to Jackie Cooper, the former Hollywood child star (1922-2011). On the other hand, this car appeared in the Rallye des Sestrières in 1951, see photo in chapter 7.

670430, 6 July 1950, to Delecroix in Paris. Sold to the American Lt Col John Simone who later owned and raced XKC-027. This is presumably the car subsequently registered in Switzerland under GE 26734 that Simone and Armand Schlee drove to eighth place in the first Tour de France Automobile in 1951.[46]

670474, 14 July 1950, to Claparede in Geneva, Switzerland. Sold to Ivo Badaracco of Lugano, who later owned and raced XKC-045.[47]

670513 KDU 161, 25 July 1950, to Hornburg in Los Angeles. Personal Export Delivery to film star Tyrone Power, who had a Pycroft hard-top fitted by Fox and Nicholl. This was panelled in aluminium over an ash frame, and covered in leathercloth.[48]

670716, 14 September 1950, to Delecroix. The 1950 Paris Motor Show car.

670798, 4 October 1950, to Hornburg in Los Angeles. Sold to film star Errol Flynn, who bought the car from Peter Satori at Pasadena.

670946, 13 October 1950, direct sale. Personal Export Delivery to HSH The Princess Antoinette of Monaco, the sister of Prince Rainier.

670968, 17 October 1950, to Fredlund in Stockholm. For Mr Fredlund's own use.

671097, 9 February 1951, to RM Overseas. For the Frankfurt Motor Show, held in April 1951.

671142, 16 May 1951, to Delecroix. Sold to M. Heurtaux, presumably Jean Heurtaux, who later owned the C-type XKC-035, in which he crashed and killed himself in 1953 (he also owned chassis 679661, see below).

671350, 28 June 1951, to RM Overseas. For the Berlin Motor Show in September 1951 (see also 671377).

671358, 29 June 1951, to Delecroix. Sold to J da Silva Ramos, who later rallied a 3.4-litre saloon.

671377, 4 July 1951, to RM Overseas. Again for the Berlin Motor Show, together with 671350. This car later ended up with an Authenrieth body (see chapter 10).

671410, 12 July 1951, to Hoffman in New York. Sold to Nash Kenosha Inc, presumably the car manufacturer.

671480, 23 August 1951, to Delecroix. The 1951 Paris Motor Show car.

671692, 8 October 1951. Although a left-hand-drive car, this was the 1951 Earls Court Motor Show car.[49] It was finished in "Red Sheen" with Red trim and was later exported to Hornburg in Los Angeles but was only despatched on 14 November 1951.

671903, 18 February 1952, to M&A Koohiji, Bahrein. A later owner believes that this car was owned by Cary Grant and used in a film, but this cannot be verified from the *Car Record Book* or other sources.[50]

671926, 27 February 1952, to Claparede in Geneva.

S 661001, MXJ 954, as raced in the 1960s by Rob Beck, by which time it had been much modified and even had a shortened chassis. (JDHT)

The 1952 Geneva Motor Show car, although later sold to a Californian owner.

The following six cars built in March-April 1952 were all entered in the "Race of Champions" held at Silverstone as part of the *Daily Express* meeting on 10 May 1952, before being exported to either Hoffman or Hornburg in the USA, but it is not certain which driver had which car in the race:
672012, 672063, 672070, 672080, 672094 and **672104** The drivers were "B Bira", Johnny Claes, Tony Gaze; "Tulo" de Graffenried, Stirling Moss and Paul Pietsch. Moss won.[51]

672019, 3 April 1952, to Hornburg in Los Angeles. Sold in Seattle to WE Boeing Jr, who can only have been a member of the aircraft manufacturing family.

672150, 7 May 1952, to Guardia & Cia in Panama. This is the first car marked "SE" for "Special Equipment" in the *Car Record Book*, although the chassis number and engine numbers lack the S prefix and suffix (compare S 672373 below).

672282 MDU 420, 27 May 1952, to Hornburg but was a Personal Export Delivery car. It was Battleship Grey. The first owner was Clark Gable, his second or possibly third XK 120. It was delivered to him by lorry while he was filming in Cornwall, hence the Coventry registration mark, and he subsequently toured Europe in the car. Despite being a standard car, it had wire wheels, and Gable later had it fitted with rear wheel spats – cut out to clear the wheel spinners – and a louvred bonnet. If you believe that Gable only had two XK 120s, this was his second car.[52]

S 672373, 13 June 1952, with engine number W 5773-8S, to Hornburg. The first car with S prefix/suffix letters in the *Car Record Book*, so it may have been the first proper SE model, but see also 672150 above.

S 672633, 24 July 1952, to Hornburg. Sold to the Harley-Davidson Sales Company. Must have made a change from motorcycles…

672844, 15 September 1952, to Delecroix in Paris. The 1952 Paris Motor Show car.

673314, 12 December 1952, to the Belgian Motor Company in Brussels. This Cream car had "special Orange trim" which suggests it may have been a show

A perhaps slightly apprehensive William Lyons looks on as the young King Feisal of Iraq tries out an XK 120 for size at the 1952 Earls Court Motor Show. The car is believed to be chassis 661028. His Majesty subsequently acquired a Mark VII saloon. (Paul Skilleter/Jaguar)

car (compare 661028). It could have been at the 1953 Brussels Motor Show, although it is recorded as going to a private owner.

S 673355, 22 December 1952, to Hoffman in New York. Sold to a very (in)famous first owner, General Rafael ("Ramfis") Trujillo Jr. The then-23-year-old playboy was the oldest son of the dictator of the Dominican Republic. A friend of the ama -teur racing driver Porfirio Rubirosa, he was supposed to have had an affair with Zsa Zsa Gabor, and later married the lesser Hollywood star Lita Milan.

S 673656, 24 February 1953, to Hoffman. Sold to CR Argetsinger, believed to be Cameron Argetsinger

At the 1951 Earls Court Show, Jaguar had two left-hand drive XK 120s on the stand. This was the UK show debut for the fixed-head, which was 679088, while the open two-seater was 671692. (JDHT)

Clark Gable in Cornwall in his second XK 120, 672282 MDU 420. (JDHT)

The "race of champions" held at Silverstone on 10 May 1952 was largely a publicity stunt. (JDHT)

who was a founder member of the Sports Car Club of America and the man who initiated motor racing at Watkins Glen.

S 673734, 11 March 1953, to Hoffman. The 1953 New York Motor Show car. It is unusual to find a note in the *Car Record Book* that a car was for a motor show in America. Presumably the choice of show car was mostly left to the American importers, who would pick a suitable car from stock.

S 674324, 20 November 1953, to Hoffman. Sold to Commander J Rutherford of Palm Beach in Florida,

presumably replacing his first XK 120, 670001 (see chapter 8).

S 674655, 12 January 1954, to Hoffman. This was a Cream car with White trim, and I believe this was the car fitted with gold-plated instead of chrome trim, which was displayed at the 1954 New York Motor Show. This was supposed to commemorate Jaguar's international speed records and race victories during 1953.[53]

S 674755, 19 January 1954, to Hoffman. Sold to Mickey Spillane, writer of the best-selling thrillers

This car, photographed outside the main entrance to the office block at Browns Lane, was the 1954 New York Show car. It has plated wire wheels, whitewall tyres, white steering wheel, white interior trim, and the brake drums seem to have been painted body colour. What does not show up is the gold plating of the bright parts! I believe this was chassis number S 674655. (Paul Skilleter/Jaguar)

featuring Mike Hammer.

S 676035, 12 July 1954, to Hornburg. Supposedly Clark Gable's fourth XK 120.[54] The *Car Record Book* unfortunately lists the first owner more prosaically as E J Heidelman, Altadena, California.

S 676108, 20 July 1954, to Hornburg. Sold to R Ginter of Beverly Hills, who may have been the racing driver Richie Ginther. He was racing a Porsche at the time but later became a Formula 1 driver for Ferrari, BRM and Honda.

676438, 26 August 1954, to Hoffman. The last LHD open two-seater. There were a total of 273 cars built in August 1954, and they qualified as "1955 models".

Fixed-head coupé, right-hand drive:

S 669003 MRW 880, 29 December 1952, to Lewis and Peat (location unknown). First FHC RHD to SE specification, and the first customer car supplied, in fact as a Personal Export Delivery. Bought by Jaguar historian Philip Porter in 1973 and restored in 1997-98.

S 669005 RKX 252, 7 January 1953, to Henlys in London. Sold to Peter Whitehead, one of the winners of the 1951 Le Mans, replacing his previous XK 120s, OTS RHD 660146 and FHC LHD 679001.[55]

669006 KSF 7, 16 February 1953, to Rossleigh in Edinburgh. Sold to Ian Stewart of Ecurie Ecosse fame, although as a road car. In the 1990s, it was restored by Nigel Dawes. As with other Dawes cars, it was uprated

and given a number of individual touches, including the fitting of chrome-plated separate side lamp housings as seen on the early OTS models, but not originally found on the FHC cars. It is believed that Nigel restored around nine FHCs to a similar specification.[56]

S 669015, 24 April 1953, to Andersons in Brisbane, Australia. On 31 January to 1 February 1954, this car won a 24-hour race at Mount Druitt in New South Wales, beating a C-type although it should perhaps be added that a Humber Super Snipe and a Holden were second and third! The car was then still owned by Andersons, and Mrs "Geordie" Anderson was one of the three drivers in the race. Later badly damaged in a crash during practice for the 1954 Australian Grand Prix, the car was rebuilt, but was at some stage fitted with a Mark VII engine. It was being restored in Australia in the 1980s.[57]

S 669024 GFE 111, 29 May 1953, to Roland C Bellamy of Grimsby. Sold to Jaguar dealer JRJ Mansbridge in Lincoln. Mansbridge won an Alpine Cup in the 1953 Alpine Rally with this car.

669066 TPJ 503, 30 September 1953, to Henlys in London. Sold to the test pilot Neville Duke, who at one time held the world air speed record. Curiously, although his car had wire wheels, it was not a Special Equipment model, according to the *Car Record Book*.[58]

669108 OLF 460, 11 December 1953, to Henlys in London. Sold to Miss P M ("Patsy") Burt of Chichester who was a well-known hillclimb competitor.[59]

The fixed-head coupé S 669015 won the 24-hour race at Mount Druitt in New South Wales. (Terry McGrath)

669120 MUS 1 later 517 KGE and 120 UAR, 13 January 1954, through Henlys in London to Coombs of Guildford. Sold to Ninian Sanderson who won the 1956 Le Mans with Ron Flockhart in the Ecurie Ecosse D-type.

669125 DVV 200, 22 January 1954, through Henlys in London to Grose of Northampton. Sold to Jack Sears in Norfolk, who raced it.

669155 PLV 9, 21 April 1954, through Henlys in Manchester to Litherland Motors, Liverpool. Sold to Gilbert ("Gillie") Tyrer who also owned XKC-059.[60]

669186 DSN 555, 17 June 1954, to Ritchies in Glasgow. Sold to D P Stewart & Son, for Jimmy Stewart, son of this Jaguar dealer, sometime driver for Ecurie Ecosse, and older brother of Jackie Stewart.[61]

669195 GJL 300, 14 July 1954, to Roland C Bellamy of Grimsby. The last RHD fixed-head, originally sold in Lincolnshire.

The Mansbridges in S 669024 GFE 111 during the 1953 Alpine Rally where they won an Alpine Cup. (JDHT)

Fixed-head coupé, left-hand drive:

679001 LWK 966, later EAN 100 (?), date not recorded. The first LHD fixed-head, probably built in November 1950 judging by its engine number W 2420-8. It was sold to the racing driver Peter White-head, who was the co-driver of the winning C-type in the 1951 Le Mans, the second of his three XK 120s. It was subsequently converted to RHD.[62]

679002, date not recorded. The second LHD car with engine number W 2945-8 (dating to January 1951), which is believed to have been the Geneva Motor Show car of 1951 and was probably the car featured in the British magazines at the time. It subsequently went to RM Overseas in Düsseldorf on 10 April 1951, and may have been at either the Frankfurt or the Berlin Motor Show in 1951. It was returned to the factory and eventually consigned to Hornburg in Los Angeles with a despatch date of 29 January 1952. It turned up in California many years later. It is now in Adelaide in Australia where it is being restored by Percy Dixon, who bought it in 1991 in the USA.

Percy states that he found a number of anomalies in the specification of the car, and started what one can only describe as a forensic examination. This led to him finding an extraordinary variety of no fewer than 280 numbers on the chassis frame, among them 660001, 660010 and 669001, apart from 679002. His theory is that the original chassis frame of 660001 was later used as the experimental chassis 660010, then for 669001, the first FHC with RHD (which at one time was fitted with a four-cylinder XK engine, see chapters 2 and 8), and finally for his car. While it is perfectly possible that the same chassis frame may have been used for a variety of experimental cars, the putative identification of the Dixon car as 660001 has been greeted with some scepticism by XK experts in Australia and elsewhere, among them Terry McGrath and John Elmgreen, who co-authored the important work *The Jaguar XK in Australia*, and Paul Skilleter. Terry has seen the car and states that it is a perfectly standard fixed-head chassis, and that the many numbers found are not stamped in but written with some sort of marker pen. It also seems likely that 669001, and possibly 660001 were still in existence while 679002 was being built, therefore precluding a hypothesis that they could be the same car. As a footnote, it may be mentioned that a car supposedly numbered 679002 was offered for sale by Nigel Dawes as "the first LHD coupé" in 1996, probably the same car that was for sale in Las Vegas by 2004.[63]

679088, 1 October 1951, to the Belgian Motor Company but only despatched on 28 November. In fact, this was the 1951 Earls Court Motor Show car and was, incidentally, the first FHC in Battleship Grey.[64]

679099, 4 October 1951, to Hoffman in New York. Sold to D Cameron Peck who until 1952 maintained an extraordinary collection of several hundred historic cars, including a Bugatti Royale. He was sometime president of the Sports Car Club of America, and of the Antique Automobile Club of America.

679282 LVC 345, 28 January 1952, works car. This car was in a non-standard two-tone colour scheme of cream and green, and was lent to Stirling Moss, who used this car to compete in rallies, including the Welsh Rally, the *Daily Express* rally and the Lyons-Charbonnières in 1952. He also used LVC 345 to tow a caravan when attending race meetings in Europe. The car still exists and was sold in a Coys auction in 2004.[65]

679661, 30 April 1952, to Delecroix in Paris. Sold to Jean Heurtaux, who also owned 671142 (see above), and who was killed driving his C-type the following year.

S 679841, 26 June 1952, to Hoffman. The first FHC LHD SE model with, unusually, engine number W 5419-9S, one of only 32 XK 120s to have had the 9:1 compression ratio from the factory.

S 679970 MHP 682, 1 September 1952, works car. Jaguar's demonstrator and press car, road tested by *The Autocar*. Later converted to RHD, now preserved in the Rosmalen Museum in Holland.[66]

S 680667, 21 January 1953, to Delecroix. Sold to the Michelin tyre company.

680863, 26 January 1953, to Hoffman. The 1953 New York Motor Show car.

681241 and **681242** were supposedly built in October 1953 but these two cars were re-numbered as **681484** and **681485**, the two final FHC LHD chassis numbers, and were only despatched in September 1954. We don't know why this re-numbering should have taken place.

S 681404, 3 March 1954, to the Belgian Motor Company. Sold to HRH Prince Jean, Hereditary Grand Duke of Luxembourg, Knight of the Garter, and ruler of his country from 1964 to 2000.

Test pilot Neville Duke with 669066 TPJ 503, a fixed-head coupé with wire wheels. (JDHT)

681422, 8 March 1954, to Delecroix. Sold to HRH Prince Saad bin Abdul, brother of the King of Saudi Arabia, whose address was a hotel in Avenue Georges V.

681451, 6 April 1954, to Hornburg in Los Angeles. Sold to André Previn, of Beverly Hills, the famous pianist, composer and conductor.

S 681485, build date uncertain, to Hoffman in New York. This was originally chassis 681242 (cp. above) of October 1953 but appears to have been finished only in July/August 1954 when it became the last LHD fixed-head.

Drophead coupé, right-hand drive:

667001 MHP 494, body number P 1001, 4 January 1952. The first RHD drophead, kept by Jaguar until sold second-hand in 1955. Apart from this car, RHD

Van Johnson in an XK 120 on the French Riviera. (JDHT)

On the corner of the 1953 Earls Court Motor Show stand, the drophead which is probably 667021. It shares stand space with, among others, that year's Le Mans winning C-type. (JDHT)

London. Reputedly once owned by Mike Hawthorn, although the *Car Record Book* does not list the first owner.[68]

667033 OHP 503, 29 September 1953. This was Jaguar's demonstrator for the 1953 Earls Court Motor Show and became a press car; it was road tested by *Autosport*.[69] Sold second-hand in 1955.

S 667040 KEA 91, 30 September 1953, to PJ Evans in Birmingham. The first right hand drive DHC to SE specification.

667182 ECP 34 (later registered 1274 EL), 15 January 1954, to Appleyards, Leeds. Sold to the Hon Patrick Lindsay, historic racing driver and subsequently owner of the D-types XKD-502 and XKD-554, among others.

667245, 26 April 1954, to Hoffman in New York. This drophead probably did not leave the UK as it was sold to Thomas Stanley Matthews at a London address. Matthews (1901-1991) was a journalist, critic and author who worked for *Time* magazine from 1929, and in 1949 he succeeded the magazine's founder, Henry Luce, as editor. Upon retiring in 1953, he moved to England. In 1954 he married Martha Gellhorn, the novelist and war reporter, who was formerly the wife of Ernest Hemingway.

S 667295, 12 August 1954, to St Helier Garage in Jersey. The last RHD drophead.

Drophead coupé, left-hand drive:

677001, 29 January 1953, to Hornburg in Los Angeles. The first LHD drophead, body number P 1002.

677008 and **677010**, 17 February and 23 February 1953, both to Hoffman. These were the two 1953 New York Motor Show cars.

S 677012, 26 February 1953, to Hoffman. The first SE model.

S 677722, 16 July 1953, to Hornburg. Sold to the film star Humphrey Bogart.

677987, 31 August 1953, to Claparede in Geneva, Switzerland. Sold to Paulette Goddard, the actress and sometime Mrs Charlie Chaplin.

678024, 3 September 1953, to Delecroix in Paris.

production only started in July 1953.

667021 UPC 8, 25 September 1953, to Henlys in London. I have tentatively identified this as the 1953 Earls Court Motor Show Car. The colour scheme, Cream with Blue trim and hood, matches the description in *The Motor*, and it may also be noted that there was a delay of three months before this car was despatched on 22 December 1953.[67]

667022 PUR 415, 25 September 1953, through Henlys in London to W M Couper of St Albans. Sold to Duncan Hamilton.

667023 TPJ 590, 25 September 1953, to Henlys in

The drophead coupés for the 1953 New York Motor Show merited a special send-off by The Lord Mayor of Coventry from the factory. This is probably 677010 which was Battleship Grey. (JDHT)

Sold to His Highness The Aga Khan.

678027, 4 September 1953, to Delecroix. Sold to the film star Danielle Darrieux.

678280, 9 April 1954, to Saad in Beirut, who were the agents in Lebanon and Syria. Sold to Al Sharif Hussein Ali whose address was The Royal Palace, Baghdad. This is probably Prince Sharif Al-Hussein bin Ali, a cousin of the Iraqi King Faisal I.

678395, 16 June 1954, to Delecroix. Sold to HRH Princess Ghislaine of Monaco, a former film actress who had married the 75-year-old Prince Louis of Monaco in 1946. Prince Louis was Monaco's ruler and the grandfather of Prince Rainier.

S 678418, 29 June 1954, to Delecroix. Sold to M. L Guevara but supposedly owned by a member of the court of the Shah of Iran, this car ended up with a strangely shaped hard top and a 3.8-litre engine from a Mark II. It was reported in France in the early 1990s, and in Barcelona in 2004. Curiously, the car has separate chrome side lamp housings, but these may, of course, not be original.[70]

678472 NRW 355, 13 August 1954, to Hutchinson in Columbia, as a Personal Export Delivery car. The last LHD drophead.

There are a number of cars that I have not been able to identify by chassis number but which are known to have had famous owners. The French novelist Françoise Sagan, who died in 2004, was photographed with two different XKs, and while her drophead coupé was an XK

140, the open two-seater was an XK 120.[71] I have mentioned Ray Milland's early alloy car. The car owned by Elizabeth Taylor and Michael Wilding was an open two-seater with left-hand drive, possibly in Silver or another light metallic colour, with ventilation flaps in the front wings but still chrome side-lamp housings. This dates it to between February 1951 and September 1952.[72]

Recently a photo has appeared showing Jayne Mansfield in a very late 1954 XK 120 open two-seater with flat horn push, a car which is believed to have been destroyed by fire while in the Barris Kustom workshop

… and here is the 1953 New York Show stand where this car and its black twin were displayed, on the right. Note also the open two-seater on the left which is a wire wheeled car fitted with the curious part-cutaway spats. The Mercedes-Benzes in the background were also part of Hoffman's display. The Le Mans trophy probably relates to the victory of the Mercedes-Benz 300SL in 1952… (JDHT)

While Elina Labourdette may not have owned this drophead, she did use it in the film To Paris with Love shot in Paris in 1954. (JDHT)

Michael Wilding and Elizabeth Taylor in their open two-seater. (JDHT)

Randolph Scott at Hornburg's showroom on Sunset Boulevard. (JDHT)

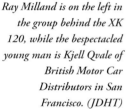

Ray Milland is on the left in the group behind the XK 120, while the bespectacled young man is Kjell Qvale of British Motor Car Distributors in San Francisco. (JDHT)

in 1957.[73] The American actor Bonar Colleano tragically met his death while at the wheel of an XK 120 drophead coupé on 17 August 1958 near Birkenhead.[74] I recently heard a rumour that Marlene Dietrich supposedly had a customised XK 120 in Paris, this awaits verification. It is also claimed that Juan Manuel Fangio and Robert Montgomery both owned XK 120s.[75]

Montgomery, together with other Hollywood stars Gary Cooper, Robert Stack and Dick Powell, was said to be awaiting delivery in December 1949.[76] An impressive list of American owners in 1950 included, apart from the names already mentioned, Charles E Bedford of Standard Oil, Briggs Cunningham, Eric Dunn, Alfred duPont, Jim Kimberly of Kleenex, Lowell Neicker, D Cameron Peck, Brookes Stevens and Jack R Vanderbilt, a fine mixture of wealthy and famous sportsmen.[77]

Of course, there were many more cars raced or rallied by private owners, abroad and at home. In fact, one begins to suspect that the majority of XK 120s sold in the home market in 1950-51 were at one point or another used in competition, but it is often difficult to link an owner's name or the registration mark with the chassis number.

1. Elmgreen & McGrath *XK in Australia* pp26-28; Skilleter in *Jaguar World* Jan/Feb 1996; *XK Gazette* no.10 Jul 1998
2. *The Autocar* 30 Sep 1949; *The Motor* 12 Oct 1949; the photo in *The Autocar* shows the car without spats, perhaps while it was still being "clamped down" to reduce apparent height, cf. Porter & Skilleter *Sir William Lyons* p135
3. *The Motor* 19 Apr 1950; *The Autocar* 21 Apr 1950, 19 May 1950; Schmid *Jaguar XK 120* p30
4. John May, who inspected this car in 1997, believes that it was originally black, he states it had "show features" such as chrome-plated cam covers and carburettor dash pots, information courtesy of John May; Michael Ware in *Classic Cars* Jun 1998

5. Elmgreen & McGrath p30
6. *XK Gazette* no.72
7. Schmid *Jaguar XK 120* p26; Skilleter in *Jaguar World* Mar 1999
8. Schmid p26
9. For the debate on Gable's car(s), see *XK Gazette* no.13 Oct 1998; Jeremy Broad in *XK Gazette* no.53 Feb 2002; John Elmgreen in *XK Gazette* no.58, Jul 2002; for the actual first Gable car, see *The Autocar* 30 Dec 1949, photo 27 Jan 1950; *Motor Sport* Jan 1950; *Road & Track* Apr 1950; Dugdale *Jaguar in America* p31; Clinton Bourke in *XK Gazette* no.60 Sep 2002; the photo of a cream car in *Jaguar Heritage* magazine no.10 Oct 2004, described as the

first Gable car, is probably of 670018 now in the Swiss Frey collection; on Caracciola see Molter *Rudolf Caracciola – Titan am Volant*; for Milland see Dugdale p35, Porter & Skilleter *Sir William Lyons* p117 citing *Jaguar Journal* Jun 1950

10. *The Motor* 7 Sep 1949; *The Autocar* 27 Jan 1950

11. Guy Broad in *XK Gazette* no.14 Nov 1998, quoted verbatim, although I cannot verify the number 2335 from other sources. Maybe Guy meant 2331; *Jaguar World* May 1999

12. Whyte *Jaguar Sports Racing & Works Competition Cars to 1953* p87; Skilleter *Jaguar The Sporting Heritage* p49

13. Schmid p26

14. Skilleter *Jaguar Sports Cars* pp106-10

15. Urs Schmid in *XK Gazette* no.57 Jun 2002; Jeremy Broad in *XK Gazette* no.58 Jul 2002; Clinton Bourke in *XK Gazette* no.60 Sep 2002

16. Photo on the cover of *Bilhistorisk Tidsskrift* no.59 summer 1979

17. Registration records, Coventry City Archives; Skilleter pp92-93; *Jaguar World* Nov/Dec 1996; Nolan *Phil Hill: Yankee Champion* pp32-36

18. Schmid p30

19. *Jaguar World* Jul/Aug 1994; Porter *Original Jaguar XK* 2nd ed. 1998

20. Elmgreen & McGrath p41, *XK Gazette* no.12 Sep 1998

21. Skilleter in *Jaguar World* May/Jun 1995

22. Elmgreen & McGrath pp42-43

23. Elmgreen & McGrath p48

24. *XK Gazette* no.13 Oct 1998, no.38 Nov 2000

25. *XK Gazette* no.54 Mar 2002; David Bentley, registrar of the XK Club, also lists the registration marks HWS 126 and HWS 201 as being on Ecurie Ecosse cars, but chassis numbers not known; *XK Gazette* no.38 Nov 2000

26. *Jaguar World* Jul/Aug 1993, reprinting an earlier article by Clark from the *XK Bulletin*; Clark in *Classic Cars* Nov 1996; Clark *Backfire* containing a 1951 article on the XK 120, posthumously reprinted in *The Daily Telegraph* 29 Sep 2001

27. Skilleter p106; *XK Gazette* no.25 Oct 1999

28. *The Motor* 12 Oct 1949

29. Boyce *Jaguar XK Series – The Complete Story* p101; *XK Gazette* no.29 Feb 2000

30. Skilleter p97; Whyte p129

31. Letter from D L Gandhi in *XK Gazette*, no.56 May 2002; Broad in *XK Gazette*, no.59 Aug 2002; no.60 Sep 2002; no.62 Nov 2002

32. *The Motor* 22 Aug 1951; Elmgreen & McGrath p67

33. *XK Gazette* no.64 Jan 2003

34. Whyte *Jaguar The History of a Great British Car* p138; *XK Gazette* no.21 Jun 1999

35. *XK Gazette* no.50 Nov 2001

36. *XK Gazette* no.61 Oct 2002

37. *XK Gazette* no.38 Nov 2000

38. Whyte (1st ed.) p220

39. Elmgreen & McGrath pp80-81

40. Information courtesy of Paul Skilleter

41. Ludvigsen *Excellence was Expected* pp91, 120

42. Information courtesy of "Doc" Peter Scadron; the author cannot vouch for it

43. Urban *Les Métamorphoses du Jaguar* pp282-85

44. *The Motor* 21 Oct 1953

45. Skilleter in *Jaguar World* Mar/Apr 1998

46. Whyte p150 – he says they were second; Viart p264

47. Schmid p26

48. *The Autocar* 6 Apr 1951; Skilleter photos between pp66-67

49 Viart p124; *Australian Jaguar Magazine* no.119 Jan 2005

50. Information courtesy of owner

51. Whyte *Jaguar Sports Racing…* pp161-62

52. Schmid p36; Schmid in *XK Gazette* no.57 Jun 2002; Clinton Bourke in *XK Gazette* no.60 Sep 2002

53. *Autosport* 19 Feb 1954

54. Schmid in *XK Gazette* no.57 Jun 2002

55. *Classic Cars* May 1998; *XK Gazette* no.17 Feb 1999

56. *XK Gazette* no.17 Feb 1999, no.85 Oct 2004

57. Elmgreen & McGrath pp83-85; Whyte p283

58. Frostick *The Jaguar Tradition* p77; Schmid p37

59. *XK Gazette* no.12 Sep 1998, no.20 May 1999

60. *XK Gazette* no.12 Sep 1998, no.22 Jul 1999

61. *XK Gazette* no.12 Sep 1998, no.24 Sep 1999

62. *XK Gazette* no.75 Dec 2003

63. *The Autocar* 2 Mar 1951; The Motor 7 Mar 1951; Les Hughes in *Australian Jaguar Magazine* no.108 2003, no.119 2005, no.120 2005; David Bentley in *XK Gazette* no.75 Dec 2003; information courtesy of Percy Dixon, Terry McGrath and Paul Skilleter

64 .*The Autocar* 24 Oct 1951; *The Motor* 26 Oct 1951; Viart p124; *Australian Jaguar Magazine* no.119 Jan 2005

65. *XK Gazette* no.15 Dec 1998

66. *The Autocar* 17 Oct 1952; XK Gazette no.25 Oct 1999; no.28 Jan 2000

67. *The Motor* 21 Oct 1953

68. *XK Gazette* no.51 Dec 2001; no.52 Jan 2002

69. *Autosport* 14 May 1954

70. Urban p310; *XK Gazette* no.80 May 2004

71. *Independent on Sunday* 5 Jul 1998; *The Guardian* 27 Sep 2004, photo credited to Lido/EPA

72. Schmid p36

73. *Jaguar Yearbook 2004* p57, photo credited to Bettmann/Corbis; Patten in *Jaguar World* Jan/Feb 1997

74. *XK Gazette* no.52 Jan 2002

75. Schmid p36

76. *The Autocar* 30 Dec 1949

77 *Speed Age* Oct 1950

Chapter Ten

Special Bodywork and "Specials"

The major work on collating information on special-bodied Jaguars was done by the French collector Roland Urban who published his findings in the book *Les Métamorphoses du Jaguar* (1993). Urban was a founder member and sometime president of the French Jaguar Drivers' Club. He collected many of the cars that he wrote about and in 1985 opened a Jaguar museum in the south of France, and yet even he was not able to trace chassis numbers of all the special-bodied cars. The following section leans very much on his work, and the research of Terry McGrath who supplied many of the photos used in Urban's book.

Part of the problem with identifying some of the special-bodied cars is that some of them were built on chassis from XK 120s that had left the factory as complete cars, rather than being supplied in chassis-only form. According to the *Car Record Books*, the following were the only seven known chassis-only deliveries, in chronological order:

660529 OTS RHD chassis, 1 January 1951, to Claparede in Geneva, Switzerland, for Hugo Frey. This became the Beutler cabriolet. The style of the car was similar to contemporary Beutler bodies on chassis from other British makers such as Bristol and Jowett. Originally pale blue, it was displayed at the Geneva Motor Show in 1952. It was quickly re-painted dark red, and registered SO 3651 – unless, of course, Beutler built two similar cars, which could account for one of the other chassis-only deliveries to Switzerland. It still exists in Switzerland, and is still dark red. Later registrations have been ZH 2366 and ZH 19495.[1]

660562 OTS RHD chassis, 8 January 1951, to Claparede. This may have been a second Beutler, but an alternative possibility is that this chassis may have been bodied by Graber. It was registered in Switzerland on 28 April 1951 to a M. Ernest Morf of La Chaux-de-Fonds (see also 660028 below).[2]

660750 OTS RHD chassis, 17 April 1951, to Shorters in Auckland, New Zealand. It was fitted with a four-seater tourer body by Abbott of Farnham in Surrey for D S Mitchell of Tauranga, New Zealand. The front end of the car was similar to the standard car and appears to have used a normal bonnet, but the windscreen was a flat one-piece type and the front wing line sloped more drastically downwards towards the rear. The rear wheel spats

The Beutler cabriolet kept a rather standard looking XK 120 grille. As first seen at the Geneva Motor Show the car was pale blue, but it was soon repainted dark red. (JDHT)

The non-standard flat windscreen and lower wing line are evident in the front three-quarter view of the Abbott car.
(Terry McGrath)

Oblin's Belgian-built coupé on chassis 660751 did look a lot like a Ferrari. Herzet drove it competitively on many occasions, here he has been stopped at the French-Italian border during the 1952 Alpine Rally (before the Schengen treaty!).
(Paul Skilleter)

The slightly ungainly, but undoubtedly very practical four-seater that Abbott of Farnham built on chassis 660750 for a New Zealand customer. The mind boggles at the idea of towing anything with an XK 120.

were elongated, like those of the Mark VII. The body was panelled in aluminium on an ash frame. Extras included a pair of fog lamps, a radio, and a tow bar. It was restored for the Dutch company Upper Classics and the finished car was displayed at the Techno Classica in Essen in 2006. While it has been suggested that there is another Abbott-bodied XK 120 surviving in Perth, Australia, this is refuted by Perth resident and XK expert Terry McGrath.[3]

660751 OTS RHD chassis, 17 April 1951, to Jaguar Car Distributors in Brussels, Belgium, finally delivered to the National SA on 22 June 1951. This is the Oblin coupé which looks like a Touring-bodied Ferrari. It ran in the 1951 Liège-Rome-Liège, driven

In the second Tour de France Automobile in 1952, Herzet and co-driver Bianchi finished thirty-eighth in the Oblin coupé. (Paul Skilleter)

660922 OTS RHD chassis, 23 October 1951, to Belgian Motor Company (the same company as Jaguar Car Distributors, just with a change of name), for G Demerbe, delivered 5 March 1952. This is the Stabilimenti Farina "Flying Jaguar" coupé. The car was displayed at the Turin Motor Show in 1952. It was part of a plan hatched by Madame Bourgeois of the Belgian importers to make a range of special-bodied Jaguars. She also commissioned Stabilimenti Farina to produce two bodies on Mark VII chassis; one a two-door saloon, the other a drophead coupé, called respectively the "Meteor" and the "Golden Arrow". The "Flying Jaguar" remained in the Demerbe family's ownership until 1985. By 2000, it had been restored and had migrated to France, in the ownership of Christophe Pund of La Galerie des Damiers who also at the time was offering the Oblin coupé and a Ghia-bodied XK 140 for sale.[5]

by Herzet and Baudouin, and finished second. It was displayed at the 1952 Brussels Motor Show. They then took part in the 1952 Lyon-Charbonnières rally and came second in class. In the Tour de France Automobile Herzet finished 38th, this time with Lucien Bianchi as his co-driver. The car was re-discovered in Belgium in the 1960s. It was for some time owned by Bob Kerr in Scotland and later by Roland Urban. By 1999, it was reported under restoration by Daniel Brooks in France, and was bought there by Jerry Montpellier by 2001.[4]

671871 OTS LHD chassis, 8 February 1952, to Emil Frey, Zürich. This was bodied by Worblaufen (also known as Ramseier) of Bern, and is given the briefest of mentions by Urban, who says it was a red cabriolet, while Viart has a photo of the car (or of 660985). It seems to have been at the Geneva Motor Show although I have failed to establish the year, probably 1953, when it featured in Worblaufen's advertising. Viart says that it was displayed together with a Mark VII-based convertible, and both cars had the Mark VII-type radiator grille and "growler" motif above it.[6]

660985 OTS RHD chassis, 16 May 1952, to Frey. This was probably also bodied by Worblaufen, presumably in the same style as 671871, and was similarly red. It was registered in Bern 1 September 1952 to the Export Agricole SA.[7]

There were many other modified, customised or special-bodied XK 120s, but for some of these cars

Above: Ramseier of Worblaufen worked in a style somewhat reminiscent of Graber, and their interpretation of the XK 120 was rather elegant. (Paul Skilleter)

Above and right: After many years of neglect, the "Flying Jaguar" has been immaculately restored for Christophe Pund. The comfortable interior is almost completely covered in leather. (Terry McGrath)

Left: One of a series of publicity shots that Madame Bourgeois sent to Jaguar of her special-bodied cars in 1952, this is the XK 120 based "Flying Jaguar". (JDHT)

the chassis numbers are not known. These other cars all left the factory in standard form, as there are no other chassis deliveries in the XK 120 *Car Record Book*s. Again, the following information is mostly based on Urban's pioneering research:

S 675360 OTS LHD, 5 April 1954, to Hoffman in New York. This became the Pinin Farina coupé which is perhaps the most famous of re-bodied XK 120s. It was shown and described in *The Autocar* in 1955, where they simply said that it was an "XK 120 … by Pinin Farina … for an American enthusiast". The car was displayed at the Turin Motor Show in May 1955. According to Urban, the car was displayed at the *1956* Geneva Motor Show – which I

This is the one-off coupé body by Pinin Farina built in 1955. Only the radiator grille retained some semblance to a Jaguar. (Paul Skilleter)

These more recent pictures shows the Pinin Farina as it is today, part restored by its German owner. The colour does it no favours! Originally it was metallic grey. The dashboard is quite advanced for 1955. (Terry McGrath)

doubt – and was bought by Max Hoffman, the Jaguar importer in New York. Although the original car was consigned to Hoffman, by March 1956 he was no longer the Jaguar importer – his contract was terminated at the end of 1955. On balance, I am inclined to favour the version from *The Autocar*.

Urban reproduces a contemporary colour photo of the car, finished in metallic grey, which seems to show a right hand drive car. However, close inspection shows this to be a mirror-printed image and the car, in fact, had left-hand drive, as is evident from other photos. Nothing is known of its subsequent history up to 1980, when the car was found in the USA by the German collector Ludwig Draxel-Fischer, who brought it back to Europe for restoration. The car is still stored in Germany, slowly undergoing restoration.[8]

A company almost as famous as Pinin Farina, Ghia built three "Supersonic" coupés on XK 120 chassis, designed by Savonuzzi, and Urban identifies two of them by chassis number. As both of the cars with known chassis numbers went to Delecroix in Paris, I speculate that this company may have commissioned them. One of these cars was photographed by *The Motor* while the body was under construction in the summer of 1954, its engine still with the normal twin SU carburettors. All three cars had chrome wire wheels, and all were present at the Concours d'Élégance in Cannes in 1954, where the white car won the Grand Prix d'Honneur.[9]

679768 FHC LHD, 12 June 1952, to Delecroix in Paris. This was the first Ghia car. It was red and the grille had just one horizontal and three vertical bars. It was fitted with a Conrero-modified cylinder head with a special aluminium intake manifold and three Weber carburettors. There is a contemporary colour photo, taken at the 1954 Montreux concours, although this, too, is a mirror image, and so appears to show it as a right-hand-drive model! A rear view taken at Montreux shows the car with a Turin trade plate. Originally it was possibly registered 66 BJ 75 but a later photo shows 69 BJ 75, and this car ended up in Roland Urban's collection. Interestingly, some photos of an XK 120 FHC in 1954 rallies in France also shows the number plate 66 BJ 75, and may be the car before it was re-bodied by Ghia; this rally car is standard, except for a modified radiator grille.[10]

The second car also had LHD, was almost certainly white and in 1954 carried the Geneva registration GE 2355. This was probably the 1954 Paris Motor Show Car, which was a light colour as seen in *The Autocar*. It had a grille similar to the first red car,

Two views of the red Ghia "Supersonic" in a museum in France. Note the number plate seen in the rear view.

The significance of this fixed-head with its modified grille and bonnet in the 1954 Lyon Charbonnières rally is the number plate, which suggests that this is the car that soon after received the first of the Ghia "Supersonic" bodies. (Paul Skilleter)

The blue car with egg-crate grille is believed to have been the third of the Ghia "Supersonic" bodies. (Paul Skilleter)

and may therefore pre-date the blue model below. This example is believed to have disappeared, although Urban suggests the body was used for the Willment Cobra Special. Ghia, incidentally, built almost identical bodies on Alfa Romeo 1900, Aston Martin and Fiat 8V chassis, and it has also been stated that the Willment Cobra used a similar body which had come from a Fiat chassis.[11]

S 675090 OTS LHD, 25 February 1954, to Delecroix, who delivered it to a M. Braydon (?) in July 1954. As re-bodied by Ghia, it was blue and had an egg-crate grille. It was originally registered under a temporary tourist registration in Paris as 9566 TT 75, later possibly under 8763 XA 69, and was owned by Michel Garçon in Lyon in the 1990s.

Another Ghia car is a left-hand-drive coupé with a very pronounced panoramic dog's leg windscreen. It has been described as an XK 120 and was, according to both Skilleter and Harvey, at the 1953 Paris Motor Show. Frostick attributed it to Ghia Aigle and his caption suggested it was an XK 140 displayed at Geneva in 1956. It is seen in all three photos with a Nash and a Chrysler in the background, both 1955

models. The same car is featured in Patrick Mennem's book. He says it was at the 1955 Paris Show, and that it was an XK 140 – and he got it right! His photo again shows a Chrysler in the background and the location is definitely Paris. In fact, Mennem's version is confirmed by a glance at *The Autocar*'s report of the 1955 Paris Show.

Urban shows a very similar car which he says was the 1955 Paris Show car and was built on XK 140 chassis 810827 (OTS LHD chassis-only delivery in January 1955). It was followed by two further cars, 815404 (FHC LHD chassis-only delivery March 1956) and a third one with an unknown chassis number. However, the 1955 car shown by Urban has a different, squarer radiator grille compared with the car in the original show photos in *The Autocar* and used by Skilleter *et al*. The latter has a distinctive curve to the top line of the grille. It could be the same car with a modified grille. Just to confuse the issue, there was a similar red Ghia body on an Alfa Romeo 1900 Super Sprint chassis at the 1954 Paris Show. This has the curved top line to the grille as seen in Skilleter *et al*, but is otherwise almost identical to the Jaguars.[12]

The Italian Ghia company should not be confused with the Swiss Ghia Aigle, which also did some work on XK 120s, as follows:

660095 OTS RHD, 25 May 1950, to Emil Frey in Zürich. This was partly re-bodied by Ghia Aigle as a coupé. It had a much more sloping roof than the standard FHC and featured external door handles of the inset flush type. The car was rediscovered in the French Alps and advertised for sale in 2004 but was then wrongly attributed to Graber. It has been suggested that

Ghia Aigle's interpretation of an XK 120 fixed-head coupé lacked the elegance of Jaguar's own version. This is probably 660095. Interestingly, it has flashing indicators fitted on the front bumpers. (Terry McGrath)

Nor was Ghia Aigle's cabriolet a great improvement on the standard car. Here it is at the Geneva Show in 1951. (Terry McGrath)

there were two cars made in this style, and certainly there are detail differences between the contemporary photo of such a car, and the recent "as found" photo.[13]

Ghia Aigle went on to build a two-plus-two cabriolet which was also based on a standard open two-seater, with higher than standard doors, and again with flush door handles. With an awkward upright windscreen, the result was not particularly elegant, but it made the Geneva Motor Show in 1951.[14] Subsequently, the same company made some bodies on Mark VII, XK 140 and XK 150 chassis.

660028 alloy OTS RHD, 2 January 1950, to Claparède in Geneva. The original owner, Victor Morf, had it rebodied (possibly after an accident) by Graber (famous for its association with Alvis; it also bodied many other British chassis) in 1951, with Graber body number 621.[15] This is most likely to be the right-hand-drive cabriolet, in typical Graber style, that is shown by both Viart and Urban. Viart shows a front view, with registration VD 2061, and he dates it to 1952. It had a seven-bar non-standard grille, XK-type front bumpers and an XK 120 badge on the bonnet. In the side views shown by Urban of the same car, it can be seen to have

XK 120 rear overriders, mounted upside down. While Urban says it was built on a Mark VII chassis, the low build of the car, the position of the steering wheel and the proportion of wheel size to wheelbase seem to confirm that it is indeed based on the XK 120.[16] It has also been suggested that 660562 (see above) was bodied by Graber.[17]

660622 OTS RHD LOE 28, 19 January 1951, to PJ Evans in Birmingham, first owner EC Witt. In 1954-55 this car was fitted with a rather rotund fastback four-seater coupé body, supposedly the work of a company called McGown in Belfast, and was advertised in this form in *Motor Sport* in 1956. It was later owned by Brian Vyse who raced it in the 1980s. The car was eventually restored to standard form.[18]

Henri Peignaux was the enthusiastic Jaguar dealer in Lyon who was one of the most prominent XK 120 drivers in France; many of his exploits are discussed in chapter 7. He commissioned the obscure coach-builder Jean Barou of Tournon in the Ardèche to re-body three XK 120s. In chronological order, the first appears to have been a fastback fixed-head coupé

Graber, as one would expect, did rather better. The side view shows the elongated rear end, while from the front can be seen the not quite standard radiator grille. The car used normal XK 120 bumpers. (Terry McGrath)

Below: The first Barou bodied coupé built on chassis 670028 was rallied, here with Radix and Laroche in the 1952 Liège-Rome-Liège. (Paul Skilleter). And (bottom) this is a modern shot of the first Barou as it is preserved today. (Paul Skilleter)

which had started out as chassis **670028**, originally an alloy OTS LHD built on 14 November 1949, that had been exported to Delecroix in Paris. It was entered by Laroche and Radix in the Liège-Rome-Liège Marathon in August 1952 where it came second. This car still exists. Urban reported it owned by one M. Tap in the Bordeaux region, and his photo of its engine shows the early tall carburettors and eight-stud cam covers, suggesting that this car is indeed 670028. The front end of the preserved car is the same as the Laroche/Radix car of the 1952 Liège.

A second coupé is believed to have been converted from a complete factory fixed-head that had been damaged in an accident, but the chassis number is not known. It is believed that the wrecked car was bought from Peignaux by a Dr Rebatel, and it was probably re-bodied in 1953, as it seems to have first appeared in the Lyon-Charbonnières rally in March 1954, driven by Rebatel and Trillat. It contested the same rally in 1955, as well as the Liège-Rome-Liège. Photos of the second Barou coupé used by Viart show the different radiator grille and position of lights at the front compared with the first car, and a different registration mark.[19] These Barou coupés reflect contemporary Italian and French styling. They were probably inspired by the work of Pinin Farina, or Jean Daninos at Facel-Metallon, as they have some resemblance to the Ford Comète bodied by Facel.

660981 OTS RHD, 2 May 1952, to Delecroix in Paris. This car went to Peignaux and was prepared by the factory for him in September 1952, prior to a record attempt at Montlhéry in October 1952 (which failed; see chapter 7). It was fitted with a number of C-type components. Peignaux still ran the Montlhéry car registered 893 AZ 38 in standard form, in the 1953 Lyon-Charbonnières rally which he won (unless the registration was transferred to another car). The story, according to Urban, is that Peignaux was unable to get hold of a C-type and so decided to build his own version. Nevertheless, in 1952-53 he *did* obtain two C-types, XKC-016 and XKC-035.

In any case, Peignaux had the car re-bodied by

The second Barou coupé differed in detail, such as the radiator grille and the arrangement of lamps. Here the first owner, M. Rebatel, is collecting the car from Henri Peignaux. (Paul Skilleter)

Barou as a two-seater barchetta, probably in 1953, and Peignaux and Devic (or Jacquin?) used the car in this form (now re-registered 1039 AE 69) in the 1954 Lyon-Charbonnières Rally. Either they did not finish, or were disqualified as it was below the minimum weight. It seems to have been its only contemporary competition appearance. Later it was fitted with three Weber carburettors, and was for a time in the Urban collection, but in 1997 was owned by Daniel Brooks in Paris, although it had several changes of ownership around this time. It was seen at the 2001 Mille Miglia and was offered by a German owner at Coys' auction on 21 July 2002, but despite a bid of £120,000, failed to reach reserve. It was later advertised by Admirals West of Cambridge, with an asking price of £175,000, and was apparently sold in the UK in 2003.[20]

Peignaux looks rather grumpy as he sits behind the wheel of the Barou barchetta in the 1954 Lyon Charbonnières rally. Perhaps he has just been told that the car has been disqualified… (Paul Skilleter)

The two coupés were followed by this barchetta, which also exists to this day. (Paul Skilleter)

The Authenrieth cabriolet, or an XK120 on steroids. Yes there is a Jaguar look but the car is rather bloated. The interior was roomy and comfortable, but why bother to change the standard instruments? (Author)

Ford Taunus. Authenrieth had hoped to build a small series of replicas, but the car remained a one-off. Herr Herbst kept the car for eight years, the next owner for two years and the third for 30, until it was re-discovered and restored by Authenrieth expert Henning Zeiss. The car was exhibited at the Techno Classica in Essen in April 2005.[21]

679239 FHC LHD, 17 January 1952, to Lagerwijs in Holland for a Mr Bloem. This was customised by an unknown coachbuilder with tail fins, headlamps relocated in raised front wings, a wider bonnet, and a rectangular egg-crate grille. It is now in the USA where one owner thought it might have been the work of Pinin Farina, but then he also thought that the car had taken part in the 1955 Le Mans…[22]

679308 FHC LHD, 31 January 1952, to Belgian Motor Company, sold to M. Lebeau of Liege. This car started life as an ordinary FHC LHD but early in life was modified with an extended roofline and a rear bench seat. The car still exists in Holland.[23]

671377 OTS LHD, 4 July 1951, to RM Overseas in Düsseldorf, and one of the two cars intended for the Motor Show in Berlin in September 1951. The first owner, a Frankfurt manufacturer called Herbst, found the car too cramped. He commissioned Authenrieth, well known coachbuilders of Darmstadt, to build a new body which resembled the standard, but was wider, with a longer cockpit and a more luxurious interior. It had specially made seats and even two children's seats in the rear. A curved, single-piece windscreen was fitted, together with wind-down door windows, and a superior hood. A new wood imitation dashboard was manufactured, with a complete set of instruments in front of the driver, cleverly fitted into two combination dials which appear to have come from the contemporary

680997 FHC LHD, 25 March 1953, to Bauloch & Reynaud in Algeria. In 1957 this car was re-bodied as a fibreglass roadster by Jacques Schwindenhammer, a paper merchant from Turckheim in Alsace. The result, named the PST, was an ugly and rather overweight car which failed to make any impression in the few races that its owner entered.[24]

Antem of Paris modified an open two-seater for Johnny Ysmael of the Philippines in 1950-51 as a cabriolet with a rear seat to carry his four children. Ysmael, who lived in the USA, also had a number of other exotic cars, including Ferraris.[25]

In Canada, John Blythe re-bodied an XK 120 in the 1970s with a fibreglass fastback coupé body, somewhat in the style of the E-type FHC. While it has been stated that htis was on an XK 120 chassis, som experts think it was on an XK 140. It was a good-looking car, although arguably of a style too modern for the chassis. The car is believed to survivie in the USA.[26]

A number of cars were inevitably modified in the USA, some of them purely for racing, others customised for road use.

670191 OTS LHD, 30 March 1950, to Hornburg in Los Angeles, but sold through Clayrich Motors of St Louis, Missouri, to one Franklin B Mayer. The chassis number quoted may therefore be incorrect, as the car in question was supposedly owned by Phil Hill's brother-in-law, Don Parkinson, who rolled it in practice at Pebble Beach on 26 May 1951. Parkinson rebuilt the car as a special with a narrow aluminium body and cycle-type wings, and competed with this special in 1951 and 1952, until he got XKC-030. The Parkinson car was many years later acquired by Terry Buffum who regularly used it in historic racing.[27]

670458 OTS LHD, 12 July 1950, to Hoffman in New York. It was rebuilt by John Fitch in the USA in 1951 as a "Le Mans Special" for Coby Whitmore with a body along the same general lines as the Parkinson car, and the owner had hopes of entering it at Le Mans. Weight was down to 2100 lbs from the 2900 lbs of the standard car, and it was fitted with wire wheels. The car still exists and took part in historic races in the USA in the 1990s. Fitch was later responsible for the Fitch Phoenix[28].

671149 OTS LHD, 17 May 1951, to RM Overseas in Düsseldorf, Germany. It subsequently moved to the USA where it was extensively re-bodied by the Barris brothers in California, but it is now in the UK where it is registered MSU 839. It is rumoured that the car was once owned by Elizabeth Taylor. This cannot be confirmed, although there is a photo of Ms Taylor with her first husband, Michael Wilding, in a standard XK 120 OTS. As it emerged from the Barris workshop, 671149 had a lowered body, "frenched" headlamps and tail lamps, and a curved one-piece windscreen, while the flat body sides of the standard car were re-modelled with a rounded section. The front bumpers were removed, and the rear overriders replaced by a strip below the boot lid in the manner of the 1948 Motor Show car.[29]

George Barris was famous as the creator of the original Batmobile in 1955. He customised several XK 120s in his shop at North Hollywood, and did one for the band leader Spike Jones, literally with bells and whistles on. He fitted a hard top to one of Clark Gable's cars, while Barry Goldwater (apparently the Arizona senator who ran unsuccessfully for President in 1964) had Buick headlamps fitted to the front wings of his XK 120. It may be the Goldwater car which is illustrated by Urban. This is photo which has been drawn over, but appears to show an XK 120 drophead coupé with Buick headlamps and bumpers, an Alfa Romeo-like grille, tail fins, and a continental spare-wheel kit.[30]

671199 (engine W 3189-8) OTS LHD, 30 May 1951, to Hoffman. This featured headlamps relocated low down in the front wings, possibly air intakes where the headlamps had been, and additional side grilles. The front bumpers were removed, and the car had wire wheels. Worse was to come at the rear where

M. Schwindenhammer with the broad grin next to his PST special, built on the basis of 680997. The body was fibreglass, and those diminutive headlamps can only be from a Citroën 2CV. (Paul Skilleter)

The dashboard and steering wheel are standard, the rest is John Fitch's vision of a potential Le Mans car, built in 1951 on the basis of 670458. (Paul Skilleter)

The restored Flajole "Forerunner" photographed at the prestigious American Pebble Beach concours event. Yes, there really is an XK 120 inside!
(Terry McGrath)

outsize tail fins were added. The original owner, a Captain Sherman Crise, is supposed to have used the car as a pace car on New York state race tracks, and also displayed the car at auto shows. By 2000 I believe that the car had gone to Denmark, but I do not know whether it retains the modified body.[31]

671226 OTS LHD, 5 June 1951, to Hornburg in Los Angeles. This seems to be the car built by Joseph Gertler for the New York beer baron Louis Ebling. It featured an egg-crate grille, additional egg-crate side grilles, headlamps moved into the wings, twin side-mounted spare wheels with covers protruding above the front wing line and Borrani wire wheels. It also had tubular frame bumpers and squared-up rear

wings topped by extravagant tail fins, although the tail fins and side-mounted spares may not originally have been on the car. Urban quotes the chassis number incorrectly as 671326 but (presumably) the correct body number, F 3036. His photo shows the car with a British-style white reflective front number plate (NG 3686) but Urban says the car eventually migrated to France, by which time it had lost the tail fins and tubular bumpers and had an XK 140 grille.

Mr Gertler Jr says the car was modified for a 1954 show and was "a brand new, zero-mileage Jaguar that my father picked up from the shipping dock in New York", which does not match the fact that the body number quoted by Urban is for a 1951 car sold in California. Of course, there could have been two

To end on a note of pure horror, this is the so-called "Batmobile" built from an XK 120 in Singapore. These days, the car has thankfully reverted to standard form.
(Terry McGrath)

similar cars, but on the whole I rather hope not! The side-mounted spares were also found in the schemes for two-plus-two XK 120s proposed by automotive designer Don Bruce in the American magazine *Auto Sport* for June 1952, and on a car customised by its owner, Sid Brody of Beverly Hills.[32]

S 673772 OTS LHD, 18 March 1953, to Hoffman in New York. This became the Flajole Forerunner, an extraordinary creation by William Flajole, a designer with the Nash company whose portfolio also included the Nash Metropolitan. His "Forerunner" design was a fastback coupé, made from fibreglass, with a removable transparent Plexiglas roof but no rear window. Headlamps hid behind a Nash-like grille, but the spare wheel was part exposed in a well in the fastback tail. The car incorporated most US 1950s styling excesses including a panoramic dog's leg windscreen, and was supposed to have several advanced safety features. It reputedly cost $8000 and took 7000 hours to build. It still exists and was restored for an American concours in 1992.[33]

The Mistral had a fibreglass barchetta-style body fitted to an XK 120 chassis in the USA in approximately 1955, but was not finished until 30 or so years later and finally appeared in action at Pebble Beach in 1992. It looks to be a workmanlike job, but its origins still seem shrouded in mystery. It could have used a proprietary fibreglass body, as these were beginning to appear in the USA around 1953. The car was reported at a classic car show in Barcelona in 2000.[34]

Walt Hansgen fitted an aluminium body somewhat in the style of the C-type to his XK 120 but with a much bigger grille *à la* Cunningham, and won a race at Watkins Glen in 1952 with the car in this form.[35]

Roger Barlow of International Motors on Wilshire Boulevard in Los Angeles commissioned the French coachbuilder Saoutchik to design bodywork for XK 120s, but these cars were never built. Barlow was a film producer, and sold a variety of European cars to a Hollywood clientele, including the 3½-litre drophead coupé which was Clark Gable's first Jaguar. For a while, Barlow was the official Jaguar importer on the West Coast, until replaced by Hornburg, and he was Phil Hill's first employer. He had imported at least one French Talbot, possibly with a Saoutchik body, and one of his pet ideas was to sell British chassis with French or Italian bodywork. He had similar plans for the MG Y-type although equally little came of this. He commissioned two Saoutchik designs for the XK 120, a drophead coupé and a fastback fixed-head that was, says Urban, a "line by line"

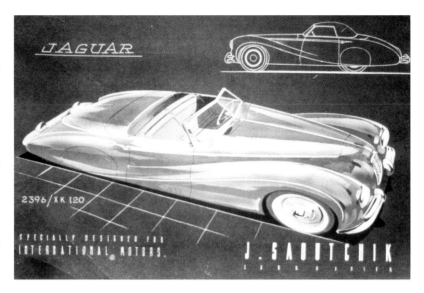

copy of a 1948 Saoutchik body on a Talbot.[36]

A fixed-head coupe was customised in the USA by the bus and coach manufacturer Fageol Twin Coach of Kent in Ohio. This had longer and more voluminous rear wings, and the rear end was remodelled to feature an external continental spare wheel. Another car was customised by none other than the famous American designer Raymond Loewy in Paris who later designed a better-known body on an XK 140 chassis, which was built by Boano in Italy.[37]

There were a number of XK 120s which were modified in Australia, mostly for racing.

660049 alloy OTS RHD, 14 February 1950, to Brylaw in Melbourne. This car was wrecked in 1959 and rebuilt in Tasmania as the Le Mans Jaguar by Bob Ford, who fitted the mechanical components from the original car in a new tubular chassis, with a

This very French cabriolet was one of two styles proposed by Saoutchik for Roger Barlow's International Motors, the other was a fastback coupé. Would such a car have found a market? (JDHT)

Apparently Raymond Loewy did this to an XK 120 but one is left wondering why he bothered. A fin in the radiator grille aperture was novel but hardly an improvement. (JDHT)

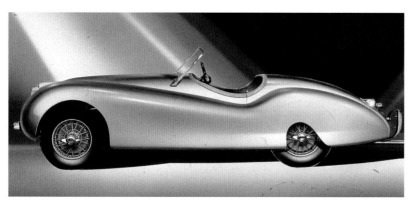

This is an interesting idea, and Hoffman actually displayed a car with this type of cut-away spat at the 1953 New York Motor Show. Similar spats were fitted to Clark Gable's second XK 120, possibly even by the factory. (JDHT)

racing body with cycle wings. It was raced in the early 1960s but had an accident in 1964, and was then rebuilt by Kerry Cox in a different form with a full-width body based on a Lotus 11 as the Paramount Jaguar. This, in turn, was destroyed in an accident in 1982. Later the car was for a time owned by Terry McGrath and is now under restoration.[38]

660181 OTS RHD, 10 August 1950, to Brylaw in Melbourne. The JRS was built by Jack Robinson in Sydney on a shortened chassis, with a single-seater racing body made by Clive Adams. Its active racing career ran from 1953 to 1955. It was later dismantled

and the engine and other parts sold off, but the remains were rediscovered in 1978 by Mike Wright, who then began a restoration job and had a new body built for it. Now complete, the car is driven enthusiastically by its owner.[39]

660226 OTS RHD, 18 September 1950, to Andersons in Brisbane. Anderson rebuilt this car as a single-seater for the Australian Grand Prix in 1954, but retained the standard bonnet. The body was the work of a local coachbuilder called Humphries. Bill Pitt finished in 12th place in the GP, and the car was later timed at 126mph (203km/h). It was broken up in 1955, although some parts were re-assembled back into a standard OTS, which was fitted with the SE (or C-type specification) engine and wire wheels from Mrs Anderson's FHC S 669015 (see chapter 9). It still survives, although without this engine and the wire wheels.[40]

660846 OTS RHD, 29 June 1951, to Brylaw in Sydney (Home Delivery to Mr White, registered LDU 718). When the original car crashed in May 1952, Larry Humphries in Sydney used the engine and other components to build a single-seater with a tubular chassis. This became the Austral-Union, also later called the Dalro Jaguar, and was raced throughout the following years, to about 1963. It has undergone many modifications over the years and from the 1970s onwards has been used in historic racing in Australia.[41]

Among other modifications made to XK 120 bodywork, a variety of hard tops were fitted to the open two-seater. The first may have been the one by Pycroft, which Fox and Nicholl fitted to Tyrone Power's car registered KDU 161.[42] Then a hard top by W M Park was fitted on the 1950 car registered JKV 116 with chassis 660082, originally owned by S Y Barsley – or Barslay. This was one of the 1950 Alpine Rally entrants, cp. chapter 7.[43] An early fibreglass hard top was offered by Universal Laminations in 1952, weighing only 26 lbs, about half that of coachbuilt hard tops.[44] The hard top by Flewitt of Birmingham looked like a permanent fixed-head coupé conversion,[45] as were the Australian conversions (for instance, by Dr Peter Crooke in Melbourne in 1954 and Les Williams of Wagga around the same time, as well as others).[46] Yet another hard top was added to a car owned by Fernand Eggenschuider in Switzerland,[47] while the German coachbuilder Rometsch is also believed to have fitted a hard top to an XK 120.[48] And many other cars were modified for racing.

Now we know why Jaguar had nothing to fear from outside designers, or may be Flewitt's fixed-head conversion was built for a very tall owner? (Paul Skilleter)

Tyrone Power had his car fitted with this coachbuilt hard top by Fox and Nicholls. (Paul Skilleter)

1. *The Autocar* 28 Mar 1952; colour photo in *Automobil Revue – Katalognummer* 1953; Frostick *The Jaguar Tradition* p79; Skilleter *Jaguar Sports Cars*, photos between p66 and p67; Urban *Les Métamorphoses du Jaguar* pp104-05; Viart *Jaguar XK Le Grand Livre* p306

2. Information courtesy of Terry McGrath

3. *The Motor* 20 Feb 1952; *The Autocar* 14 Mar 1952; Frostick p78; Skilleter photos between p66 and p67; Elmgreen & McGrath *XK in Australia* p250; Urban p70; *XK Gazette* no.56 May 2002; information courtesy of Terry McGrath

4. *The Autocar* 14 Mar 1952; Frostick p79; Whyte *Jaguar Sports Racing and Works Competition Cars to 1953* pp150, 193; Urban pp250-53 – he quotes the chassis number erroneously as 660051; Viart p328; *XK Gazette* no.8 May 1998, no.16 Jan 1999 and no.43 Apr 2001

5. Frostick p79; Urban pp145-47 – he quotes the chassis number erroneously as 660992; Viart p307; *Classic Cars* Dec 2000; and information courtesy of Mike Riedner

6. *Automobil Revue – Katalognummer* 1953 p38; Urban p67; Viart p322; Frostick p101, photo of the Worblaufen Mark VII which he attributes to Beutler

7. Urban p67; information courtesy of Terry McGrath

8. *The Autocar* 1 Apr 1955; Frostick p79; Frostick *Pinin Farina – Master Coachbuilder* p163; Harvey *The Jaguar XK* p209; Urban pp271-73; Viart p319; information courtesy of Terry McGrath

9. *The Motor* 21 Jul 1954; *The Autocar* 15 Oct 1954; *Annual Automobile Review* 1954-1955 opp. p50; Urban pp170-76; Viart pp308-09; Burgess-Wise *Ghia* pp 50, 54, 68; Georgano (ed) *The Beaulieu Encyclopædia of the Automobile – Coachbuilding* p167

10. Information courtesy of Terry McGrath

11. Mills *Essential AC Cobra* p67

12. *The Autocar* 12 Oct 1955; *Annual Automobile Review* 1954-1955 opp. p188; Skilleter, photos between pp66-67; Harvey p209; Frostick *The Jaguar Tradition* p85; Mennem *Jaguar An Illustrated History* p112; Urban p177; Burgess-Wise p67; *Beaulieu… Coachbuilding* p167

13. Urban p160; *XK Gazette* no.86 Nov 2004, no.89 Feb 2005

14. *The Autocar* 16 Mar 1951; Skilleter, photos between pp66-67; Urban p160

15. Information courtesy of Urs Haehnle, Jaguar Drivers Club Switzerland, and Urs Ramseier

16. Urban pp182-83; Viart p313

17. Information courtesy of Terry McGrath

18. Urban p315; *XK Gazette* no.46 Jul 2001

19. Urban p90; Viart pp270, 282, 301-02; Whyte p197; information courtesy of Terry McGrath

20. Memo from P Weaver to FRW England dated 15 Sep 1952, JDHT; Whyte pp247, 280; Urban pp86-91; Viart pp282, 300 (the two French authors do not agree

with each other); Larson *C-type Register* pp27, 54; *XK Gazette* no.8, May 1998, no.46 Jul 2001, no.60 Sep 2002, nos 67 to 71 Apr to Aug 2003

21. Schrader in *Beaulieu … Coachbuilding* p75; information courtesy of Henning Zeiss, owner of the car and author of *Authenrieth – eine Darmstädter Karosserielegende*

22. Stagg in *Jaguar Journal* (USA) summer 1979; information courtesy of Terry McGrath

23. *XK Gazette* no.75, Dec 2003; and information courtesy of the owner

24. Viart pp293, 322

25. Urban p71, citing *Road and Track* for May 1951; information courtesy of Terry McGrath

26. Harvey p210; Urban p306; information courtesy of John Elmgreen and Terry McGrath

27. Urban pp267-69; Chris Jaques in *XK Gazette* no.78 Mar 2004

28. Fitch in *Auto Sport Review* May 1952; Urban pp148-49

29. Patten in *Jaguar World* Jan/Feb 1997; Jonathan Radgick in *XK Gazette* no.80 May 2004

30. Bruce Carnachan in *XK Gazette* no.82 Jul 2004; Urban p113

31. Information courtesy of Terry McGrath, quoting former owner Mr Beck of Florida, and of Johan Bendixen

32. Urban pp306, 340-41; Joe Gertler Jr. in *XK Gazette* no.54 Mar 2002; *Auto Sport* Jun 1952; *Road & Track* May 1953; information courtesy of Terry McGrath

33. Urban pp152-54; *Motor Trend* Sep 1955; information courtesy of Terry McGrath

34. Urban pp248-49; *XK Gazette* no.30 Mar 2000

35. Urban p314

36. Urban p287; Clausager *MG Saloon Cars* p102

37. Information courtesy of Terry McGrath

38. Elmgreen & McGrath p175; Urban p260

39. Elmgreen & McGrath p172; Urban p203

40. Elmgreen & McGrath p174; Urban p84

41. Elmgreen & McGrath p171; Urban pp130-31; information on Australian cars generally courtesy of Terry McGrath

42. *The Autocar* 6 Apr 1951; Skilleter photos between pp66-67

43. *The Motor* 30 Apr 1952; *The Autocar* 9 May 1952; Frostick p78; Urban p312; registration records, Coventry City Archives; *Car Record Book*, JDHT; Whyte p109

44. *The Motor* 23 Jul 1952

45. *The Autocar* 12 Sep 1952

46. Elmgreen & McGrath pp63, 65, 67, *et passim*

47. Harvey p211; Urban p307

48. Information courtesy of Terry McGrath

Afterword

"…is a joy for ever?"

The book that you have now read is a history of the XK 120. It is a historian's book, even an archivist's book. I have aimed to provide an objective account, by researching primary and secondary sources. My book is not an intimate guide to the pitfalls and pleasures of restoration or ownership today; something I have neither the knowledge nor experience to produce nor, for that matter, the inclination. There are also more detailed guides to originality available, if this is what you seek.

But, at the end, let me take a look at where the XK 120 stands today. As indicated in my introduction, it has a solid following, and prices are holding up well, with "condition 1" cars being typically valued around £40,000 in the UK in 2005. (As always with classic cars, open cars are more highly valued than coupés.) The early alloy cars are more sought after by the *cognoscenti* and command a hefty premium, while selected examples with outstanding provenance or history come on the market only at substantial six-figure sums.

If you are looking to buy an XK 120, there are at any time a lot of cars to choose from. This is not surprising, as a very high percentage of the 12,000 cars made are believed to survive; while estimates vary, there could be as many as half of them still in existence. Even now, they are still being re-discovered, and new restoration projects are being started. Much dedicated effort by club registrars is being put into tracking XK 120s round the world, and one day we

Thirty years on, an XK 120 prepares to climb Prescott during the Lombard RAC "Golden Fifty" rally in 1982. (JDHT)

may have a complete listing of confirmed survivors; or perhaps never, if they keep on turning up!

The XK 120 enjoys a wide net of support. As well as the established general clubs – in the UK the Jaguar Drivers' Club (with its XK Register, founded by David Lethbridge and Paul Skilleter in 1967) and the Jaguar Enthusiasts' Club – there is the more recent XK Club, founded by Jaguar XK historian and owner Philip Porter. This is dedicated exclusively to the XK models, and the club's monthly magazine, *XK Gazette*, is a most valuable source of information. In the USA, as well as the numerous local area clubs united under the banner of the Jaguar Clubs of North America, there is – also within the JCNA – the Classic Jaguar Association with its own XK section. Most other countries where Jaguars are found have at least one national Jaguar club. There are a great number of specialists, for restoration as well as parts, and there are several dealers who specialise in XKs, or in Jaguars generally. These are mostly in the UK but also exist in the USA, and increasingly in many European countries.

One phenomenon that may merit comment in the early part of the 21st century is the current condition of many XK 120s. As will be realised from many references in this book, improvements and modifications to XK 120s were made even in the early years, then often to keep them competitive in racing. Now, however, a substantial part of the XK 120 "industry" (it would be demeaning to call a *cottage* industry) is dedicated to producing heavily modified cars. Very many XK 120s in regular use have been updated in a variety of ways in an effort to overcome those aspects of the car that are now considered handicaps, either because of modern driving conditions or because they are in the hands of a later generation of drivers.

Cars are now routinely fitted with modern braking systems, with discs on all four wheels and power assistance. Rack and pinion steering is used, sometimes again with power assistance. Conversions to five-speed, all-synchromesh gearboxes are common. Transplants of later, more powerful, XK engines – fuel injected 4.2-litre units, for instance – are regularly undertaken. Then there is a host of less drastic modifications which are now routine, such as installing electric fans, modern headlamps, conversions to wire wheels and bigger carburettors. There are also improvements to the driving position to make it possible for tall people to drive an XK 120 in comfort, usually by means of seats re-located rearwards to the detriment of the battery boxes or smaller steering wheels, plus a rainbow of non-original paint colours. Cylinder head conversions to use lead-free petrol are *de rigueur*, and there is inevitably a demand for conversions from left-hand drive to right-hand drive – or *vice versa*. Never mind seat belts…

Engine transplants on XK 120s are not uncommon either. Judging by the water outlet from the cylinder head this is an XK 150 3.4 engine (despite the cylinder head being red). The drophead XK 120 did not have the small separate air filters on the carburettors, but a single air filter in front of the radiator.

All this is assisted by the availability of an almost complete range of spare parts, even including new aluminium two-seater bodyshells. As a result, there are now a lot of cars that are somewhat remote from their original specification, and we can almost talk about the development of a new generation of "silhouette" XK 120s, since if there is one original aspect of the car that is usually left intact, it is the basic styling. You can have a "new" XK 120 tailor-made to your desired specification, for road use or racing, and you can easily spend a lot more money than any current price guide suggests these cars are worth. A leading XK restorer confided to me that he found it much more interesting to build a modified car or special than just to restore a car to its original specification.

In these circumstances, however, you also begin to wonder whether there are not cars out there which are, in effect, complete replicas, even if they may benefit from an original identity, log book, chassis number plate, and the much-vaunted "matching numbers" for engine, body and gearbox, which were all originally stamped on the plate. Even if the numbers appear to match, are the actual components still the original ones?

I don't blame owners who modify their XK 120s;

you fall in love with the looks and the glamour of the car, but it is at the same time nice to be able to *use* it, without necessarily having to put up with irritating shortcomings. I would not go as far as a well known classic car writer who, a few years ago in print, questioned whether a modified XK 120 was "an expensive lash-up? Probably". He also advised you *not* to buy an XK 120, although he was probably right in saying that an XK 140, XK 150 or an E-type are better bets for modern motoring in unmodified form. And, in all fairness, there are just as many enthusiasts who do value the XK 120 as it was, warts and all, and who prefer to restore the car to its *original* specification and preserve it like that. The choice is yours, and the important thing above all is that you value and enjoy your XK 120.

I still wonder, however, what the future holds. We who own classic cars today are, after all, only the temporary custodians of a particular piece of four-wheeled heritage. Perhaps we are unwittingly creating problems for future owners or restorers who may take a different view of what constitutes the proper conservation of an historic motor car.

In whatever form, the XK 120 will surely still be the car to have for many enthusiasts.

Appendix 1: The Alloy-Bodied XK120 Cars

Right Hand Drive Cars

Date man.	Chs. no	Paint colour	Trim colour	Original Destination	Date desp.	Status
Not recorded	660001	Bronze changed to Birch Grey; Blue for 1949 Silverstone race	Biscuit	Jaguar Cars Ltd; reg. HKV 455; 1948 Motor Show; Bira 1949 Silverstone race; later Mark IV (XK140) fhc prototype; disc brake test car?	Not recorded	Claimed to be under restoration by Tom Zwakman in Holland 2004
July 1949?	660002	Cream	Red	Brylaw, Sydney, Australia	21/07/1949	Exists in the UK, reg. ESJ 563
January 1950	660003	Black	Biscuit and Red	Hoffman, New York, USA (the *second* car)	18/01/1950	Found in USA 1997, now in UK
12/10/1949	660004	Cream	Red and Biscuit	Brooking, Perth, Australia	02/11/1949	Exists in Australia
13/10/1949	660005	Cream	Biscuit and Red	Dominion, Adelaide, Australia	23/11/1949	Exists in Australia
14/10/1949	660006	Olive Green	Suede Green	Hoffman, New York, USA	05/11/1949	
21/10/1949	660007	Cream	Biscuit and Red	Brylaw, Melbourne, Australia	24/11/1949	Exists in the UK
25/10/1949	660008	Mid Brunswick Green	Suede Green	Gilman, Hong Kong	08/11/1949	
26/10/1949	660009	Bronze	Biscuit	Shorters, Auckland, New Zealand	12/11/1949	Exists in the UK, reg. FSK 729
26/10/1949	660010	Not recorded	Not recorded	Jaguar Cars Ltd experimental department	Not recorded	
01/11/1949	660011	Cream	Biscuit and Red	Andersons, Brisbane, Australia	23/11/1949	
01/11/1949	660012	Pastel Blue	Duo-Blue	Brylaw, Melbourne, Australia	28/11/1949	Exists in Australia
07/11/1949	660013	Pastel Blue	Duo-Blue	Pearey Lal, New Delhi, India	02/12/1949	
07/11/1949	660014	Bronze	Biscuit and Pigskin	Brooking, Perth, Australia	24/11/1949	Exists in the UK
10/11/1949	660015	Pastel Blue	Duo-Blue	Andersons, Brisbane, Australia	03/01/1950	Destroyed in fire in 1952
10/11/1949	660016	Pastel Blue	Duo-Blue	Brylaw, Sydney, Australia	25/11/1949	Stolen and broken up in 1960
11/11/1949	660017	Cream	Biscuit and Red	Brylaw, Sydney, Australia	07/12/1949	Exists in Australia
11/11/1949	660018	Cream	Biscuit and Red	Dominion, Adelaide, Australia	12/12/1949	Exists in Australia or the UK?
24/11/1949	660019	Pastel Blue	Duo-Blue	Independent, Wellington, New Zealand	09/12/1949	Exists in New Zealand
28/11/1949	660020	Silver	Red	Brylaw, Sydney, Australia	09/12/1949	Exists in Germany
28/11/1949	660021	Silver	Red	Gilman, Hong Kong	20/12/1949	Exists in the UK, reg. YVS 477, ex-Robert Danny collection
29/11/1949	660022	Black	Biscuit and Pigskin	Lagerwijs, The Hague, Holland	30/01/1950	Exists in Holland, reg. PT-10-40
09/12/1949	660023	Cream	Biscuit and Pigskin	Emil Frey, Zurich, Switzerland	04/01/1950	
12/12/1949	660024	Pastel Blue	Duo-Blue	Claparede, Geneva, Switzerland	04/01/1950	Exists in Switzerland
20/12/1949	660025	Silver	Red	Brinkman, Singapore, Malaya; PED, orig. reg. JRW 828	11/01/1950	Exists in the UK, reg. 97 DLA
20/12/1949	660026	Silver	Red	Brylaw, Sydney, Australia	02/02/1950	Exists in the UK
22/12/1949	660027	Silver	Red	Emil Frey, Zurich, Switzerland	20/01/1950	
02/01/1950	660028	Silver	Red	Claparede, Geneva, Switzerland	17/01/1950	Re-bodied by Graber in 1951
03/01/1950	660029	Silver	Red	Garware, Bombay, India; PED reg. JRW 663	14/03/1950	
03/01/1950	660030	Red	Biscuit and Red	Brylaw, Melbourne, Australia	03/02/1950	Exists in Australia
03/01/1950	660031	Black	Biscuit and Red	Claparede, Geneva, Switzerland	03/02/1950	Exists in the UK, reg. NSL 407
04/01/1950	660032	Red	Biscuit and Red	Lagerwijs, The Hague, Holland	13/02/1950	Exists in the UK, reg. OXK 7
13/01/1950	660033	Cream	Biscuit and Red	Sagers, Bulawayo, Rhodesia	03/02/1950	
26/01/1950	660034	Pastel Blue	Duo-Blue	Brylaw, Melbourne, Australia	13/02/1950	Exists; stolen but rediscovered in Queensland, 1980s
27/01/1950	660035	Pastel Blue	Duo-Blue	Emil Frey, Zurich, Switzerland	14/02/1950	Exists in Switzerland, reg. SO 31677
27/01/1950	660036	Pastel Blue	Duo-Blue	Claparede, Geneva, Switzerland	14/02/1950	Exists in Austria
27/01/1950	660037	Pastel Blue	Duo-Blue	Jaguar Car Distributors, Brussels, Belgium	16/02/1950	Stolen in Belgium 1981

Date man.	Chs. no	Paint colour	Trim colour	Original Destination	Date desp.	Status
30/01/1950	660038	Pastel Blue	Duo-Blue	Andersons, Brisbane, Australia	22/02/1950	
01/02/1950	660039	Black	Biscuit and Red	Hoffman, New York, USA	16/02/1950	Exists in the UK
01/03/1950	660040	Cream	Pigskin Grain	Jaguar Cars Ltd for Leslie Johnson; reg. JWK 651	17/03/1950	Exists in the UK, for sale by Gregor Fisken, 2004
01/03/1950	660041	Pastel Blue	Pigskin	Jaguar Car Distributors, Brussels, Belgium; but raced by L H "Nick" Haines	28/03/1950	Returned to the UK, reg. MHJ 79 exists in the UK, owner Pearson
01/03/1950	660042	Olive Green	Suede Green	Jaguar Cars Ltd for Peter Walker; reg. JWK 977	26/04/1950	Exists in the UK
01/03/1950	660043	Red	Biscuit and Red	Jaguar Cars Ltd for Clemente Biondetti; reg. JWK 650; sold second-hand 29/10/1952	23/03/1950	Exists in the UK
01/03/1950	660044	Cream	Duo-Blue	Appleyard, Leeds for Ian Appleyard; reg. NUB 120	12/04/1950	Exists in the UK, owner JDHT
01/02/1950	660045	Cream	Biscuit and Red	GH Koch, Vienna, Austria; PED reg. JWK 20	20/02/1950	Exists in Austria, ex-Robert Danny collection
02/02/1950	660046	Black	Biscuit and Red	Brylaw, Sydney, Australia	20/02/1950	Exists in Australia
02/02/1950	660047	Black	Biscuit and Red	Brylaw, Melbourne, Australia	15/02/1950	Exists in Australia
10/02/1950	660048	Cream	Biscuit and Red	Emil Frey, Zurich, Switzerland	08/03/1950	Exists in the UK, reg. PPP 120 L
14/02/1950	660049	Black	Biscuit and Pigskin	Brylaw, Melbourne, Australia; PED reg. JWK 191	02/03/1950	Original car wrecked; some parts used for the "Paramount Jaguar" special; being rebuilt in Australia
15/02/1950	660050	Silver	Duo-Blue	Brylaw, Sydney, Australia; PED reg. JWK 376	14/03/1950	Exists in Australia
15/02/1950	660051	Black	Biscuit and Red	Delecroix, Paris, France	28/02/1950	Exists in Liechtenstein
16/02/1950	660052	Silver	Red	Auto Omnia, Oporto, Portugal	07/03/1950	May exist in France
16/02/1950	660053	Silver	Red	Hoffman, New York, USA	06/04/1950	Exists in the UK; reg. 5470 AP?
21/02/1950	660054	White	Blue	Claparede, Geneva, Switzerland	28/02/1950	Exists in Austria
01/03/1950	660055	Pastel Blue	Duo-Blue (or Red?)	GH Koch, Vienna, Austria; PED reg. JWK 377	07/04/1950	Exists in Germany or the USA?
02/03/1950	660056	Pastel Blue	Red	Compagnia Generale, Milan, Italy	18/04/1950	Exists in France?
02/03/1950	660057	Apple Green	Biscuit	Henlys, London, for Tommy Wisdom; reg. JWK 988, Moss' 1950 TT winning car	14/04/1950	Exists in the UK, ex-Robert Danny collection, owner Bamford?
03/03/1950	660058	Silver	Red	Brinkmann, Singapore, Malaya	01/05/1950	Exists in Singapore

Left Hand Drive Cars

Date man.	Chs. no	Paint colour	Trim colour	Original destination	Date desp.	Status
Not recorded	670001	Bronze changed to White, but Red for 1949 Silverstone race	Biscuit and Red	Jaguar Cars Ltd, Walker in 1949 Silverstone rave, then Hoffman, New York, USA	15/12/1949	Exists in the USA, owner until 2004 Walter Hill Collection
Not recorded	670002	Red changed to White	n/r	Jaguar Cars Ltd, reg. HKV 500; the Jabbeke car; changed to RHD for 1949 Silverstone race (Johnson); last raced 1951, taxed to end of 1951. Reduced to produce.	24/03/1950	
August 1949?	670003	Cream	Biscuit and Red	Hornburg, Los Angeles, USA	05/09/1949	Last reported in the UK, claimed to be ex-Clark Gable
August 1949?	670004	Pastel Blue	Blue	James L Cooke, Toronto, Canada	10/08/1949	Exists in Holland (Zwakman)
August 1949?	670005	Blue sheen	Blue	Hoffman, New York, USA	17/08/1949?	Exists in the USA
August 1949?	670006	Cream	Biscuit	Hornburg, Los Angeles, USA	15/08/1949	Broken up; parts in Holland 2005
August 1949?	670007	Cream	Biscuit and Red	Hoffman, New York, USA	29/08/1949	
August 1949?	670008	Cream	Biscuit and Red	Hoffman, New York, USA	02/09/1949	Exists in Germany
13/09/1949	670009	Cream	Biscuit and Red	Delecroix, Paris, France; Paris Show Car	25/09/1949	Exists in Belgium

Date man.	Chs. no	Paint colour	Trim colour	Original destination	Date desp.	Status
13/09/1949	670010	Cream	Biscuit and Red	Hornburg, Los Angeles, USA	16/09/1949	Exists in the USA
13/09/1949	670011	Cream	Biscuit and Red	Hoffman, New York, USA	23/09/1949	
13/09/1949	670012	Pastel Blue	Duo-Blue	Gilman, Hong Kong; PED reg. JHP 648	07/10/1949	Exists
11/10/1949	670013	Pastel Blue	Duo-Blue	Hornburg, Los Angeles, USA	05/11/1949	May exist in the USA?
17/10/1949	670014	Pastel Blue	Duo-Blue	Hornburg, Los Angeles, USA	08/11/1949	Exists; in Denmark or Germany?
18/10/1949	670015	Pastel Blue	Duo-Blue	Hoffman, New York, USA; PED reg. JRW 117	11/11/1949	Exists in Canada or the USA?
20/10/1949	670016	Gunmetal	Red	James L Cooke, Toronto, Canada	14/11/1949	
20/10/1949	670017	Cream	Biscuit and Red	Hoffman, New York, USA	14/11/1949	Exists in Italy, owner Collezione Koelliker
21/10/1949	670018	Cream	Biscuit and Red	Hornburg, Los Angeles, USA	02/12/1949	Exists in Switzerland, owner Frey Collection
25/10/1949	670019	Pastel Blue	Duo-Blue	Hoffman, New York, USA	11/11/1949	Exists in Germany or Holland?
27/10/1949	670020	Pastel Blue	Duo-Blue	Hoffman, New York, USA	14/11/1949	Exists in Switzerland
28/10/1949	670021	Cream	Biscuit and Red	Thomas Plimley, Vancouver, Canada	18/11/1949	Exists in the UK or Holland?
02/11/1949	670022	Cream	Biscuit and Red	Ehlert Motors, Buenos Aires, Argentina	29/11/1949	Exists
03/11/1949	670023	Pastel Blue	Duo-Blue	Hoffman, New York, USA; first owner Briggs S Cunningham	24/11/1949	
04/11/1949	670024	Pastel Blue	Duo-Blue	Hoffman, New York, USA	24/11/1949	Exists in the USA
09/11/1949	670025	Black	Red	Hoffman, New York, USA	24/11/1949	Exists
09/11/1949	670026	Pastel Blue	Duo-Blue	Ehlert Motors, Buenos Aires, Argentina	29/11/1949	Exists
14/11/1949	670027	Silver	Duo-Blue	Hoffman, New York, USA	29/11/1949	Exists in the UK
14/11/1949	670028	Battleship Grey	Red	Delecroix, Paris, France	28/11/1949	Became Barou coupé
15/11/1949	670029	Gunmetal	Pigskin	Hornburg, Los Angeles, USA	28/12/1949	
15/11/1949	670030	Yellow	Red	Seiglie, Havana, Cuba	16/12/1949	
16/11/1949	670031	Pastel Green	Suede Green	Budd & Dyer, Montreal, Canada	02/12/1949	
16/11/1949	670032	Gunmetal	Red	Hornburg, Los Angeles, USA	28/12/1949	
17/11/1949	670033	Cream	Biscuit and Red	Hoffman, New York, USA	07/12/1949	
17/11/1949	670034	Cream	Biscuit and Red	CAMAV, Caracas, Venezuela	28/12/1949	
18/11/1949	670035	Red	Red	Hoffman, New York, USA	07/12/1949	Exists in the UK, reg. KGH 769 A
21/11/1949	670036	Blue (Duco)	Blue and Biscuit	Hornburg, Los Angeles, USA	28/12/1949	
21/11/1949	670037	Silver	Red	James L Cooke, Toronto, Canada	13/12/1949	Exists in the UK, reg. AL 120
22/11/1949	670038	Red	Black	Hornburg, Los Angeles, USA	28/12/1949	
22/11/1949	670039	Black	Biscuit and Red	Thomas Plimley, Vancouver, Canada	06/01/1950	
23/11/1949	670040	Black	Biscuit and Pigskin	Hoffman, New York, USA	12/12/1949	Exists in the USA
24/11/1949	670041	Black	Biscuit and Pigskin	Hornburg, Los Angeles, USA	29/12/1949	Exists in the USA, ex-Harrah Collection
25/11/1949	670042	Cream	Biscuit and Red	Goodwin Cocozza, Rio de Janeiro, Brazil	29/12/1949	Exists in Brazil or Holand?
30/11/1949	670043	Cream	Biscuit and Red	Pablo Aicardi, Montevideo, Uruguay	01/02/1950	
30/11/1949	670044	Silver	Red	Hoffman, New York, USA	20/12/1949	
02/12/1949	670045	Silver	Red and Silver	Jaguar Car Distributors, Brussels, Belgium	05/01/1950	
05/12/1949	670046	Red	Biscuit and Red	Hoffman, New York, USA	21/12/1949	
05/12/1949	670047	Silver	Red	Hoffman, New York, USA	03/01/1950	Exists in the USA, ex-Brooks Stevens Museum
06/12/1949	670048	Bronze	Biscuit and Pigskin	Hornburg, Los Angeles, USA	15/01/1950	Exists in the USA or UK; reg. LYP 918?
06/12/1949	670049	Red	Biscuit and Red	Seiglie, Havana, Cuba	28/12/1949	

Date man.	Chs. no	Paint colour	Trim colour	Original destination	Date desp.	Status
07/12/1949	670050	Gunmetal	Grey	Hornburg, Los Angeles, USA	11/01/1950	
07/12/1949	670051	Pastel Blue	Duo-Blue	Goodwin Cocozza, Rio de Janeiro, Brazil	30/12/1949	Exists in Brazil
09/12/1949	670052	Pastel Blue	Duo-Blue	Seiglie, Havana, Cuba	30/12/1949	
12/12/1949	670053	Suede Green	Suede Green	Hoffman, New York, USA	03/01/1950	Exists in Canada
12/12/1949	670054	Suede Green	Suede Green	Hornburg, Los Angeles, USA	05/01/1952	Exists in the USA
14/12/1949	670055	Red	Biscuit and Red	Goodwin Cocozza, Rio de Janeiro, Brazil	27/01/1950	Exists in Brazil
14/12/1949	670056	Silver	Red	Hoffman, New York, USA	03/01/1950	Exists in France
15/12/1949	670057	Silver	Red	SM Kauppa, Tampere, Finland	26/01/1950	Exists in the UK
15/12/1949	670058	Lavender Grey	Suede Green	Hornburg, Los Angeles, USA	12/01/1950	
16/12/1949	670059	Red	Biscuit and Red	James L Cooke, Toronto, Canada	13/01/1950	Exists in Canada
19/12/1949	670060	Black	Biscuit and Pigskin	Hornburg, Los Angeles, USA	11/01/1950	
19/12/1949	670061	Cream	Biscuit and Red	Hoffman, New York, USA	10/01/1950	Exists; in the UK?
20/12/1949	670062	Cream	Biscuit and Pigskin	Universal Motors, Cairo, Egypt	20/01/1950	Exists in Germany, owner Lang
21/12/1949	670063	Bronze	Biscuit and Tan	Emil Frey, Zurich, Switzerland	12/01/1950	Exists in Switzerland, owner Urs Schmid
22/12/1949	670064	Black	Biscuit and Tan	Delecroix, Paris, France; PED reg. JRW 771	09/01/1950	
23/12/1949	670065	Pastel Blue	Duo-Blue	Hoffman, New York, USA	10/01/1950	
28/12/1949	670066	Black	Biscuit and Red	Hornburg, Los Angeles, USA	13/01/1950	Exists
29/12/1949	670067	Silver	Biscuit and Red	Hoffman, New York, USA	10/01/1950	
29/12/1949	670068	Pastel Blue	Duo-Blue	Universal Motors, Cairo, Egypt	20/01/1950	Later bought by Dick Protheroe, reg. in UK GPN 635, exists in the UK; "The Ancient Egyptian"
30/12/1949	670069	Silver	Biscuit and Red	Hornburg, Los Angeles, USA	20/01/1950	Exists in Canada
30/12/1949	670070	Cream	Biscuit and Red	Fenix, Lima, Peru	27/02/1950	Exists in the USA?
02/01/1950	670071	Cream	Cream	Delecroix, Paris, France; converted from the original RHD chassis 660003	31/03/1950	
03/01/1950	670072	Bronze	Biscuit and Tan	Hoffman, New York, USA	25/01/1950	Exists in the UK?
04/01/1950	670073	Bronze	Biscuit and Tan	Hoffman, New York, USA	24/01/1950	Exists in Canada
02/01/1950	670074	Silver	Biscuit and Red	Hornburg, Los Angeles, USA	10/02/1950	
05/01/1950	670075	Cream	Biscuit and Red	Hoffman, New York, USA	18/01/1950	
06/01/1950	670076	Bronze	Biscuit and Tan	Hoffman, New York, USA	24/01/1950	
06/01/1950	670077	Pastel Blue	Duo-Blue	Hoffman, New York, USA	25/01/1950	
06/01/1950	670078	Cream	Biscuit and Pigskin	Hornburg, Los Angeles, USA	26/01/1950	Exists in France or the USA
09/01/1950	670079	Pastel Blue	Duo-Blue	Budd & Dyer, Montreal, Canada	02/02/1950	Exists in the USA
09/01/1950	670080	Pastel Blue	Duo-Blue	Goodwin Cocozza, Rio de Janeiro, Brazil	27/01/1950	
10/01/1950	670081	Black	Biscuit and Red	Jaguar Car Distributors, Brussels, Belgium	23/01/1950	
10/01/1950	670082	Pastel Blue	Duo-Blue	Hornburg, Los Angeles, USA	10/02/1950	
11/01/1950	670083	Black	Biscuit and Pigskin	Hoffman, New York, USA	25/01/1950	
11/01/1950	670084	Black	Biscuit and Pigskin	Hoffman, New York, USA	24/01/1950	Exists; in the USA?
11/01/1950	670085	Suede Green	Suede Green	Henlys, London; PED reg. JRW 835	08/02/1950	Exists in the USA
11/01/1950	670086	Black	Biscuit and Tan	Hoffman, New York, USA	25/01/1950	
12/01/1950	670087	Gunmetal	Blue	Hornburg, Los Angeles, USA; first owner WF Harrah (of the Harrah Collection)	31/01/1950	Exists in the UK, reg. PGY 189 L; Was PED reg. JWK 169
12/01/1950	670088	Gunmetal	Biscuit and Suede Green	Hornburg, Los Angeles, USA	10/02/1950	
12/01/1950	670089	Gunmetal	Red	CAMAV, Caracas, Venezuela	27/02/1950	Exists in the USA
13/01/1950	670090	Silver	Red	Thomas Plimley, Vancouver, Canada	16/02/1950	Exists in the USA

Date man.	Chs. no	Paint colour	Trim colour	Original destination	Date desp.	Status
13/01/1950	670091	Silver	Red	Hoffman, New York, USA	08/02/1950	
16/01/1950	670092	Bronze	Biscuit and Tan	Hornburg, Los Angeles, USA	10/02/1950	Exists in the UK, reg. OSU 136
16/01/1950	670093	Bronze	Biscuit and Tan	Hornburg, Los Angeles, USA	10/02/1950	Exists in the USA or Germany?
17/01/1950	670094	Bronze	Biscuit and Tan	Fenix, Lima, Peru	10/03/1950	
17/01/1950	670095	Silver	Red	Goodwin Cocozza, Rio de Janeiro, Brazil	09/02/1950	
18/01/1950	670096	Silver	Red	Hornburg, Los Angeles, USA	10/02/1950	Exists
18/01/1950	670097	Silver	Red	Hoffman, New York, USA	01/02/1950	Exists
19/01/1950	670098	Silver	Red	Hornburg, Los Angeles, USA	10/02/1950	
19/01/1950	670099	Silver	Red	Hornburg, Los Angeles, USA	10/02/1950	
20/01/1950	670100	Silver	Red	Hoffman, New York, USA	02/02/1950	Exists in the UK, reg. XKR 120
20/01/1950	670101	Silver	Duo-Blue	Jaguar Car Distributors, Brussels, Belgium	09/03/1950	Exists in the UK
23/01/1950	670102	Black	Biscuit and Red	Hoffman, New York, USA	08/02/1950	Exists in the USA
23/01/1950	670103	Black	Biscuit and Pigskin	Hoffman, New York, USA	08/02/1950	Exists in the USA, owner Indianapolis Speedway Museum
23/01/1950	670104	Black	Biscuit and Red	Hoffman, New York, USA	08/02/1950	
24/01/1950	670105	Cream	Red	Fredlunds, Sweden (ex-Sommer, Denmark; was 1950 Copenhagen Motor Show car)	07/02/1950	
24/01/1950	670106	Black	Biscuit and Pigskin	Hornburg, Los Angeles, USA	10/02/1950	Exists in Italy but is now "Parravano Special"
25/01/1950	670107	Black	Biscuit and Red	Thomas Plimley, Vancouver, Canada	16/02/1950	
25/01/1950	670108	Cream	Red	James L Cooke, Toronto, Canada	20/02/1950	
25/01/1950	670109	Red	Biscuit and Red	Hoffman, New York, USA	16/02/1950	
26/01/1950	670110	Pastel Blue	Duo-Blue	James L Cooke, Toronto, Canada	17/02/1950	Exists in the USA
26/01/1950	670111	Red	Biscuit and Red	CAMAV, Caracas, Venezuela	10/02/1950	Exists in the USA or the UK?
30/01/1950	670112	Silver	Blue	Hoffman, New York, USA	16/02/1950	
31/01/1950	670113	Silver	Red	Hoffman, New York, USA	16/02/1950	Exists in the USA
01/02/1950	670114	Suede Green	Biscuit and Suede Green	Hornburg, Los Angeles, USA	20/03/1950	
01/02/1950	670115	Red	Biscuit and Red	Hoffman, New York, USA	16/02/1950	Exists in the USA
01/02/1950	670116	Red	Biscuit and Red	Hoffman, New York, USA	21/02/1950	Exists in the UK
03/02/1950	670117	Red	Biscuit and Red	Hoffman, New York, USA	16/02/1950	Exists in the USA
03/02/1950	670118	Red	Biscuit and Red	Hornburg, Los Angeles, USA	21/02/1950	
03/02/1950	670119	Pastel Blue	Duo-Blue	Hoffman, New York, USA	21/02/1950	Exists in the USA
03/02/1950	670120	Pastel Blue	Duo-Blue	Hornburg, Los Angeles, USA; first owner HM Manney (motoring writer)	22/03/1950	Exists in the USA or the UK
06/02/1950	670121	Pastel Blue	Duo-Blue	Hoffman, New York, USA	23/03/1950	Exists in Switzerland
06/02/1950	670122	Pastel Blue	Duo-Blue	Hoffman, New York, USA	08/03/1950	
06/02/1950	670123	Pastel Blue	Duo-Blue	Hornburg, Los Angeles, USA	22/02/1950	Exists in the USA; owner Walter Hill Collection until 2004
07/02/1950	670124	Birch Grey	Biscuit and Red	Hornburg, Los Angeles, USA	20/02/1950	Exists in the USA
07/02/1950	670125	Pastel Blue	Duo-Blue	Hoffman, New York, USA	22/02/1950	
08/02/1950	670126	Lavender Grey	Biscuit and Suede Green	Hornburg, Los Angeles, USA	20/02/1950	Exists in Holland
08/02/1950	670127	Birch Grey	Biscuit and Red	Hoffman, New York, USA	14/03/1950	Exists in the UK?
10/02/1950	670128	Birch Grey	Biscuit and Red	Hornburg, Los Angeles, USA	20/02/1950	Exists in the UK, reg. LWK 19
10/02/1950	670129	Bronze	Biscuit and Pigskin	Hornburg, Los Angeles, USA	21/03/1950	Exists in the UK
10/02/1950	670130	Bronze	Biscuit and Tan	Hoffman, New York, USA	22/03/1950	
10/02/1950	670131	Black	Biscuit and Tan	Hornburg, Los Angeles, USA	22/03/1950	
13/02/1950	670132	Black	Biscuit and Pigskin	Jaguar Car Distributors, Brussels, Belgium	06/03/1950	Exists in the USA
13/02/1950	670133	Silver	Red	CAMAV, Caracas, Venezuela	02/03/1950	Exists in the USA
13/02/1950	670134	Silver	Red	Hoffman, New York, USA	23/03/1950	Exists in the USA

Date man.	Chs. no	Paint colour	Trim colour	Original destination	Date desp.	Status
15/02/1950	670135	Cream	Biscuit and Red	Delecroix, Paris, France	06/03/1950	May exist in France?
15/02/1950	670136	Cream	Biscuit and Red	Delecroix, Paris, France	28/02/1950	Exists in Italy
16/02/1950	670137	Red	Biscuit and Red	Luzon Industrial Corporation, Philippines	21/03/1950	Exists in the Philippines
17/02/1950	670138	Black	Biscuit and Red	Hornburg, Los Angeles, USA; First owner Phil Hill; PED reg. JWK 496	29/03/1950	Exists in the USA
17/02/1950	670139	Black	Biscuit and Red	Hoffman, New York, USA	07/03/1950	
17/02/1950	670140	Silver	Red	Jaguar Car Distributors, Brussels	20/03/1950	Exists in the UK, reg. EJD 33 D?
20/02/1950	670141	Silver	Red	Hoffman, New York, USA	23/03/1950	Exists in the USA
20/02/1950	670142	Silver	Duo-Blue	Hornburg, Los Angeles, USA	21/03/1950	
20/02/1950	670143	Silver	Duo-Blue	Hornburg, Los Angeles, USA	21/03/1950	
21/02/1950	670144	Silver	Blue	RM Overseas, Düsseldorf, Germany	07/04/1950	Later owned by Paul Skilleter, reg. LXK 48, exists in the UK
21/02/1950	670145	Suede Green	Suede Green	RM Overseas, Düsseldorf, Germany	07/04/1950	
21/02/1950	670146	Birch Grey	Biscuit and Red	RM Overseas, Düsseldorf, Germany	14/04/1950	Exists in the USA
22/02/1950	670147	Red	Biscuit and Red	Hoffman, New York, USA	28/03/1950	
22/02/1950	670148	Red	Biscuit and Red	Hornburg, Los Angeles, USA	22/03/1950	
22/02/1950	670149	Pastel Blue	Duo-Blue	Fenix, Lima, Peru	18/04/1950	
23/02/1950	670150	Birch Grey	Biscuit and Red	Hoffman, New York, USA; fitted with an Arnott (or Wade?) supercharger for the first owner	24/03/1950	Exists in Germany, but body now rebuilt on chassis from 660369
23/02/1950	670151	Pastel Blue	Duo-Blue	Hoffman, New York, USA	31/03/1950	Exists in the UK or the USA?
23/02/1950	670152	Pastel Blue	Duo-Blue	Jaguar Car Distributors, Brussels, Belgium	16/03/1950	
24/02/1950	670153	Pastel Blue	Duo-Blue	James L Cooke, Toronto, Canada	13/04/1950	Exists in Canada
24/02/1950	670154	Lavender Grey	Suede Green	Hoffman, New York, USA	23/03/1950	Exists in Canada or the USA?
24/02/1950	670155	Black	Red	Hornburg, Los Angeles, USA	21/03/1950	Exists in the USA
27/02/1950	670156	Silver	Red	Hoffman, New York, USA	14/03/1950	
27/02/1950	670157	Cream	Biscuit and Red	Auto Omnia, Oporto, Portugal	30/03/1950	Exists in Portugal or Italy?
28/02/1950	670158	Black	Red	Hoffman, New York, USA	28/03/1950	Exists in the UK, reg. MVS 823
28/02/1950	670159	White	White	Hoffman, New York, USA	23/03/1950	
28/02/1950	670160	Pastel Green	Suede Green	Hoffman, New York, USA	23/03/1950	
28/02/1950	670161	Silver	Red	Hornburg, Los Angeles, USA	27/03/1950	
01/03/1950	670162	Pastel Blue	Duo-Blue	Hoffman, New York, USA	29/03/1950	Exists in the USA
01/03/1950	670163	Pastel Blue	Duo-Blue	Auto Omnia, Oporto, Portugal	31/03/1950	
01/03/1950	670164	Silver	Red	Hoffman, New York, USA	28/03/1950	Exists in the UK
02/03/1950	670165	Red	Biscuit and Red	Hornburg, Los Angeles, USA	27/03/1950	Exists in the UK or Germany
03/03/1950	670166	Silver	Red	Hoffman, New York, USA	29/03/1950	Exists in Germany
06/03/1950	670167	Pastel Blue	Duo-Blue	Hoffman, New York, USA	04/04/1950	Found in USA 2002, now in UK
06/03/1950	670168	Silver	Red	Hoffman, New York, USA	05/04/1950	Exists in the USA or the UK?
07/03/1950	670169	Silver	Red	Hornburg, Los Angeles, USA; PED, reg. JWK 752	12/04/1950	Exists in the USA
08/03/1950	670170	Birch Grey	Biscuit and Red	Hornburg, Los Angeles, USA	12/04/1950	Exists in the USA or the UK
08/03/1950	670171	Birch Grey	Biscuit and Red	Hornburg, Los Angeles, USA	12/04/1950	
08/03/1950	670172	Pastel Blue	Duo-Blue	Jaguar Cars Ltd; reg. JWK 675; first steel body, dismantled and reduced to produce	23/03/1950	But the car escaped and exists in the UK?
08/03/1950	670173	Birch Grey	Biscuit and Red	Coulentianos, Athens, Greece	05/05/1950	Exists in the USA
10/03/1950	670174	Pastel Green	Suede Green	Importadora Fisk, Santiago, Chile	14/04/1950	Exists in the USA
10/03/1950	670175	Birch Grey	Biscuit and Red	Hornburg, Los Angeles, USA	12/04/1950	
14/03/1950	670176	Black	Biscuit and Red	Hoffman, New York, USA	25/04/1950	
14/03/1950	670177	Black	Biscuit and Red	Hornburg, Los Angeles, USA	12/04/1950	Exists in Switzerland
16/03/1950	670178	Silver	Red	Hornburg, Los Angeles, USA	21/04/1950	Exists in the USA, owner Bob Tucker, "1000 mile car"

Date man.	Chs. no	Paint colour	Trim colour	Original destination	Date desp.	Status
16/03/1950	670179	Silver	Red	Hornburg, Los Angeles, USA	21/04/1950	
17/03/1950	670180	Cream	Biscuit and Red	Hornburg, Los Angeles, USA	12/04/1950	Exists in the UK?
17/03/1950	670181	Cream	Biscuit and Red	Hoffman, New York, USA	18/04/1950	Exists in the UK with FHC body
20/03/1950	670182	Cream	Biscuit and Red	Waverley Motors, Ottawa, Canada	13/04/1950	
21/03/1950	670183	Cream	Biscuit and Red	Hoffman, New York, USA	18/04/1950	Exists in the USA
22/03/1950	670184	Cream	Biscuit and Red	Lagerwijs, The Hague, Holland	12/04/1950	

The total of chassis numbers in this table is 58 RHD and 184 LHD cars. However, as 660010 was an experimental chassis and as 670172 was the first steel-bodied car, this leaves 57 RHD and 183 LHD cars, for a total of 240 alloy-bodied cars. Around 40 RHD cars and 100-plus LHD cars are believed to exist, over half of the total production.

The main sources for the information included in the above table include:

The original Car Record Books kept in the archive of the Jaguar Daimler Heritage Trust, and Heritage certificates issued by the JDHT, 1991-2005
Coventry registration ledgers, Coventry Transport Museum and record cards for cancelled registrations, Coventry City Archives
XK in Australia by John Elmgreen and Terry McGrath, published Sydney, Australia, 1985
XK Le Grand Livre by Bernard Viart, published Paris, France, 1993
Jaguar World Jan/Feb 1995, "*The XK 120 Story*" containing a partial list of surviving alloy-bodied cars ©Terry McGrath
Jaguar XK 120 Anatomie eines Kultobjekts by Urs Schmid, published Solothurn, Switzerland, 2000
XK Gazette, monthly magazine of the XK Club, various issues 1997 to date
The website www.thanoa.com/jaguar as checked in 2004; this contains a list of some of the surviving alloy-bodied cars, based on Terry McGrath's work

It should be noted that locations and owners where quoted may not be up to date and are more likely to represent the latest information which was available at the time of writing.

Appendix 2: Dating and Identification

CHASSIS NUMBERS
The following were the XK 120 chassis number ranges by calendar year:

	OTS RHD	OTS LHD	FHC RHD	FHC LHD	DHC RHD	DHC LHD
1948	660001 only					
1949	660002-660027	670001-670070				
1950	660028-660521 (1)	670071-671096				
1951	660522-660934 (2)	671097-671796	669001-669002 (5)	679001-679214		
1952	660935-661045	671797-673388	669003-669004	679215-680571	667001 only	
1953	661046-661153 (3)	673389-674591	669005-669111	680572-681308 (6)	667002-667168	677001-678102
1954	661154-661176 (4)	674592-676438	669112-669195	681309-681485	667169-667295	678103-678472

Notes:
(1) Excluding 660519; also, chassis number 660111 was probably not completed until January 1951
(2) And 660519
(3) Excluding 661099
(4) And 661099
(5) 669001 probably built during 1950
(6) Excluding 681241 and 681242 which were not completed until July 1954 and were then re-numbered as chassis 681484 and 681485

The chassis number ranges give the following production figures:

			Less		Notes
Open two-seater*	RHD	1176	7	1169	1 experimental chassis, 6 chassis only
Open two-seater	LHD	6438	1	6437	1 chassis only
Fixed-head coupé	RHD	195	1	194	1 experimental "XK 100" car
Fixed-head coupé	LHD	2485	2	2483	2 cars re-numbered
Drophead coupé	RHD	295		295	
Drophead coupé	LHD	1472		1472	
		12,061	11	12,050	

*including 12 CKD cars for Ireland

If we include everything except the two re-numbered cars, we get an overall production figure of 12,059 XK 120s. This is also the total figure for the tables detailing Sales by Agent found in chapter 6. (I have counted cars with RHD or LHD as they were built, and have not accounted for the conversions of a few early cars.)

On the Special Equipment (SE) models, the chassis number was prefixed with the letter S. This version became available in general production in August 1952 and from then on accounted for the majority of left-hand-drive cars (see also chapter 5).

The chassis number was stamped in the top face of the left-hand chassis side member, and just about visible from above as here. In the photo the section of the exhaust after the down pipes have joined up can be seen above the number.

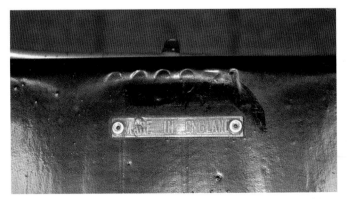

The chassis number was similarly stamped in the front cross member of the chassis, just visible by looking down right in front of the radiator.

There were the following numbers of SE cars (with S prefix, but sometimes missing the S suffix to the engine numbers):

Open two-seater	RHD	43
Open two-seater	LHD	2194
Fixed-head coupé	RHD	57
Fixed-head coupé	LHD	751
Drophead coupé	RHD	36
Drophead coupé	LHD	706
Total		3787

OTHER IDENTIFICATION NUMBERS:

Engine Numbers:

From W 1001 (1948) to W 9999 (Oct/Nov 1953)	8999 engines
Then from F 1001 to F 4090	3140 engines
And from F 4201 to F 4250 (to Aug 1954)	50 engines
Total number of engines (theoretically)	12,139

So an estimated 80 engines were not used in production cars.

The engine numbers were suffixed with the compression ratio, -7, -8 or -9. The 7:1 ratio was initially standard on home-market cars but as the low-octane "pool" petrol was replaced by higher-octane branded petrol, from the start of 1953 most home-market cars had the 8:1 compression ratio. 8:1 was always standard on cars for the USA and other markets where high-octane petrol was commonly available. The 9:1 ratio was most unusual and was only supplied to special order; not more than 32 cars, mostly LHD Special Equipment models, had this higher compression in 1953 and 1954. The higher-tuned engines fitted to SE models had a suffix letter S after the compression ratio.

The first 20 engines went into the following cars:

W 1001-7	was fitted in 660001, replacing the original prototype engine 248/03 in this car
W 1002-8	was fitted in 670006
W 1003	not found, see below
W 1004-8	was fitted in 670003
W 1005-8	was fitted in 670630, in August 1950
W 1006-8	was fitted in 670004
W 1007-8	was fitted in the first 660003 but was replaced in this car by W 1026-8, and W 1007-8 ended up in 660015; the second 660003 ended up with W 1137-8
W 1008	not found, see below
W 1009-7	was fitted in 660002
W 1010-8	was fitted in 670008
W 1011-8	was fitted in 670005
W 1012-8	was fitted in 670015
W 1013-8	was fitted in 670007
W 1014-8	was fitted in 670009
W 1015-8	was fitted in 670012
W 1016-8	was fitted in 670001, replacing the original prototype engine 249/01 in this car
W 1017-8	was fitted in 670013
W 1018-7	was fitted in 660008 but was replaced in this car by W 1037-7; W 1018-7 went into 660031 instead (the alloy car featured in this book)
W 1019-7	was fitted in 660007
W 1020-8	was fitted in 670016 but was replaced in this car by W 1099-8 and ended up in 670064, with a 7:1 compression ratio

The numbers stamped on the ID plate were often as wobbly and uneven as they appear here. From the numbers we deduce that this is the 31st open two-seater with right-hand drive, it has the 120th body, but only has the 18th engine, with the 7:1 compression ratio; in fact this engine had originally been fitted in an earlier car.

The location of the ID plate in front of the radiator on LWK 707 is unusual. It may just be possible to read the numbers on this typically poorly-stamped Jaguar ID plate.

Of the missing engine numbers 1003 and 1008, it is likely that 1003 was fitted in either 660019 or 660027 (these two cars both have engine number 1035 in the Car Record Book), while 1008 remains a mystery. It did, unfortunately, sometimes happen that engine and other component numbers were duplicated in the Car Record Books.

BODY NUMBERS:

Open two-seaters	from F 1001 to F 6502 (Nov 1953)	5502 bodies
	and from F 6603 to F 8723	2121 bodies
Total number of open two-seater bodies		7623 bodies

There is no way to account for the odd gap of 100 numbers in the two-seater body number sequence, unless the man with the stamp in the factory simply made an error!

Comparing body numbers and chassis numbers:

Open two-seater:	Chassis numbers: RHD 1176, LHD 6438	Total	7614
Cars not bodied:	Experimental chassis 660010	1	
	Chassis-only deliveries	7	
	Two of the lightweight cars	2	
	(the third lightweight car originally had a standard body)		

So, ten OTS chassis were not bodied, leaving 7604 cars that were fitted with bodies. This gives a surplus of 19 OTS bodies, and there are also 19 body numbers which have not been found in the *Car Record Books*. All of the 240 alloy bodies with numbers from F 1001 to F 1240 are accounted for in the *Car Record Books*, as are all the early steel bodies; the first "missing" body number is F 1687, in July 1950.

Fixed-head coupé from J 1001 to J 3680   2680 bodies

There were also 2680 fixed-head coupé chassis numbers issued, but two of these numbers were issued to cars that previously had another chassis number, which leaves 2678 chassis. The two surplus body numbers were not issued in production.

Drophead coupé from P 1001 to P 2769   1769 bodies

There were 1767 drophead coupé chassis numbers, and again it can be confirmed that the surplus of two body numbers were not issued in production.

GEARBOX NUMBERS:

These are more confusing, as the basic design of the XK 120 gearboxes, and thus the number series, was shared with the Mark V and later Mark VII saloon models, although XK 120 gearboxes are not directly interchangeable with those of the saloon models. There were four different gearbox number prefixes and number ranges:

JH	from 1948/49 to November 1951*, numbers up to 8338-plus, also used on Mark V and Mark VII
SH	used (rarely) May 1951 to November 1951*, numbers on XK 120s from approx. 879 to approx. 2703; this type of 'box was more often used on the "Mark IV" models, the Mark V and the early Mark VIIs
JL	from January 1952* to August 1954, numbers from 8806 to approx. 24584 (these numbers appear to continue the number range from the JH series); the basic JL type continued to be used through to end of production of the XK 150 and Mark IX models
OSL	(with suffix letter B) used (rarely) from May to August 1954, numbers up to approximately 1997; this type of gearbox is more commonly associated with the XK 140 model but was also used on some Mark VIIs

*Note that there was a break in XK 120 production from November 1951 to January 1952

Philip Porter in *Original Jaguar XK* explains the significance of the different gearbox types as follows:

• All are versions of the Moss-type gearbox; the SH prefix stands for "Single Helical"
• S in prefix indicates made by Moss, J in prefix indicates made by Jaguar
• JH and SH are similar but JH 'boxes have an assembly of individual gears on the layshaft whereas SH have a one-piece gearcluster on the layshaft
• JL and OSL 'boxes have a shorter mainshaft, and a modified rear-end cover without a separate cover to the rear extension; cars fitted with these 'boxes use a shorter propshaft

The gearbox serial numbers quoted in the *Jaguar XK 120 Spare Parts Catalogue* for the JH and SH series 'boxes bear little resemblance to the numbers found in the *Car Record Books*. From January 1954, cars with a close-ratio gearbox were identified with the suffix CR to the gearbox number in the records, but this was very rare on the XK 120, and I have found only 18 cars in the *Car Record Books* with the CR suffix to the gearbox number.

Appendix 3: Colour Schemes

The XK 120 was originally launched in 1948-50 in 10 different paint colours. Of these, Birch Grey, Black, Cream, Gunmetal (metallic) and Suede Green were established Jaguar colours, while the remaining shades were new, including Bronze, Pastel Blue, Pastel Green, Silver (all metallics), as well as Red. That meant the original range comprised five metallics and five solid colours. It is believed that the original type of paint was "Zofelac" cellulose.

Two further well known Jaguar colours, Battleship Grey and Lavender Grey, were introduced in regular production in September 1951, after a few earlier cars (including some of the alloy-bodied cars) had been painted in these colours. In March 1952 they were followed by the new colours British Racing Green, Dove Grey and Twilight Blue (a dark metallic blue). The latter colour remained rare on the XK 120 and was more often seen on the Mark VII, and was in any case short-lived in the range.

In October-November 1952, co-incident with the new paint plant in the then-new Browns Lane factory coming into use, the original cellulose paints were replaced by synthetic ones. In fact, Jaguar was probably the first British specialist car manufacturer to adopt synthetic paint for its production. At this time, all of the six metallic colours were discontinued, although there were new non-metallic versions of Pastel Blue and Pastel Green, and the shade of Red was changed.

The fixed-head and drophead coupé models were available in the same paint colours as the open two-seaters. However, the metallic colours were found only on the early LHD fixed-heads as they were discontinued before the RHD fixed-head, or the dropheads, went into production.

The range was now of 11 colours, with only one further change to come, as in March 1954 Dove Grey was discontinued, to be replaced in June 1954 by Light Grey. Although short-lived on the XK 120, and mostly found on LHD two-seaters, this may have been the same colour that was subsequently standardised on the XK 140 under the name of Pearl Grey.

After 1952, the suppliers of synthetic paints were either British Domolac (BD) or Pinchin Johnson (PJ). In the main, BD colours included Battleship Grey, Black, Lavender Grey, Light Grey, Pastel Green, Red and Suede Green, while PJ supplied Birch Grey, British Racing Green, Cream (now also known as Old English White), Dove Grey and Pastel Blue. Some colours were dual-sourced, and some Black paint came from Glasso.

The interior trim colour schemes included a number of two-tone designs, such as Biscuit and Pigskin, Biscuit and Red, Biscuit and Tan, and Duo-Blue, but also the single colours of Biscuit, Blue (Dark Blue), Red, Suede Green and, from 1951, Tan. Over the years, two-tone trim became less common and more cars had single-colour interiors. Fixed-head and drophead coupé models normally had single-colour trim. In 1954, both Black and Grey trims also appeared, but were rare and found mostly on LHD cars.

There were five standard hood colours available throughout, these being Black, Fawn, French Grey, Gunmetal and Sand. On 1954 models, they were briefly joined on a small number of mostly LHD cars by Blue, which later became a standard hood colour on the XK 140.

There were many examples of non-standard paint, trim and hood colours, or combinations of these. I have identified around 300 different colour schemes on XK 120 models, many of which were used only on a single car. It is, however, possible to rationalise this somewhat by identifying a smaller range of what we may call standard colour combinations.

The first three of the tables below have therefore been based on an analysis of all the cars. They include those paint and trim combinations which are statistically the most common, with the distribution of the standard hood colours for each of these combinations.

Open two-seater:

Paint	Interior trim	Hood							Total
		Black	Blue	Fawn	French Grey	Gunmetal	Sand	Other or n/r	
Battleship Grey	Biscuit and Red	74			1	19			94
	Red	40			4	117		2	163
Birch Grey	Biscuit and Red	27		16	194	32	2	6	277
	Duo-Blue	1		2	2	7			12
	Red	39		15	264	52	1	11	382
Black	Biscuit	20		2				1	23
	Biscuit and Pigskin	14		1	1		4	1	21
	Biscuit and Red	411		20	2	4	13	9	459
	Biscuit and Tan	75		9	1		14	7	106
	Red	282		8	2	1	7	8	308
	Tan	12		1	1		1		15
Brit. Rac. Green	Suede Green	68		4	3	95		1	171
	Tan	106		4		19		2	131
Bronze	Biscuit and Tan	4		174	3		70	6	257
	Tan			14					14

Paint	Interior trim	Hood Black	Blue	Fawn	French Grey	Gunmetal	Sand	Other or n/r	Total
Cream	Biscuit	1		16			1	1	19
	Biscuit and Pigskin			12				2	14
	Biscuit and Red	52		269	5		50	38	414
	Biscuit and Tan	8		73	5		22		108
	Black	28							28
	Blue/Dark Blue	18	11	24	7			4	64
	Red	321		203	15	1	22	5	567
	Suede Green	20		49	1		1		71
Dove Grey	Biscuit and Red			18					18
	Biscuit and Tan			18					18
	Red						9		9
	Suede Green			23					23
	Tan			50	5		5		60
Gunmetal	Red	1		1	2	66		2	72
Lavender Grey	Biscuit and Red	2		17	8				27
	Red			99	20				119
	Suede Green			9	10		4		23
	Tan			8	3				11
Light Grey	Black	10							10
	Blue/Dark Blue	5	10		4				19
	Grey	12							12
	Red	31		2					33
Pastel Blue	Blue/Dark Blue	26	4	21	254	35		1	341
	Duo-Blue	72	1	96	235	48	3	34	489
	Red	17	1	44	40	5	1	2	110
Pastel Green	Biscuit			6	25				31
	Red			8	10				18
	Suede Green	20		322	102	12	41	11	508
Red	Biscuit	62		120	6		2	5	195
	Biscuit and Red	33		161	5		42	5	246
	Black	34							34
	Grey	3		7		6	1		17
	Red	23		22			1		46
Silver	Blue				9	3		1	13
	Duo-Blue	13		16	85	38		11	163
	Red	41		66	228	146	4	30	515
Suede Green	Suede Green	33		66	309	15	2	21	446
	Tan				9				9
Twilight Blue	Duo-Blue				7	31			38
		2059	27	2116	1887	752	324	226	7391

This selection accounts for 97 per cent of the open two-seaters. Of the remaining 223 cars, 121 had 43 other combinations of the standard paint and trim colours, none of which were used on more than, at the most, seven cars; 54 had standard paint colours with non-standard trim colours (see below); 20 were in special paint colours (see below), sometimes also with special trim colours; and the final 28 cars were not painted, including 12 CKD cars, eight chassis and eight cars supplied in primer.

Fixed-head coupé models:

Paint	Trim Biscuit	Blue	Grey	Red	S. Green	Tan	Total	Notes
Battleship Grey			13	144			157	
Birch Grey			6	284			290	
Black	30		6	295	10	45	386	
Brit. Rac. Green					65	117	182	
Bronze						76	76	Mostly LHD
Cream		31		210	26	27	294	
Dove Grey				19	22	59	100	
Gunmetal				45			45	LHD only
Lavender Grey				63	7	20	90	

Paint	Trim							Notes
	Biscuit	Blue	Grey	Red	S. Green	Tan	Total	
Pastel Blue		195	13	39			247	
Pastel Green				7	186		193	
Red	37		7	65			109	
Silver		43		142			185	LHD only
Suede Green					173	8	181	
Twilight Blue		40		6	26	27	46	LHD only
Total	67	309	45	1319	489	352	2581	

This accounts for over 96 per cent of fixed-head models. Of the remaining cars, for one Birch Grey LHD car the trim colour was not recorded. 50 had other combinations of standard paint and trim colours, none of which was found on more than four cars; 40 had non-standard trim colours (including two-tone trim; see below); six were in non-standard paint colours, or primer (see below).

Drophead coupé models:

Paint	Interior trim	Hood							Total
		Black	Blue	Fawn	French Grey	Gunmetal	Sand	Other or n/r	
Battleship Grey	Grey	3				7			10
	Red	75		1	8	81	1		166
Birch Grey	Blue/Dark Blue	6	1		9			1	17
	Red	31	2		153	12			198
Black	Biscuit	12		1	2		4		19
	Grey	4					1		5
	Red	162		2	4	1	21		190
	Tan	23		1		1	64	1	90
Brit. Rac. Green	Biscuit	5		1					6
	Red	6							6
	Suede Green	41		7		30	3	2	83
	Tan	44		7		42	5		98
Cream	Black	5							5
	Blue/Dark Blue	5	21	18					44
	Red	67		58	11	2	8	2	148
	Suede Green	2		9	1				12
Dove Grey	Tan			48	5		17		70
Lavender Grey	Red	1		28	26				55
	Suede Green			4	5				9
	Tan				2		5		7
Pastel Blue	Blue/Dark Blue	9	2	4	158	2	1		176
	Red	10		7	6	1			24
Pastel Green	Suede Green	4		97	18		2	1	122
Red	Biscuit	11		8				1	20
	Black	5							5
	Grey	9		4	4		2		19
Suede Green	Suede Green	1		3	80		1		85
		541	26	308	492	179	135	8	1689

In the case of the drophead coupés, the 1689 cars in the table account for over 95 per cent of all production. Of the remaining cars, 53 were in various other combinations of standard paint and trim colours, none of which were used on more than four cars. This group includes the seven dropheads in Light Grey, and it is questionable whether this can be described as a "standard" colour on the drophead. 22 had special trim colours (see below, including those with two-tone trim) and the final three cars were in special paint colours (see below, including the only drophead painted Bronze). One of these also had special trim.

The following table shows when the standard paint colours were used and how many cars were painted in the different colours:

	From	To	OTS RHD	OTS LHD	FHC RHD	FHC LHD	DHC RHD	DHC LHD	Total
Battleship Grey*	Sep-51	Aug-54	13	255	16	145	38	145	612
Birch Grey	Feb-50	Aug-54	93	588	34	267	35	190	1207
Black	Sep-49	Aug-54	190	758	45	351	55	253	1652
Brit. Rac. Green*	Mar-52	Aug-54	17	296	24	164	43	153	697
Bronze	Oct-48	Nov-52	63	228	1	93	1		386
Cream	Jun-49	Aug-54	184	1147	17	285	41	184	1858
Dove Grey	Mar-52	Mar-54	3	125	2	99	10	65	304
Gunmetal	Oct-49	Oct-52	6	73		50			129
Lavender Grey*	Sep-51	Aug-54	6	183	8	83	14	60	354
Light Grey	Jun-54	Aug-54		78			1	6	85
Pastel Blue**	Jun-49	Aug-54	144	809	19	241	24	183	1420
Pastel Green**	Nov-49	Aug-54	54	505	7	189	12	117	884
Red***	Jan-49	Aug-54	67	476	2	114	2	45	706
Silver	Nov-49	Nov-52	195	505		187			887
Suede Green	Dec-49	Aug-54	103	357	19	163	17	71	730
Twilight Blue*	Mar-52	Oct-52	3	42		47			92
Special colours			11	9	1	3	2		26
Not painted			24	4		2			30
Total			1176	6438	195	2483	295	1472	12,059

*also on a few earlier cars

**metallic to Oct-Nov 1952, then solid

***change of shade in 1952-53; including 20 open two-seaters marked "Red Sheen" (mostly in August 1952 with numbers from 672664 to 672681) and three "Special Red", as well as seven fixed-head coupés in "Red Sheen" (from 679894 to 679900 in August 1952), all left-hand-drive cars

Special non-standard paint colours:

Open two-seater: There were 11 RHD cars and nine LHD cars in non-standard colours, as well as a total of eight cars in primer, as follows:

Alpine Mist	661174	Tan/French Grey			
Blue	660802	Red/Fawn			
Olive Green	660006	Suede			
Primer	660116 660118 660132 661161	Biscuit and Tan/Fawn Biscuit and Tan/Fawn Biscuit and Pigskin/Fawn Biscuit/Sand	672975 673794 674326	Red/French Grey Red/Black Biscuit/Sand
White	660054 660741	Blue/Black Blue/unknown Special	670159	White/unknown
Yellow	660920	Black/unknown	670030	Red/Black Red/Black

Fixed-head coupé:

669001, RHD: White, trim unknown.

679282, LHD: Green and Cream two-tone, Suede Green trim.

679467, LHD: Black and Cream two-tone, Grey trim.

680111, LHD: Connaught Green, Suede Green trim.

679209 and 680987, LHD: Primer, Red trim.

Also note 669002, RHD: Bronze, Tan trim – the only RHD car in Bronze.

Drophead coupé:

667068, RHD: Bronze, Tan trim, Sand hood.

667177, RHD: Pink, White and Dark Blue trim, Blue hood.

667195, RHD: Midnight Blue, Biscuit trim, Black hood.

Trim colours:

	From	To	OTS RHD	OTS LHD	FHC RHD	FHC LHD	DHC RHD	DHC LHD	Total
Biscuit	Aug-49	Aug-54	15	273	10	80	20	38	436
Biscuit and Pigskin	Nov-49	Jun-50	15	24					39
Biscuit and Red	Jan-49	Apr-54	390	1156		10		8	1564
Biscuit and Tan	Dec-49	Jul-54	112	390		15		1	518
Black*	Mar-54	Aug-54	2	73		1		11	87
Blue incl. Dark Blue**	Jun-49	Aug-54	24	434	21	299	46	199	1023
Duo-Blue***	Sep-49	Aug-53	179	536		11	3	6	735
Grey*	Jan-54	Aug-54	4	40	6	45	15	27	137
Red	Oct-49	Aug-54	233	2138	96	1231	120	677	4495
Suede Green	Nov-49	Aug-54	166	1091	40	452	54	262	2065
Tan*	Jul-51	Aug-54	20	233	21	334	36	239	883
Special trim			9	47		4	1	4	65
Not trimmed/not known			7	3	1	1			12
Total			1176	6438	195	2483	295	1472	12,059

*also on a few earlier cars

**Dark Blue specified on some cars from Sep 1952 onwards, on 38 OTS LHD, one FHC RHD and eight DHC LHD

***also on a few later cars

For some cars especially in 1954, there is a specific contrast colour quoted for the trim piping, including 86 OTS LHD, one FHC RHD, three DHC RHD and five DHC LHD.

Special non-standard trim colours:

Open two-seaters: Nine RHD cars and 47 LHD cars, as follows:

	RHD	Paint/hood colours	LHD	Paint/hood colours
Biscuit and Suede Green			670088 670114, 670260 670126	Gunmetal/Gunmetal Suede Green/French Grey Lavender Grey/French Grey
Biscuit and White			674261	Cream/Fawn
Black and Red			675277	Cream/French Grey
Black and White	660223	Cream/Black	675826	Black/Black
Blue and Biscuit			670036	Blue Duco/unknown
Cream	660694	Cream/Fawn	670071, 670358, 671419	Cream/Fawn
Cream and Black			670033, 670936, 670939, 670941	Cream/Fawn
Dark Blue and Grey			674480	Birch Grey/French Grey

Colour	RHD	Paint/hood colours	LHD	Paint/hood colours
Light Blue			670556 673200 675994	Pastel Blue/Black Silver/Gunmetal Pastel Blue/French Grey
Grey and Red	660987	Gunmetal/Gunmetal		
Green (special)	661026	White/unknown		
Orange	661028	Cream/unknown	673314	Cream/Black
Pigskin	660040 660041 660123	Cream/Fawn Pastel Blue/Fawn Black/Black	670029 670415 672333	Gunmetal/Grey Black/Black Battleship Grey/French Grey
Red and Biscuit*	660004	Cream/unknown	670710	Silver/French Grey
Red and Silver			670045	Silver/Grey
Red and Tan			675366	Red/Black
Tan and Black			676126	Cream/Black
White			670159 674043 674567, 674655 674852, 675632 675487 675559, 675560, 675561, 675593, 675607, 675640	White/unknown Orchid Blue/French Grey Cream/Fawn Black/Black Pastel Blue/Blue Cream/Black
White and Biscuit			674166, 674575 674333	Cream/Fawn Cream/Sand
White and Black			674791, 675269	Cream/Black
White and Red			674298	Cream/Fawn
White and Green			674109	Cream/Fawn

*this may be an error for Biscuit and Red

Fixed-head coupé:

40 LHD cars had special trim, as follows:

10 cars in various paint colours with Biscuit and Red trim.
15 cars in various colours with Biscuit and Tan trim.
11 cars in Pastel Blue or Silver with Duo-Blue trim.
679835 and 680100 in Black had Light Blue trim.
681483 in Red had Red and Pale Blue trim.
681282 in Cream had White and Emerald Green trim.

Drophead coupé:

23 cars had special trim, as follows:

667127, 667155 and 667159, RHD, all in Pastel Blue with Duo-Blue trim and Dark Blue hoods.
667177, RHD in Pink had White and Dark Blue trim and a Blue hood.
Eight LHD cars in various paint colours with Biscuit and Red trim.
Six LHD cars in Cream or Pastel Blue with Duo-Blue trim.
677570, LHD, in Cream had White and Biscuit trim and a Fawn hood.
677600, LHD, in Cream had Biscuit and Tan trim.
678244, LHD, had White trim and a Black hood.
678279 and 678420, LHD, both British Racing Green, had Biscuit and Suede Green trim, with a Black and a Fawn hood respectively.

Hood colours:

There were five standard hood colours used throughout the production run, joined by Blue from September 1953 on drophead coupé models and from January 1954 on the open two-seater.

	OTS RHD	OTS LHD	DHC RHD	DHC LHD	Total
Black	259	1862	93	477	2691
Blue incl. Dark Blue	0	29	16	16	61
Fawn	303	1864	55	270	2492
French Grey	293	1632	64	441	2430
Gunmetal	133	637	49	134	953
Sand incl. Dark Sand	71	262	13	131	477
Special hood colours	38	49	2	0	89
Not known	79	103	3	3	188
	1176	6438	295	1472	9381

Special hood colours:

Open two-seaters: 87 cars

Golden Brown on one RHD car (661039), and on 12 LHD cars (numbers between 673179 and 673213), all in November 1952.
Two early RHD alloy cars (660020, 660021) and 10 LHD cars (including seven alloy cars) have "Grey" hoods which may simply be the standard French Grey.
In October and November 1950, a batch of 35 RHD cars were fitted with hoods in Grey or French Grey plastic (numbers between 660311 and 660356), as well as three LHD cars (670865, 670879, 670946). This seems to have been an experiment which was not repeated.
Also in October 1950, 23 LHD cars (numbers between 670944 and 671051) had hoods in Fawn or Light Fawn "Mellohide" or plastic.
One LHD car (674993) had a Red hood, unless this is an error in the records.

Drophead coupés:

667180, RHD, hood in Fawn PVC.
667268, RHD, hood in White "tonneau cover material".

Sometimes hood colours are referred to as "Dark Blue" (674612, three DHC RHD and two DHC LHD) or "Dark Sand" (660057, and nine LHD OTS) but it is thought that these are simply the normal Blue or Sand colours.

Appendix 4: Coventry Registration Marks

The following is a list of the letter combinations issued for Coventry-registered motor vehicles during the XK 120 years:

Letters	From	To	Notes
HKV	May-49	Jun-49	HKV 455, HKV 500: May 1949
JDU	Jun-49	Aug-49	
JHP	Aug-49	Oct-49	
JRW	Sep-49	Jan-50	First in 1950: JRW 712
JWK	Jan-50	Apr-50	
JVC	Apr-50	Jun-50	
JKV	Jun-50	Jul-50	
KDU	Jul-50	Oct-50	
KHP	Oct-50	Dec-50	
KRW	Dec-50	Feb-51	First in 1951: KRW 140
KWK	Feb-51	Apr-51	
KVC	Apr-51	May-51	
KKV	May-51	Jun-51	
LDU	Jun-51	Jul-51	
LHP	Jul-51	Sep-51	
LRW	Sep-51	Nov-51	
LWK	Nov-51	Jan-52	First in 1952: LWK 540
LVC	Jan-52	Mar-52	
LKV	Mar-52	May-52	
MDU	May-52	Jul-52	
MHP	Jul-52	Sep-52	
MRW	Sep-52	Nov-52	
MWK	Nov-52	Jan-53	First in 1953: MWK 791
MVC	Jan-53	Apr-53	
MKV	Apr-53	Jun-53	
NDU	Feb-53	Aug-53	HDES only*
NHP	Aug-53	Jun-54	HDES only
NRW	Jun-54	Apr-55	HDES only
ODU	Jun-53	Aug-53	
OHP	Aug-53	Oct-53	
ORW	Oct-53	Dec-53	
OWK	Dec-53	Feb-54	First in 1954: OWK 50
OVC	Feb-54	Apr-54	
OKV	Apr-54	May-54	
PDU	May-54	Jul-54	
PHP	Jul-54	Sep-54	

*HDES: Home Delivery Export Scheme, relating to new vehicles sold tax-free to overseas visitors (or UK residents moving abroad), on the condition that these cars were exported within 12 months, also known as "Personal Export Delivery". In such cases, a pink rather than a buff Log Book was issued. Up until 1953, such vehicles registered in Coventry had been given marks from within the normal run of issues.

Cars registered locally by Jaguar Cars Limited fell mostly in two categories: Firstly the cars used by the company itself (prototypes, experimental cars, press cars and demonstrators, and finally company cars for senior management). Secondly, cars sold directly by Jaguar to private customers, but these were almost inevitably Personal Export Delivery cars; ordinary home market customers would place an order in the usual way through a dealer or distributor, and the cars would be registered in the locality of the selling dealer, or the first owner.

The PED cars were often delivered to their first owners at the factory, but some were ordered and delivered through Henlys in London, or provincial distributors, or in case of the frequent sales to US Service Personnel, via the US Forces Post Office UK Exchange Service. Some PED cars were direct sales, others were consigned to the overseas importer or distributor through whom the order had been placed, even if the point of delivery was in the UK.

Jaguar in common with other motor manufacturers and traders was pre-allocated batches of registration marks, which means that the dates of first registration for individual cars do not completely follow the sequence of numbers from 1 to 999. The Jaguars sold through the local distributor S H Newsome were also registered in Coventry, but there were far fewer of these than there were cars registered by the company. There are two sources for details of Coventry registered cars. One is the Coventry Transport Museum, which keeps the original issue ledgers of Coventry registrations from 1949 to 1975. The other is the Coventry City Archive, which keeps the "cancellation cards" for Coventry registrations for the period 1921 to 1963. A "cancellation card" was the final (and only) record kept by the registration authority, once a vehicle was declared exported or scrapped, and the log book returned (if it was), or if the vehicle had not been taxed for five years. If a vehicle continued to exist and to be taxed, there will not be a cancellation card. On the other hand, there are cancellation cards for most of the PED cars, which were exported before their year of grace was out.

These original registration records are interesting as they contain the chassis number and engine number, and (on the cancellation cards) colour, first registered owner, last known owner, and date of expiry of the last tax disc. If you have a Jaguar with a Coventry registration or have any interest in these records, you can make an appointment to visit the archive or museum to have a look at the record for your car. The sources for the information above are *Glass's Index of Registration Numbers 1929-1965* (1965) and Philip Riden's *How to trace the History of Your Car* (2nd edition 1998).

Bibliography

Primary unpublished sources:
In the JDHT archive: *Car Record Books* 1948-54 vols. 8 to 13; Competition Department files (Phil Weaver); England competition files; Experimental Department test reports; Jaguar sales statistics, various years; Lyons files: Speech at Mark V convention 30 Sep 1948; ditto, telegram from Sutton 14 Apr 1949; ditto, List of Development Department Cars 28 Oct/1 Nov 1949; photographic department negative registers; SS Cars Limited and Jaguar Cars Limited, minutes of the board of directors.

In other archives: Coventry City Archives: Registration cards for cancelled registrations; Coventry Transport Museum: Coventry Registration Ledgers; Public Record Office, Kew: SUPP 14/332 "The Market for British Cars in America".

Primary printed sources – newspapers, journals and annuals:
Annual Automobile Review (*Automobile Year*) 1954-55 (Switzerland); *Automobil Revue – Katalognummer* (Switzerland; various years); *Automobile Engineer*; *Autosport*; *Auto Sport Review* (USA); *Motor Sport*; *Motor Trend* (USA); *News Chronicle*; *Road and Track* (USA); *Speed Age* (USA); *Sportscar Illustrated* (USA); *Sportscar Quarterly* (USA); *The Autocar*; *The Economist*; *The Motor*; *The Motor Industry of Great Britain* (SMM&T annual handbook, various years); *The Times*; *The Times Survey of the British Motor Car Industry* (various years).

Published papers:
WM Heynes "The Jaguar Engine" 1953; WM Heynes "Milestones in the Life of an Automobile Engineer" 1960; TP Newcomb and RT Spurr "Jaguar XK 120" *Proceedings of the Institution of Mechanical Engineers* vol. 202 no. D3 (1988).

Jaguar Cars Limited publications:
Jaguar Apprentices' Magazine; *Jaguar Journal* employee magazine; *Jaguar XK 120 and Mark VII Service Manual*; *Jaguar XK 120 Handbook*; *Jaguar XK 120 Spare Parts Catalogue*; *Service Bulletins*; "Statement to Shareholders" by W Lyons 1950; various Jaguar circular letters, press releases, price lists and dealer lists; various Jaguar and XK 120 sales brochures.

Secondary sources – published books:
Anon *50 Years of American Automobiles from 1939* (Yeovil, Somerset 1989)
Anon *Jaguar Yearbook 2004* (Coventry 2005)
Boyce, Jeremy *Jaguar XK Series – The Complete Story* (Marlborough 1996)
Burgess-Wise, David *Ghia – Ford's Carozzeria* (London 1985)
Clark, Alan *Backfire* (London 2001)
Clausager, Anders *MG Saloon Cars* (Bideford, Devon 1998)
Dugdale, John *Jaguar in America* (Otego, NY 1993 and later edition)
Elmgreen, John and McGrath, Terry *The Jaguar XK in Australia* (Sydney 1985)
Frostick, Michael *The Jaguar Tradition* (London 1973)
Frostick, Michael *Pinin Farina – Master Coachbuilder* (London 1977)
Harvey, Chris *The Jaguar XK* (Oxford 1978)
Jenkinson, Denis *From Chain Drive to Turbocharger* (Cambridge 1984 and London 1985)
Gardner, Col ATG *Magic M.P.H.* (London 1951)
Georgano, GN (ed.) *The Beaulieu Encyclopaedia of the Automobile – Coachbuilding* (London 2001)
Georgano, GN (ed.) *The Encyclopaedia of Motor Sport* (London 1971)
Glass's Index of Registration Numbers 1929-1965 (Weybridge, Surrey 1965)
Hassan, Walter, with Robson, Graham *Climax in Coventry* (Croydon 1975)
Larson, Terry *The C-type Register* (Coventry 2001)
Ludvigsen, Karl *Porsche: Excellence was Expected* (Princeton, NJ 1977 and later editions)
Mennem, Patrick *Jaguar – An Illustrated History* (Marlborough 1991)
Mills, Rinsey *Essential AC Cobra* (Bideford, Devon 1997)
Moity, Christian and Tubbs, DB *The Le Mans 24-hour Race 1949-1973* (Lausanne, Switzerland 1974, and Radnor, PA 1975)
Molter, Günther *Rudolf Caracciola – Titan am Volant* (second edition, Stuttgart 1997)
Montagu of Beaulieu, with Sedgwick, Michael *Jaguar – A Biography* (London 1961 and later editions)
Murray, David *Ecurie Ecosse* (London 1962)
Newcomb, TP, and Spurr, RT *A Technical History of the Motor Car* (Bristol and New York 1989)
Nolan, William F *Phil Hill: Yankee Champion* (second edition, Carpinteria, CA 1996)
Porter, Philip *Jaguar Sports Racing Cars* (Bideford, Devon 1995)
Porter, Philip *Original Jaguar XK* (second edition, Bideford, Devon 1998)
Porter, Philip *The Jaguar Scrapbook* (1989)
Porter, Philip and Skilleter, Paul *Sir William Lyons* (Yeovil, Somerset 2001)
Plowden, William *The Motor Car and Politics in Britain* (Pelican edition, Harmondsworth, Middlesex 1973)
Price, Barrie *The Rise of Jaguar* (Dorchester 2004)
Riden, Philip *How to trace the History of Your Car* (second edition, Cardiff 1998)
Schmid, Urs *Jaguar XK 120: Anatomie eines Kultobjekts* (Band 1) (Solothurn, Switzerland 2000)

Sedgwick, Michael *Cars of the 1930s* (London 1970)
Simons, Rainer *From Roadster to Legend* (Munich 1996)
Skilleter, Paul *Jaguar Saloon Cars* (Yeovil, Somerset 1980 and later editions)
Skilleter, Paul *Jaguar Sports Cars* (Yeovil, Somerset 1975 and later editions)
Skilleter, Paul *Jaguar – The Sporting Heritage* (London 2000)
Skilleter, Paul *The Jaguar XKs – A Collector's Guide* (London 1981, and later editions)
Stein, Jonathan A *British Sports Cars in America* (Kutztown, PA 1993)
Urban, Roland *Les Metamorphoses du Jaguar* (Cannes and Paris 1993)
Viart, Bernard F *Jaguar XK – Le Grand Livre* (Paris 1993)
Walker, Nick *A-Z of British Coachbuilders 1919-1960* (Bideford, Devon 1997)
Wilkinson, WE, with Jones, Chris *"Wilkie"* (Olney, Bucks. 1987)
Whisler, Timothy R *At the End of the Road* (Greenwich, CT, and London 1995)
Whyte, Andrew *Jaguar Sports Racing and Works Competition Cars to 1953* (Yeovil, Somerset 1982 and later edition)
Whyte, Andrew *Jaguar – The History of a Great British Car* (Cambridge 1980 and later editions)
Zeiss, Henning *Authenrieth – eine Darmstädter Karosserielegende* (Germany)

Later newspapers and journals:
Australian Jaguar Magazine (Australia); *Bilhistorisk Tidsskrift* (Denmark); *Collector's Car*; *Coventry Evening Telegraph*; *Classic Cars*; *Independent on Sunday*; *Jaguar Heritage*; *Jaguar Journal* (USA); *Jaguar Quarterly*; *Jaguar World*; *The Daily Telegraph*; *The Guardian*; *The XK Gazette* (XK Club publication)

Apart from the authors of the works listed above, I would also like to acknowledge and thank the following who have been quoted directly or indirectly or who have assisted in writing this book, including colleagues and volunteers at the JDHT:

Ian Appleyard, Claude Baily, Johan Bendixen, David Bentley (XK Club), John and Ruth Sands Bentley, Bob Berry, Clemente Biondetti, William Boddy, Lucio Bollaert, Joska Bourgeois, Clinton Bourke, Ken Bowen, Derek and Margaret Boyce, Guy Broad, Jeremy Broad, Richard Brotherton (BMIHT), MJ Bubbert, Den Carlow, Bruce Carnachan, Morris B Carroll, Barry Collins (Coventry Transport Museum), Mike Cook (Jaguar Cars North America), Coventry City Archives staff, Sir Stafford Cripps, Nigel Dawes, Norman Dewis, Percy Dixon, Alan Docking, John Dowdeswell, Tony Dron, J Emerson, FRW "Lofty" England, John Fitch, Paul Frère, Clark Gable, DL Gandhi, Joe Gertler Jr., AE Goldschmidt, Penny Graham née Griffiths formerly Woodley, Gregor Grant, Urs Haehnle, LH "Nick" Haines, Ann Harris, Richard Hassan, Harold Hastings, Tom Hendricks, William Munger Heynes, Walter Hill, Max Hoffman, Cyril Holland, Les Hughes, Dr James Hull, Chris Jaques, Bob Knight, Gerd-Rüdiger Lang, Don Law, John Lea, Sir William Lyons, Neil McPherson, Richard Mason, Dennis May, John May, Karen Miller, Gilbert Mond, Stirling Moss, Tony O'Keeffe, Jim Patten, John and Ursula Pearson, Sue Pearson, Gloria Pedati (Jaguar Cars North America), Laurence Pomeroy Jr., François Prins, Pat Quinn née Lyons formerly Appleyard, Jonathan Radgick, Urs Ramseier, Ernest "Bill" Rankin, Mike Ridley, Mike Riedner, "Doc" Peter Scadron, Donald R Severson, Julia Simpson, Dick Skipworth, Howard and Sue Snow, Richard Soans, Ole Sommer, Heiner Stertkamp, Ron "Soapy" Sutton, Montague Tombs, Bob Tucker, Michael Ware, Phil Weaver, Derek Bovet White, John Woods, Tom Zwakman, and probably others to whom I apologise for not mentioning them by name.

Photographic acknowledgements:

Many of the photos used in this book came from the JDHT archive, thanks to the invaluable assistance of Karam Ram. The colour photos specially taken for this book are by Rowan Isaacs, and feature cars owned by Philip Haslam, Jeff Hine, Dr James Hull, and the JDHT. Other archive photos came from Paul Skilleter (including the former Bernard Viart collection), Mike Cook of the archives of Jaguar Cars North America, Terry McGrath, and the collection of Herridge and Sons (including the collection of the late David Hodges). The author and publisher apologise if individual photos remain unattributed or incorrectly attributed. We thank all contributors for allowing images to be used.